EXERCISES
IN RELIGIOUS UNDERSTANDING

Exercises
in
Religious Understanding

DAVID B. BURRELL, C.S.C.

UNIVERSITY OF NOTRE DAME PRESS
NOTRE DAME   LONDON

Copyright © 1974 by
University of Notre Dame Press
Notre Dame, Indiana 46556

Chapter 1 originally appeared in the *Journal of Religion*
50 (1970), as "Reading *The Confessions* of Augustine:
An Exercise in Theological Understanding" (327-51).
Reprinted here by permission of the University of Chicago.

Library of Congress Cataloging in Publication Data

Burrell, David B
  Exercises in religious understanding.

  Includes bibliographical references.
  1. Religion—Philosophy. I. Title.
BL51.B858   200'.1   74-12566
ISBN 0-268-00548-6
ISBN 0-268-00549-4 (pbk.)

Manufactured in the United States of America

To my Companions

Contents

Preface

These essays were inspired by a desire to grapple with the multiple relations among faith and reason, and to try to show in the process that there are helpful ways to use one's head in matters religious. The essays themselves pay homage to the original thinkers whom I count my mentors. I would like to acknowledge here my gratitude to friends who have helped me to this expression, notably John Gerber, Michael Novak, and David Tracy. I am indebted to my colleagues at Notre Dame, some of whose names appear herein: Kenneth Sayre, Ralph McInerny, Ernan McMullin, and Vaughn McKim. I am grateful in particular to Sister Mary Rachel Dunne, whose dissertation on Kierkegaard helped bring him into philosophical focus for me, to Sister Elena Malits, who urged me to greater clarity in presenting Augustine, Aquinas, Kierkegaard and Jung, and to Morton Kelsey, who has assisted mightily in the journey. Finally, to Edgar Whelan and to those who formed the receptive communities at Land-o-Lakes and Bennington in the summers of 1971 and 1972: thanks for offering the time and space that exercises like these demand. To these companions and to others along the way, I offer this work in some recognition for the tangible company they form.

The labors of many have contributed to shaping these reflections from manuscript to book. I am grateful to them all, and especially to Roger Burrell and to Shirley Schneck, who saw to the execution of various stages of typescript; to Paul Tracey for his care in reading proofs and organizing the index, and finally to John Ehmann for easing the entire work to press.

INTRODUCTION
On Hermeneutic Exercises

Each essay in this work is designed to be a workout. The book itself responds to a common recognition that metaphysics is inescapable, yet does so by offering a way to escape many a metaphysical pretension. The way must be taken, however, to experience the relief it promises. For stating it risks sounding pretentious. Each exercise intends to develop a definite set of skills. These skills are exhibited by the particular thinker in focus. The men are chosen as examples for us: examples of individuals who tried to understand what they were experiencing as religious men. Examples are to be imitated. And he imitates best who attends more to what a master does than to what he says.

So these exercises are offered to help us develop particular skills—the skills which these individuals exhibit in executing their own projects. In each case their experience with issues religious in scope raised questions for them, faced them with problems. They were forced to use their wits to unravel the conceptual tangles involved, to resolve the problems so they could pursue the questions. They proposed distinctions, adapting or inventing a set of linguistic tools to meet the challenge in the terms it presented itself to them. Since their conceptual apparatus and techniques were developed to that end, we can hardly hope to learn them if we ignore what each of them is up to in employing the tools he does. So we have no other way to learn from thinkers like these except to learn how to do what they did so well. And why learn *about* someone unless we can learn *from* him? The nub of the pressure for relevance is protection against pedantry.

What has all this to do with metaphysics? Everything, if we take metaphysics to consist primarily of a set of philosophical skills. Exercises are designed to develop skills. These exercises concentrate on negotiating obstacles to understanding in religious matters. To become skilled oneself in doing what others do well is to assimilate what they have to offer. To acquire these skills with an awareness of the purpose they serve can even mark an advance over the masters. Then we find we cannot only do what they did but grasp why they did as they did. Often we find ourselves in a position to articulate their purposes better than they. By standing on the shoulders of giants from the past we can increase their stature as well as our own.

A philosophical skill, then, is like other skills in that it is more a knowing-how than a knowing-that. Yet in practice it demands a degree of awareness far exceeding most other skills. For it is a highly conscious skill, and meant to be employed in as finely discriminating a way as possible. This quality of conscious discrimination is built into the set of skills we call metaphysics.

So the metaphor does not prove so innocuous as it may have initially appeared. There are many sorts of skills, and different skills demand to be possessed differently. The difference lies in a quality of consciousness which includes self-awareness. So it will not suffice even to have mastered what the masters do so well. In trying to understand what they were up to, we are constantly invited to become aware of what *we* are doing. To respond to that invitation is to assimilate oneself in assimilating a tradition. To fail to respond means failing to understand the tradition as well. For the noise of our own preoccupations can keep us from hearing clearly what they are saying. Any commentary contributes to the entropy of the total situation by a factor equal to our initial lack of awareness. For when we are unaware of the hold our own preoccupations have on us, we normally assume the channel to be clear.

Exercising a set of logical skills expertly enough to be doing metaphysics, then, demands something more than keenness. It requires self-awareness, and a level of self-awareness that is difficult to sustain. These exercises are designed to elicit that awareness in us as we try to master the skills of these masters, and so come to appreciate the discriminating way in which they employed the tools available to them. The aptitude called metaphysical, then, can be neither contained nor exhibited in a set of propositions. It can only be *displayed* in the manner in which one proposes distinctions, and accommodates or adopts a language to clarify conceptual confusion. And I wager that so keen a skill can only be acquired by consciously imitating those we recognize to be expert at it. A discipline demands apprenticeship, since the know-how's essential to it cannot be conveyed by statement.

It may prove useful to contrast *discipline* with *method.* Descartes' ideal of a method, at least, comprised a set of steps, one following another and each unambiguous in intent. A perfect method would be one which required no further skill to execute and whose execution demanded no interior change in the operator. Verification procedures could be carried out by a laboratory assistant of average intelligence willing to follow instructions. A discipline, on the other hand, allows for more self-expression and also asks more from the performer. Think of playing a guitar or piano, dancing or yoga. Where the description of *method* offers the ideal for scientific procedure, metaphysics demands something more akin to a *discipline.*

One reason why this is so lies in the key terms employed in philosophical assessments. They are nearly always analogous. Hence one can only grasp their meaning in a particular context by understanding how this use is related to other uses in related contexts. Since any bit of understanding we might glean could be expressed as relating the contexts in an ordered way, these terms and the understanding they convey has been dubbed "analogous," from the Greek term for proportion.[1]

The upshot of all of this is that the set of skills known traditionally as metaphysics is better understood as demanding a discipline than a method, and a highly conscious discipline. And since, *method,* as I have been using it, is associated with normal science, and normal science offers a paradigm for *theory,* this set of philosophical skills must be something other than *theory.* And if this is so, its goal would presumably be something different from *explanation.*

Both these conclusions are true, and they help one appreciate why I am offering exercises, and apprenticing myself to paradigm figures in the history of philosophical theology in the hope of enticing others to do the same. For if philosophy's secret lies in doing it, and in doing it consciously so that one ferrets out the resistances and confusions within himself, then only living examples will help us learn it. And we can only make historical figures live by figuring out with them how they did the remarkable things they did.

Bernard Lonergan, whose extended workbook, *Insight,* set me off on this route some time ago, has expressed the difference in his latest work, *Method in Theology.* "As science develops," he says, "philosophy is impelled to migrate from the world of theory to find its basis in the world of interiority."[2] That means, for him, moving to a clarity of consciousness whence one becomes increasingly aware of what he is up to when he is understanding something to be the case.[3] Concretely it involves taking different instances of knowing as examples of knowing something to be the case, and grasping the proportional likenesses among them. That grasp demands that one's own perspective be factored in, hence "one has not only to read *Insight* but also to discover oneself in oneself."[4]

All this is astonishingly similar to Wittgenstein of the *Investigations* and to contemporary followers of his. I am thinking particularly of Paul Holmer and his essay on "Kierkegaard and Philosophy," where he outlines how S.K. does philosophy by judiciously using examples.[5] With the skills at his disposal Kierkegaard is able to dramatize the further step which I have referred to as "consciousness" or "awareness" and which Lonergan intends by "interiority." S.K. displays this discriminating factor, normally not susceptible of formulation, by adopting diverse standpoints in his pseudonymous writings. And all of his expressly philosophical examinations of theological issues are pseudonymous.

So the *genre* to which these essays aspire is that of an exercise—a finger-exercise, if you will. Anyone who works through them should be in a better position to exercise those discriminating philosophical skills summarily called metaphysics. In Lonergan's scheme of functional specialties for doing theology this work is properly *dialectical*. It seeks to develop the critical skills needed to adjudicate among conflicting theological standpoints by watching others proceed in similar situations, and taking their moves into our repertory by imitating them. Correlatively, it prepares each one of us who sets out to acquire these skills for the conversions which attend so interior a discipline. As Lonergan seems it, "dialectic contributes to [conversion] by pointing out ultimate differences, by offering the example of others that differ radically from oneself, by providing the occasion for a reflection, a self-scrutiny, that can lead to a new understanding of oneself and one's destiny."[6] In this sense, of course, conversion is never a once-for-all thing. "It is ever precarious, ever to be achieved afresh, ever in great part a matter of uncovering still more oversights. . . . ."[7] One continues to apprentice himself to others whose wit and discriminating quality he admires.

And that is precisely what links these thinkers together: each uses his head to untangle those confusions which tended to block the understanding of matters religious in his age. Augustine proposed a way of understanding that was personal as well as archetypal, offering an accounting for one's personal history which the *Platonici* managed to overlook with their fixed set of ideals for the *humanum*. Anselm was concerned to harness logic to the service of God, using it to highlight what is uniquely divine about Him. Aquinas needed to transcend language while rigorously respecting its limits, and managed to find a way of ascertaining the limits so that he could do so. Kierkegaard was convinced that intelligence is versatile enough to rid itself of its own pretense and to bring the power and majesty of faith into sharp relief. In the wake of the Enlightenment such a project taxed the virtuosity of his immensely versatile intelligence to its limit. Jung found the canons of rationality prevailing at the end of the nineteenth century to be thoroughly dehumanizing, and even destructive in their one-sidedness. A science of the psyche would demand an entirely new method, something more like a discipline. Furthermore, the symbols that proved fruitful to the *self* questing for wholeness turned out to be intrinsically religious in their range and scope.

Each of these exercises, then, provides an object lesson in interpretation. I offer them as examples of what it means to *do* hermeneutics. Like any set of exercises, these are meant to train apprentices. Yet even a master performer never stops practicing, and his practice is ingredient in every virtuoso performance. So the next stop is already adumbrated in these exercises. For it consists not in formulating a theory but in a discriminating performance, be it in reading or teaching or simply understanding how it is things are. The goal of exercising one's native wit is not to try to surpass it, but to come to trust it. Zen reminds us how healthy an attitude this can be in religious matters. These essays offer the witness of some Western religious thinkers in behalf of that testimony of Zen.

NOTES

1. See my *Analogy and Philosophical Language* (New Haven, 1973) for an historical and analytic study of these uses, and for a perceptive summary of medieval practice, see Yves Simon, "Order in Analogical Sets," *New Scholasticism* 34 (1960).

2. Bernard J. F. Lonergan, *Insight* (London, 1957); *Method in Theology* (London, 1972) 259.

3. As he puts it summarily in *Method:* "Once such an account of knowledge is attained, one can move from the gnoseological question (What are we doing when we are knowing?) to the epistemological question (Why is doing that knowing?) and from both to the metaphysical question (What do we know when we do it?)" (260).

4. *Method,* 259. I have spelled out some consequences of *Insight* as a performative exercise in "Judgment and Sensibility: Novak's Debt to Lonergan," *Journal of the American Academy of Religion* 40 (1972) 349-67.

5. In Ralph McInerny (ed), *New Themes in Christian Philosophy* (Notre Dame, 1968).

6. *Method,* 253.

7. *Method,* 252.

PART ONE

Beyond Explanations

1: AUGUSTINE
Understanding as a Personal Quest

This essay is intended not to swell the bulk of Augustiniana but rather to assist anyone who would engage himself in a work as engaging as the *Confessions* with some hope of advancing his theological understanding. The essay offers assistance in two ways: by leading one to take up the text once again, and by leading the same person to examine what he continues to bring to that text. For one advances in theological understanding in the measure that he understands a little better what counts as understanding in matters religious. Hermeneutic or interpretation or, more simply, understanding is more secure the more reflective it is; this essay proposes to display that thesis. Hence the initial and final justification I shall offer for considering Augustine's *Confessions* to be primarily an exercise in theological understanding lies in the fact that they can be read that way with unsuspected fruitfulness. The thesis of the chapter, then, concerns hermeneutics more than it does Augustine, but the benefits of a fresh understanding of Augustine are more than incidental.

11

1. Use and Interpretation

The tools offered for helping us to understand an historical figure often seem to interpose themselves in the way of the very quest they are designed to assist. How can we use them to help us achieve the quality of understanding we are after? It is one thing to learn enough about the various currents which have influenced an author to be able to offer a plausible reconstruction of his world view. Yet something more is needed if this understanding is to advance us in our quest for self-understanding as well. The scholar may argue that this second kind of understanding is not relevant to his work; and the querying individual will then be tempted to wonder what end the scholar's work. When claims of irrelevance invite charge of irrelevance, one suspects that illumination, if at all possible, lies elsewhere.

Yet illumination is possible. The plethora of scholarly material surrounding Augustine and the *Confessions* in particular plays a distinct and specifically ancillary role in understanding that work.[1] It can bring us to a sharp appreciation of the schemes which dominated Augustine's shaping of the work. These schemes provide the material rules of inference which license some implications and restrict others. To identify them is to explain why questions are posed in the terms in which they are, and why certain issues are taken up and others dropped. For purposes of discussion I should like to call this contribution "dialectical" in the straightforward sense of positioning the issues. Anything which helps us to understand why the discussion is framed as it is clearly claims our interest and contributes to our enlightenment.

Beyond the interesting, however, lies the critical. How does Augustine structure the book—given the influences which parameter his decision—and why? How does he use the schemata offered to him? And a correlative question: what do the obstacles I feel in approaching the text tell me about what is going on in the unfolding of Augustine's exposition, or in myself? When a question is posed in what seems to be an untoward way, it could be that a scheme is operating in Augustine's exposition of which I am innocent—or that I am employing a scheme in my reading which inhibits my following what is a quite linear path for Augustine. One could easily show that these two ways of describing a difficulty in interpretation come to the same thing. In fact, they do: such is the reciprocity between text and reader. Yet their sense is different, and this difference determines what steps we will take to correct the distortion. The road from Athens to Piraeus is the same that leads from Piraeus to Athens, yet it usually helps to know which direction we are traveling.

Granted that Augustine's world view is vastly different from my own, how can I read him not only to understand what he is saying but also to come in greater measure to grips with what I wish to say? Is it not hard enough to expect someone living today to understand what Augustine was saying, without expecting him to have something to say to me? The challenges posed by a consciousness of historical and cultural relativity contain the elements of their own response. For it is clear that we can never hope to understand what Augustine is saying until we become aware that we are reading him in a certain way. The very factor that tends at first to paralyze us actually turns out to empower both kinds of understanding—the historical and the critical. Once we realize that what looks like a straightforward question is already a reflective one, then the task of reflective understanding does not seem so prohibitive. The trick is surely to discover whence the misreading comes and so where to direct the therapy: to Augustine and his world view or to me and to mine?

Points of conflict, then, turn into points of contact, as I become aware of my own canons of interpretation in attempting to lay hold of Augustine's. What we have in common are the issues we each must face. But we will most probably differ in the formulation we give to them. Once we have been able to voice some of these differences, we are free to turn our attention to the way we each work with the conceptual apparatus available to us. For what we share with each other and with Augustine are the skills required to meet an issue. The way we handle the frameworks we have indicates the quality of judgment we possess; and as Wittgenstein has reminded us, "To share a language is to share in . . . judgments."[2]

To test this observation, consider what reading Augustine's text adds to reading a summary account in any history of philosophy. Assuming that the summary is an accurate one, we will learn little more from the actual text. Yet the text, we feel, gives us more of the man. The manner in which he comes to grips with questions shows us how much the question is his question. If we respect this fact, we will be less and less tempted to take home what he says as an "answer." For what Augustine says, he has worked out in response to his question. Yet in compensation we will have learned a little better how to meet our questions, by participating in his attempt to formulate his. In this manner, reading becomes exercising, as learning passes over from learning about to learning how. Let us bring these reflections to bear on the *Confessions*.

Plan of Exposition. The clues we have to follow in understanding another and coming to grips with the obstacles we erect to such an understanding are invariably structural or logical clues. Even relatively "straight" questions of historical influence, we are told, cannot be answered uniquely by finding literal citations from one author in another.[3] It seems natural to speak of the "sense and structural unity of the work," as if in the same breath. The reason attention to form is so telling is at once simple and profound. Both fourth- and twentieth-century authors must organize their work. Hence, the task is an understandable and a comprehensible one, no matter what general set of views one espouses. The manner in which a work is organized can be counted on to shed light on the set of judgments which control what a person does with the schemes at hand. The order decided upon says something about relative weighting and this will prove all the more true in the case of Augustine's *Confessions,* where the mode itself is not inherited but consciously adopted.

In what follows, I shall begin by proposing some general and hypothetical remarks about the role of the *Confessions* in Augustine's life and literary output. I shall then propose a way of reading the work suggested by paying careful attention to some obvious structural features of its composition. Bringing these two sorts of observations together will allow me to present the *Confessions* as a project in understanding. Finally, I should like to compare and contrast this way of proceeding with some recent psychological analyses. This specific comparison with another method of interpretation is offered as a test of the hermeneutic remarks proposed in the section on "Use and Interpretation."

The Role of the Confessions in Augustine's Life and Writings. The difference between the *Confessions* and other work of Augustine is immediately and dramatically evident. Linguistically, the *Confessions* is a carefully and a highly constructed work. It is fashioned and chiseled more like a work of art than an account. It is clear from comparative studies that this work not only differs from the rest of Augustine's output but stands without any clear precedent, initiating a novel literary genre.[4] The choice of form illustrates better than anything else Augustine's feel for theological understanding. What is remarkable about the choice is its apparent naturalness; to adopt an autobiographical form in the way he does is to exhibit its appropriateness. It is not so much to credit Augustine with a special insight as to charge others with oversight. For what we have is a crafted response to the biblical recommendation that we praise God for what he has done in and to our lives. The format is central to the Jewish blessing and consequently to the Christian anaphora.[5] It forms a standard motif for celebration and for increasing the faith which triggers celebration. Augustine adapted the recom-

mendation from the arena of God's people to the field of
his own personal history: Where fathers were to relate the
great deeds of God to their children, Augustine recalls his
own childhood to relate God's deeds there to himself
now—for the child is the father of the man.[6]

In this way Augustine finds a recommended way of
coming to grips with the question central to every Christian life, but nettling for a professionally religious person—
the question of faith. I speak not of the neurotic desire to
find certitude where none will be forthcoming, but of the
troublesome issue of one's own genuineness. As bishop and
as theologian, he must speak of God and the things of
God. But where does he himself stand? How can he responsibly speak of such things, as distinguished from ana-
lytically or defensively? Perhaps this is too modern a
hypothesis to foist upon Augustine, but I think not. For
the very manner in which he undertakes the *Confessions*
suggests it, as well as the way he organizes the material. He
undertakes it publicly, as befits his character, and as he
must, being a magisterial figure in a church whose founder
resented being called "master." The irony of such a position could not be lost on a psyche as sensitive as Augustine's. Furthermore, the double sense of "confession" is
well served by this hermeneutic hypothesis—praising God
for all that He has made him and confessing how much he
yet remains in need of purification.

That part of the authenticity question which can be
tackled in a work of human crafting might be roughly
called establishing the criteria or the warrants for speaking
responsibly of God. How, on what evidence, do you say
what you do? By choosing the autobiographical format
Augustine could show how a person's understanding of
God is interwoven with his personal development. Certain
questions arise at certain times, and until they do, a
language crafted to respond to them remains idle. Correlatively, this logic feeds back on the writer to apprise him of
where he now stands. This special understanding of where
he stands comes to an author directly as he retraces his
own steps up to the present. But the form also allows him

to have a reflective insight, were he to try to ascertain why he selected one episode rather than another, and why he organizes his history in the stages that he does.

To look carefully at the genre is to appreciate its severe demands. What Augustine undertakes is to trace his way to God, the manner in which the relatedness of every creature to the Creator was exhibited in his case. Here the plan betrays a metaphysical scheme: for the Christian, "to be" is "to be related to God the Creator." Yet Augustine continued to frustrate the operation of this scheme; his innate propensity to be autonomous kept preventing this (true) scheme from being true. The sign that he was bucking a metaphysical fact was, of course, its revenge; every effort at autonomy resulted in increased dependency and enslavement. Metaphysical schemes become dramatized when the context is the history of human subjectivity. So runs Augustine's genius.[7]

Furthermore, by focusing on his intellectual development Augustine was able to unfold one hypothetical scheme after another, showing what made them look plausible and how he came to reject them. Exercise in revealing the springs of one's judgments along the way allows him to examine the judgments upon which he is presently operating. This is Plato's recommendation for dialectic: that it exercise itself in becoming aware of the hypotheses which it has adopted, that it become skilled in bringing them up for examination. It is significant that this recommendation does not lend support to the search for a definitive scheme or a foundation for understanding. Nor does Augustine propose anything like that. He rather casts his work into a format which will illustrate the relatedness of all things to God by unfolding the drama within his spirit, which can become all things. By exposing his life right up to the moment of composing he places himself in an admirable position for taking stock of the premises governing his thought and life at present.

We are clearly in the presence of someone who cherishes and relies upon intellectual skill. Yet these skills are just as clearly placed at the service of living one's life, of helping

one to understand, and to live into that primary relatedness which being alive is. The autobiographical form shows
this fact more easily than it could be said. For we are not
speaking of a yet higher scheme, but of the manner in
which any scheme may be utilized. The form will also
exhibit how Augustine is driven to adopt an epistemological model quite different from that available to him in
neo-Platonism. The model he proposes is the very one, of
course, when led him to adopt the developmental format
of an autobiography. Understanding what something is
demands more than insight or vision; it will also require an
appropriate discipline so that we can articulate what we
understand in a word which faithfully expresses our present situation. In things that matter there is no knowing
short of becoming, no articulation short of a faithful
expression of where it is that one is.

The reason for this, as we shall see below, is that the
hypothetical scheme one is employing is not nearly as
important as the manner in which one employs it. This
fact imposes itself in "things that matter," because this
phrase describes those subjects of inquiry which are presupposed to any inquiry, those topics toward which we
cannot help but be positioned whether we have taken a
position or not. Hence, understanding cannot escape self-
understanding, and taking a position often involves dis-
engaging oneself from the position in which he already
stands. To say that Augustine succeeds in dramatizing
metaphysics is another way of noting how he firmly sub-
ordinates conceptualization to living, schema to us, understanding to judgment, and judgment to action. For if "to
be" is "to be related," then any affirmation of what I am
includes an assessment of what I must become. Let us
illustrate these general contentions in the unfolding of the
work.

Mode of Composition. The divisions in the work are
clearly demarcated and more or less adequately announced
by the initial chapter in each book. This chapter acts as a

prelude, summarizing and projecting the theme of the ensuing book. On this pattern, book I occupies a special place, hence it is the first five chapters which serve to introduce not simply the first book but the themes of the entire work. The development of the work may then be elaborated into an introduction and four parts as follows:

Introductory I.1-1.5
Growing Up:
    1. Childhood
    2. Youth
    3. Adolescence
    4. Young Bachelor
    5. Transitional

Focusing on Conversion:
    6. A Despairing State
    7. Intellectual Enlightenment
    8. Conversion and Return

From Conversion to Present:
    9. Ecstatic Liberty of Spirit
    10. Present Posture

Understanding Along the Way:
    11. Critical Appraisal of God's Relation to Men
    12. Removing Obstacles to Speaking of God
    13. Unity of Creation and Redemption

The closest Augustine comes to anything like a theological treatise can be found in the final three chapters of the *Confessions*. It is as though he dare not undertake anything so risky as the interpretation of Scripture until he has brought himself to an awareness of where he stands and whence he has come. Something of the same may be said for us. We can only understand what Augustine is able to write in the measure that we undertake his journey ourselves. And yet we could not be required to have traversed the same distance. We can understand what he is up to, just as he was able to see what he had to do long before he was able to bring himself to do it.

It is perfectly characteristic that his philosophical reflections should be entirely at the service of our reading the Scriptures. The work of the theologian will be to overcome obstacles which may stand in the way of others reading and profiting by the Scriptures. For all understanding is meant to show us a little more of the way, and the Scriptures are the ideal food along the way. Nor can he hope by philosophical analysis to remove those obstacles to reading the Scriptures which we may share with the young Augustine. He can only hope that the earlier part of his own book has prepared us to meet our obstinacy and pride so that we have done what is possible on our part to remove those obstacles to understanding.

The division which I have presented of the book is an uncomplicated and immediate one, except for the section comprising books 9 and 10. It would seem more natural here to follow Albert Outler's suggestion that book 9 completes Augustine's personal history, placing it all in proper perspective with the death of his mother and the severance of his strongest earthly tie. The rest of the work would then be seen as exploring two closely related problems:

> First, how does the finite self find the infinite God (or, how is it found of him)? And, secondly, how may we interpret God's action in producing this created world in which such personal histories and revelations do occur? Book X, therefore is an explanation of *man's way to God,* a way which begins in sense experience but swiftly passes beyond it, through and beyond the awesome mystery of memory, to the ineffable encounter between God and the soul in man's inmost subject-self. But such a journey is not complete until the process is reversed and man has looked as deeply as may be into the mystery of creation on which all our history and experience depends.[8]

Outler then goes on to show how in book II "in the
beginning God created the heaven and the earth" is the
basic formula of a massive Christian metaphysical world
view. Then books 12 and 13 allow Augustine to elaborate
the mysteries of creation until he is able to relate the
entire round of creation to the point where we can view
the drama of God's enterprise in human history on the vast
stage of the cosmos itself. In this fashion, Augustine can
show how the Creator is the Redeemer, and man's end and
the beginning meet at a single point.

The division which I have adopted is quite compatible
with Outler's, for book 10 is clearly a transitional effort
and can be read as part of the more theological writing or
(as I have) more closely linked to Augustine's personal
history—as he sums up the confessional section: "This,
then, is my present state" (10.33). The long section on
memory or consciousness then becomes his explicitly reflective glance back over the endeavor he has just completed. Were he not so composed, neither could the work
be. I have chosen to link books 9 and 10 together to make
evident an epistemological structure which I consider to
be one of the most useful explicitly philosophical con-
tributions of the *Confessions*. This division also has the
advantage of creating a new section precisely at the moment of newness, his baptism. But I have remarked that
such a scheme is compatible with Outler's, precisely because a work like the *Confessions* itself is capable of being
diversely schematized. It is meant to be put to use in the
same manner Augustine puts intellectual schemes to
work—to assist human understanding along the way.

2. Understanding as Becoming, Knowing as Knowing How

It has been remarked that Augustine admirably formulates the crucial dictum of the existentialists—knowing is
becoming. I have suggested that the very form of the
Confessions illustrates this contention, and have tried to

show in a schematic manner why the concluding theological sections depend for their efficacy on our participating in Augustine's personal journey. Yet it is possible to
come a good deal closer to elaborating Augustine's epistemological position than simply to remark that knowing is
becoming.

It will prove fruitful to speak in terms of knowing how
to use a particular language, feeling at home in employing
it, and realizing the consequences that follow from speaking it. Although Augustine will not put it in these terms,
and even though his own remarks about language are
rather simplistic and stereotyped (I.8, II.20), the manner
in which he uses prose belies the remarks he may make
about using it. The simple fact is that he finds it necessary
from his own experience to supplement the Platonist
modeling of knowing on a flash of vision or insight. For his
experience found him seldom short of insight, yet often
unable to respond: "I was astonished that although I loved
you and not some phantom in your place, I did not persist
in enjoyment of my God." (7.17)

Many have also remarked how Augustine invariably introduces important figures in his life some time before he
details their influence upon him. It is as though insight
merely introduces us to a new understanding, and that
something else must intervene before that understanding
becomes our own. What must intervene is on the one hand
a gift and on the other hand a struggle. The first we can
always count on, the second requires time and effort.
Before we can possess what we have glimpsed, we must
undertake a style of life which embodies some of the
syntax of the new language adumbrated in the original
insight.

It is as though Augustine realizes that mere insight must
be filled out by expression before we can possess what we
have seen. And since expression demands language and
language brings with it a structure of consequences, those
entailments must reach into the organization of one's life
before he can be said to understand in a way that gives him

facility with a new language. I have already noted that the couplet books 9 and 10 form a unit on this interpretation. The ecstatic liberty experienced in book 9 is comparable to a flash of insight, while the probing and confessions of book 10 recount the way of life which must follow upon the experience of liberation in order that one continue to act freely.

Yet perhaps the most pointed illustration of the progressive laying hold of a new language, first by insight and then by grace and discipline, can be found in the couplet of chapters 7 and 8. Chapter 7 recounts Augustine's intellectual enlightenment, and specifically his breakthrough to a new and appropriate language for God, the language of origin or principle: "I entered into the depths of my soul, . . . and with the eye of my soul, such as it was, I saw the Light that never changes casting its rays over the same eye of the soul, over my mind" (7.10). Similarly, for all of creation: "I looked at other things too and saw that they owe their being to you. . . . They are in you because you hold all things in your truth as though they were in your hand, and all things are true insofar as they have being" (7.15). Yet the net effect of this new insight was to "realize that I was far away from you" (7.10).

The same pattern is condensed in an account of a dialectical ascent in classical neo-Platonic terms:

> So, step by step, my thoughts moved on from the consideration of material things to the soul, which perceives things through the senses of the body, and then to the soul's inner power. . . . This power of reason, realizing that in me it too was liable to change, led me on to consider the source of its own understanding. . . .And so, in an instant of awe, my mind attained to the sight of God who IS. . . . But I had no strength to fix my gaze. In my weakness I recoiled and fell back into my old ways, carrying with me nothing but the memory of something that I loved and longed for, as though I had sensed the fragrance of the fare but was not yet able to eat it. [7.17]

In these highly reflective passages at the end of book 7 Augustine is delineating a twofold intellectual conversion. The first stage recognizes the manner in which "the Platonists" allowed him to find a new direction in his central endeavor of discovering how one might conceive of God. Yet in the very same breath he notes that the same books which led him to this new understanding failed to enlighten him how to put it into practice—although they were replete with the Word, they could not bring themselves to give it flesh (7.9). At one and the same time Augustine must acknowledge his debt to the neo-Platonists and seek to enlarge the pattern for understanding which they offered to him. The inspiration for a new pattern is manifestly Christian—the difference between a disembodied word and a word made flesh is precisely the increment which discipline adds to insight. And the inward side of discipline is, of course, a gracious gift of God. So the impetus of the twofold intellectual conversion to Platonism and beyond remains the grace of God, and grace gives this conversion its specific form.

This revolution in models for understanding is carefully catalogued in the following passages collated from the last two chapters of book 7—the chapters which sum up Augustine's intellectual enlightenment and set the stage for the decisive moment of conversion.

> By reading these books of the Platonists I had been prompted to look for truth as something incorporeal, and I caught sight of your invisible nature, as it is known through your creatures. I was certain both that you are and that you are infinite, though without extent in terms of space either limited or unlimited. I was sure that it is you who truly are, since you are always the same, varying in neither part nor motion. I know too that all other things derive their being from you, and the one indisputable proof of this is the fact that they exist at all. I was quite certain of these truths, but I was too weak to enjoy you. [7.20]

> By the gift of grace he is not only shown how to see

you, who are always the same, but is also given the strength to hold you. By your grace, too, if he is far from you and cannot see you, he is enabled to walk upon the path that leads him closer to you, so that he may see you and hold you. [7.21]

It is one thing to descry the land of peace from a wooded hilltop and, unable to find the ways to it, struggle on through trackless wastes where traitors and runaways, captained by their prince, who is lion and serpent in one, lie in wait to attack. It is another thing to follow the high road to that land of peace, the way that is defended by the care of the heavenly Commander. Here there are no deserters from heaven's army to prey upon the traveller, because they shun this road as a torment. [7.21]

Language: A Way of Life. It is noteworthy that those chapters of book 8 which express the tension of conflict between what Augustine saw and what he was prepared to do (chaps. 5-10) employ the expressions "intellect" and "will." It seems as if this way of speaking, which opposes the two ingredients of understanding—insight and discipline—is most appropriate to capture the felt hiatus between seeing what must be the case and bringing oneself into line with that train of thought. Yet the language of intellect and will is strictly speaking provisional on Augustine's new-found model for understanding. For the organization of the book and the specific remarks we have collated certainly will not support linking intellect with understanding and will with doing. It is rather that certain things cannot be understood unless we are prepared to incarnate them. The language model allows this point to be made quite precisely: The rules of inference which govern a particular language must become the rules of one's life if he is to use that language with confidence and alacrity. Is this perhaps why, when the tension of opposition between insight and his way of life is released, Augustine quite naturally has recourse to a more primitive mode of expression: "The light of confidence flooded into my heart and all the darkness of doubt was dispelled" (8.12).

To understand something means to be able not simply to mention it but to go on and speak about it. Hence to understand something is to be able to integrate what we can say about it into a working framework which allows us to say yet other things about what we understand. This, I take it, is at least part of what understanding something amounts to. What Augustine helps us to see is that understanding certain things—things which bear upon our own existence—also means going on to live in a manner every bit as consistent and consequential as is our ability to speak about them. Language is a way of life, and a confident use of language demands a consonant way of living. Furthermore, in the arena of religious discourse, where the things understood challenge our penchant to go on to speak about them in our settled idioms, the way of life becomes decisive. On the model suggested, one can easily satisfy himself that a manner of living consonant with the language he has taken up will feed back on that language to confirm him in its use. The evidence is to be found in the sensitivity with which one detects possible trains of thought and the keenness with which he tracks them down.

Yet in the religious arena, where discourse about God must break through settled habits and rules of inference, a new way of life may need to establish consistencies existentially which will then be embodied in discourse. This, I take it, is the burden of Augustine's complaint that he could not—until book 7, chapter 10—conceive of God as spirit. That is, he had no other language than the ordinary descriptive one, but to use it of God would turn Him into an object in the world. Yet the new language of origin or principle, which is adumbrated in book 7, chapter 15; certainly appears vacuous until one undertakes to live "entirely devoted to the search for truth" (6.11). And this way of living requires a complete turnabout—something which Augustine does not execute until the end of book 8, and whose consequences he continues to plumb in the life which follows that moment of conversion. I am suggesting that Augustine not only improved upon a simple insight model for understanding, but also provided us with a pattern for religious understanding which will be of considerable help in determining precisely how one establishes criteria for religious discourse. If language entails and is entailed by a way of life in the manner in which Augustine demands that it be, then some revolutionary consequences are in store for contemporary analytic philosophy of religion. And the further fact that these consequences can be illustrated on the model of language and language use suggests that this new breakthrough is not a simple evocation of "experience" but rather contains the seeds of a disciplined inquiry into criteria.

3. Understanding or Explanation?

The observations about a new epistemological model have been gleaned from a critical, reflective reading of Augustine. They are clearly exhibited in the *Confessions,* but nowhere argued to. Their warrant, as the choice of style indicates, is not a further set of statements, but Augustine's own life. Yet that life itself has recently come under a type of scrutiny which challenges the presumed authority of sainthood. In the terms of the challenge, what Augustine hailed as insight simply gives testimony to a conditioned mode of response, for the heart of the matter lies in a struggle between Augustine and Monica.[9] What he reports as a conversion is a surrender, and what looks like discipline following upon insight is rather a behavior pattern confirming his dependency.

Like any explanatory framework, this one pretends to completeness. And Augustine is especially vulnerable. First, because he has made himself so: the warrant for what he says is what he has become, the great deed God has made of him and which he speaks. Beyond this fact, however, he simply is vulnerable to psychoanalytic probings: There is much evidence to support a "surrender to Monica" reading. The brilliant account of the painful turmoil which issued in the release of his conversion—"it was as though the light of confidence flooded into my heart"—culminates with:

> Then we went in and told my mother, who was overjoyed. And when we went on to describe how it had all happened, she was jubilant with triumph and glorified you, *who are powerful enough, and more than powerful enough, to carry out your purpose beyond all our hopes and dreams.* For she saw that you had granted her far more than she used to ask in her tearful prayers and plaintive lamentations. You converted me to yourself, so that I no longer desired a wife or placed any hope in this world but stood firmly upon the rule of faith, where you had shown me to her in a dream so many years before. And you *turned her sadness into rejoicing,* into joy far fuller than her dearest wish, far sweeter and more chaste than any she had hoped to find in children begotten of my flesh. [7.12]

This passage placed where it is reveals already a great deal. But taken together with the description of the mystical experience he shares with Monica at Ostia (9.10), and reinforced by his own perception of steady indulgence countered by repeated blows for freedom, the possibility that Augustine could have acted other than he did grows more and more remote. He simply lost a long and violent tug-of-war, falling at last into the arms of Monica and of mother church. Think, for example, how little mention there is of Christ the mediator in the *Confessions,* and how prominent is the church.[10] And it will become even more prominent, as his ill-resolved oedipal tendencies appear refracted into doctrinal disputes with Donatus and Pelagius. The sufficiency of church and of God's grace is at issue in these instances, and Augustine responds by extolling man's dependency. In each case it is man who depends and whose glory lies in utter surrender.

One seldom knows what to do with "explanations" like

these; they prove (or disprove) so much. Yet it would prove perilous to reject them wholesale. Consider by contrast the following explanation offered for Augustine's frequent use of *fovere:*

Gods fostering care is something depicted in the medicinal image of the Omnipresent as "bathing or fomenting" either the wounds of Augustine's sinfulness or the spiritual eyes which need clearing so that he can come to "see." That medicinal care is often accompanied by therapeutic pain, giving it a paternal character. At other times, it takes a more maternal form. Then God is like the mother-bird already mentioned, beneath whose wings the chick finds both protection and nourishment to fledge it for mature flight, or like a mother or a nurse, feeding the believing "little one" from what Isaias terms the "breasts of His great consolation," or (in another meaning of the term) "caressing" and "fondling" him, patiently teaching him to walk, then run, along the road of the spiritual life.

But before maternal omnipresence can teach the soul to walk, it must bring it back from wandering; before the fallen soul can be strengthened to run and fly, it must be little enough to "confess" that until now it has been fleeing, running away from where it most profoundly wished to go. Augustine's mother for years had to watch her son pursue life's journey with presumptuous, grown-up confidence, his back to the Light, his eyes upon the empty realities that Light enlightened. She had to listen to him as, sick with sinfulness, he blamed his sores upon a primitive catastrophe for which he claimed to bear no guilt; the sufferings of mortal life he never ceased complaining of, not counting them as salutary, therapeutic chastisement for his own primordial sinful choice, but as the doing of a hostile "race of darkness." He was like a child, tired of her maternal attentions, running off impatiently to seek distraction with his playmates. Playmates, alas, can be cruel, their games can end in loss, frustration, scraped knees, and scalding tears. She could have told him that, but children never listen. Headstrong is the word for them.

But mothers know how to wait their moment. Knees scraped, eyes streaming, even the most headstrong child comes back again, wailing that life has cheated, deluded him, failed to live up to its deceptive promise. Back now he comes, content to climb upon her waiting lap; for one last protest he looks back upon the way on which he ventured forth so hopefully in the morning brightness. This is her moment: with tender maternal hand she caresses his fevered head, gently turns his eyes away from what had been the cause of his complaining, placed his head against her breast. Calmed, he sleeps, and wakes, and finds that all is well again.[11]

Fortunately, the issues need not be polarized about a rhapsodic outburst or a psychoanalytic reduction. On balance, the psychoanalytic scheme, no matter how crudely employed, offers a firmer grip for understanding. In fact, the greater one's psychological awareness in approaching the text, the more courageous will he find Augustine. Lesser men would never have attempted the task. The utter candor and relentless analysis with which Augustine executes it should give pause to a latter day analyst, however orthodox his persuasion. For the same candor and analytic power which provide material of fine enough grain and sharp enough focus to tempt reasonable psychologists into profering a diagnosis testify in their own behalf. A man so courageous and so perceptive, we are tempted to say, must do more than instantiate a psychological typology. There is no doubt, as we shall see, that psychological tools can sharpen our image of the man, but it is difficult to suppress the suspicion that working on the image present in the *Confessions* should help hone those very tools as well. An inquiry as reflective as Erikson's into Luther would seem to be called for; one which takes the opportunity to improve one's tools as well as to display them in use.[12] For as one writer remarks: "Augustine, like other men of unusual gifts, *used* his conflicts.[13]

What were those conflicts? How did he use them? How did they handicap him? Can we understand his writings any better if we can answer these questions? Would we

be any better equipped to ferret out systematic consequences, recognize them to be distortions and be able to
say why they were? The initial psychological inquires
available allow some tentative responses to each of these
questions, suggesting that more reflective and comprehensive investigation would prove immensely illuminating. But
before using the investigations we have, and to signal the
caution with which I shall employ them, a summary observation is in order. If, as intimated, Augustine's "conversion" is really (i.e., can be satisfactorily explained as) the
belated surrender of an indulged child to the indulging and
devouring mother, it should spell the end of the line—psychological death. Yet the movement itself is not only
experienced as a great release, but also triggers an outburst
of theological and cultural explorations of astounding fertility and creativity. (I am thinking not merely of the sheer
volume of work but notably of his treatise on the Trinity,
his discussions of teaching, or freedom and grace, as well as
his monumental essay in sociopolitical criticism, *The City
of God.*) The very terms of psychological analysis itself
warn against doctrinaire diagnosis in a case as challenging
as this.[14]

Autonomy versus Dependency. Certainly the most
comprehensive of the psychological studies is that of
Dittes, who proposes to link Augustine's account of his
own life together with his prevailing doctrinal positions. [15]
And this is, of course, what Augustine himself invites. Nor
is Augustine entitled to take issue with Dittes's summary
of his doctrine nor with Ditte's analysis of the manner in
which his life contributes to the positions he assumed in
matters of doctrine. For Dittes is proposing a depth-analy-
sis, which could well be utterly revelatory to the individual
concerned. But we are entitled to take issue, if we can,
with the manner in which Dittes employs his analytic
tools.

In summary, Dittes finds that Augustine conceives God
more as an impersonal force and power from which every-

thing emanates, rather than as a person in his own right. Furthermore, the church rather than Christ is mediator for Augustine. Freedom is characteristically resolved with a firm insistence on the unqualified authority and power of the creating God. A man's role is utterly and absolutely dependent upon the intentions of God. Hence the overall picture which Augustine leaves us of God and the world involves "the utter dependence of man on God, [and] his own virtual impotence and ineffectiveness before God." God, on the other hand, is characterized by "remoteness, aloofness, absoluteness, impersonality, and unapproachability—except in the abject humility of confession [before] this controlling God."[16]

One could certainly contest this summary account of Augustine's thought. It seems especially tied to a literal reading of the *Confessions,* wherein the very literary form of the piece is overlooked and hence undue weight given to the statements made therein. Augustine cannot be blamed for having recourse to the only conceptual framework available to him—Neoplatonism—but it is incumbent on his readers to detect the ways in which he puts this framework to use. Hence, for example, the only manner in which Augustine may have been able to "conceive God" would be in some formula of emanation, but the fact that the entire work is itself a prayer addressed in the first person to God would certainly modify the way in which we receive his explicit emanationist formulas.

What is more important to our considerations, however, is the manner in which Dittes "explains" this particular doctrinal complexion. That it takes the unique shape it does may be traced to a prolonged struggle for autonomy in the face of an overweening mother—a struggle which Augustine finally lost as he settled for dependency. [17] There are abundant clues in the *Confessions* which would lead us, as we have seen, to be sympathetic to this explanation. The indulgent mother who has transferred her own sexual longings from husband to favorite son may well so threaten him with her seductive and protective overtures that he will resolve (without even knowing it) never to let intimacy encroach upon his life. Hence the only plausible figure for God would be an utterly autonomous one. In fact, Augustine's bid for autonomy—a move so violent that it induced a nearly fatal illness (5.9)—was met by Monica's journeying herself to Milan. Hence the only practical solution for Augustine was to give in to that same overweening presence, forsaking autonomy for dependency.

Characteristically, this defeat would be unable to resolve the earlier fears of intimacy, and hence would have to be covered with a celibate life style. Furthermore, in anyone as passionately desirous of unity as Augustine, his own capitulation would inevitably lead him to extirpate striving after autonomy in others. Enter Augustine the champion of mother church against Manichee, Donatist, and Pelagian. Nor did Augustine have many scruples about pursuing a vigorous persecution of heresy and heretic, for the terms of his own capitulation had already led him to subordinate the goodness of God to his power.[18] Such would inevitably be the result of a surrender sacrificing both autonomy and any hope of intimacy.

Dittes's account is at once perceptive and persuasive. Yet it succeeds as well as it does by a customary mirror trick. One the one hand is a summary of Augustine's thought which prepares the way for the analysis, and on the other a disarmingly simplistic use of the categories, "autonomy" and "dependency," as though they were polar opposites. As for the summary of his theology, I have already mentioned the way in which Dittes overlooks how utterly personal are the *Confessions* as a work. With regard to the emphasis on church he sees as against Jesus, one could reasonably argue that Dittes's expectations are themselves peculiarly Protestant. The *Confessions* more plausibly represent an implicit Christology where Jesus' life in His Church was the experienced reality. What distinguished the Christian would not then be his "relation to Jesus" but rather his new-found access to God as father in the community of brothers which is Christ. Certainly Augustine's

Commentary on the Psalms is replete with this form of implicit Christology.

But more important for our purposes is the manner in which Augustine's inner conflict is represented as a tug-of-war between two opposing forces—autonomy and dependency. On this scheme, the end of the eighth book would prove decisive: Augustine surrenders to his mother. Yet we have already seen that this simple solution runs counter to the obvious creativity of Augustine's subsequent life. Drawn up short by this fact, we are tempted to ask whether autonomy and dependency are really that simply opposed one to another. Can it not be argued that the genuinely autonomous person is precisely the one who has come to accept the basic parameters of his life? Does not the person who acknowledges his dependency stand more of a chance for genuine autonomy and creativity? In Augustine's own case must we not modify Dittes's scheme with a time vector, so that Augustine gradually rehearses an unentailed autonomy until he can sustain accepting a deeper dependency, and so find his way through to the autonomy which is his? Would not an interpretation like this be closer to the facts of the case as well as more faithful to the inner dynamics of autonomy and dependency?

Wholeness. Yet if Dittes does not in the end offer an explanation, he does bring a good deal of illumination. His observations about Augustine's childhood correlate carefully with those of Woollcott, Bakan, and Kligerman: Augustine was definitely an indulged child. Here we have a useful clue to his formulation of the freedom question: *Homo non liber est nisi liberatus.* For the indulged child never senses himself to be free; with good reason he is ever worried about indulging himself. One thinks immediately of the latter portion of book 10, where Augustine recounts his present state and reproaches himself for following the inclination of his own appetites. Woollcott calls attention to Augustine's narcissism, and notes his inability to "integrate his own masculine strivings."[19] Bakan, distinctly more critical, takes up the theme of reproach, and links it with an unentailed narcissistic ego which is itself alienated from existence, "and which leads Augustine to build an image of God essentially alienated from existence—a God whose primary activity is reproach."[20] All this leads Augustine to overrate a simple tree-stripping episode, attach himself to the church as mother, live a life compulsively reacting against sexuality, and finally be overtaken by a "Jesus-complex."[21] For Bakan, his major sin is to undo the work of God.

What strikes the reader about Bakan's analysis is the utter confidence with which it is uttered. It is quite obvious that Bakan brings to the work a set of definite and differing religious views which make it difficult for him to enter into Augustine's views with sympathy. The best clue to this insensitivity is the way in which he misses the pear-tree episode, where Augustine is relating a paradigm case of senseless activity. Woollcott, whose reading is far more sensitive, himself completely misreads the crucial passage where Monica (presumably) sends Augustine's mistress home. Woollcott has it that he "sent his mistress packing without remorse."[22] But the text reads:

> The woman with whom I had been living was torn away from my side as an obstacle to my marriage and this was a blow which crushed my heart to bleeding, because I loved her dearly. . . . Furthermore the wound which I had received when my first mistress was wrenched away showed no signs of healing. At first the pain was sharp and searing, but then the wound began to fester, and though the pain was duller there was all the less hope of a cure. [6.15]

In each case there is evidence that those features of the *Confessions* which cater to the respective theories received more attention than less palatable passages.

Augustine's Self-Reproach . . . Nothing seems more obvious to a modern reader of the *Confessions* than the author's inveterate tendency to reproach himself from infanthood on. Yet, interestingly enough, this observation seems compatible with Pruyser's remarking "the relative absence of self-directed aggression" and "a peculiar absence of true remorse."[23] In fact, these shrewd observations of Pruyser help to explain how Augustine could continue in his attitude of self-reproach in the face of God's affirming mercy toward him. One feels that the grace of God which Augustine celebrates so generously should in ten years have worked a greater self-acceptance than the continued tone of self-accusation betrayed in the *Confessions*. Yet this tone would be more understandable were Augustine constitutionally unable really to accuse himself. And this Pruyser suggests is the case: "Indeed, very little guilt feeling is expressed directly."[24] Is it that Augustine tended to view himself in his past (and present) activities rather than simply acknowledge. That was/is *me*? Were he so unable to present himself available for forgiveness, continued self-reproach in the face of forgiveness believed would be that much more understandable.

Pruyser's reading would also account for the emphasis Augustine places on the necessarily complementary prayers: "Master me, God!" and "Thank you for allowing me to live with your life and to love with your love." In response to Dittes's surrender theory, I would insist that Augustine's theology of grace is compatible with either or both of these attitudes, although we find the first more prominent in his writings, especially in the *Confessions*. There is further evidence to show that this incapacity to acknowledge his own sinfulness quite simply and directly is linked with a lingering unwillingness to surrender, still present at the time of writing the *Confessions*. I suggest this interpretation in view of the obvious stoic ideal of self-control operating as he assesses his present state in book 10. Predilection for such an ideal would certainly characterize the indulgent child, precisely because self-control suffered such frequent defeats. To speak in this way, of course, demands a more subtle use of "surrender" than

Dittes's simple opposition with "autonomy." Yet the ability to use "surrender" in this fashion is another argument for a more relative employment of that opposition.

4. Beyond Explanations to Interpretation

It should be clear by now that a simple application of orthodox psychoanalytic doctrine does not prove very useful in understanding Augustine. However, some degree of illumination has certainly been offered by the preliminary attempts available to us. By illuminating the sources and shape of his personal conflicts, this style of investigation allows a sensitive reader to remark how Augustine managed to put those conflicts to use, as well as how they continued to handicap him. A similarly sensitive reader with theological training will be able to recognize in many cases how these conflicts may have introduced specific distortions into the manner of formulating and illustrating major themes in Christian theology. Precisely because the theologian, and above all this theologian, is so intimately involved in his work, studies of this sort seem a hermeneutic necessity.

On the other hand, the main intent of his major theological breakthroughs is hardly deflected. I am thinking particularly of his staunch anti-Pelagian position and its crucial role in the history of doctrine. For one can grasp the heart of this series of affirmations announcing the primacy and sufficiency of God's grace in a form which remains quite neutral to the manner in which we conceive God: that the standards of human excellence no longer conform to a pattern which we might conceive, but rather are themselves transformed to the point where no patterns are left (see *Confessions*, 13.22).

Nor need we be worried that Augustine "describes a mystical ecstatic experience he shares with his mother . . . in a rhythm, flow and imagery (which) strike the reader as passionately orgastic."[25] For what other lan-

guage can a human being employ? Furthermore, our critical reading of the psychological critics confirms that a
religious and psychological viewpoint are hardly incom-
patible, if such confirmation were necessary. (One would
have thought that viewpoint-language offers itself precisely
to suggest compatibility, but one of the writers in the
symposium finds it "evident that Augustine's life cannot
be viewed through both perspectives simultaneously without contradiction."[26] The discussion here is a response in
content as well as in form to such a contention.) Yet we
were able to acknowledge that the two viewpoints, religious and psychological, were compatible specifically by
showing how psychological explanations are most useful
when clipped of their endemic pretentions to completeness.

In fact, the central methodological principle of Augustine's *Confessions* has proven useful in assessing assessments of it. That is, if we recall that we should bemisled in
our quest for understanding were we simply to rely on our
efforts to identify the conceptual frameworks he is employing by tracing down the major influences upon his
thought. Beyond this historical sophistication we are asked
to become more and more conscious of the manner in
which he put the frameworks which he had to use. The
simplest way to awaken this consciousness is to become
more responsible in employing the interpretative frameworks which we possess. The inspiration comes from Augustine; we can only hope to bring our human quest for
understanding to term by engaging our all-too-human
selves upon it. This means trusting the insights we are given
and not fearing to take up a form of life consonant with
the formulation we give those insights. Living consistently
with the consequences of thse words made flesh will invite
and guide whatever correction becomes necessary.

In matters religious, understanding demands that we
attempt to live what we are trying to speak. The demand is
a logical one, and is borne in upon anyone the moment he
realizes that man has no way of speaking straightforwardly

and coherently of God. Augustine's conscious manner of constructing the *Confessions* displays this demand of logic and provides some practical hints how to carry it out. Hence in its role as a work of edification the *Confessions* succeeds in laying out an epistemology as well. The task of this essay has been to remove some of the obstacles that may have prevented us from laying hold of what Augustine is doing. Some of the difficulties arise from ourselves; some reflect flaws in his execution of the project.

And since the project extends through word to flesh, locating certain obstacles to understanding amounts to identifying weaknesses in Augustine himself.[27] Need we remind ourselves that we are in a position to make this identification precisely in the measure that Augustine has proven faithful to his own epistemological demands? Yet whether we are reminded or not, these results in fact enhance the *Confessions* as a hymn of thanksgiving and praise to the Creator who revealed himself in Jesus: "I have cheerfully made up my mind to be proud of my weaknesses, because they mean a deeper experience of the power of Christ" (2 Cor. 12:9). Although Augustine does not seem to be able to bring himself to speak these words with the alacrity of a Paul, he acknowledges their force in undertaking the *Confessions* and displays that force in executing them. By a rigorous application of his own epistemology, we should have expected the *Confessions* to show even more than they are able to say.

NOTES

1. Among the more useful works I have found are Pierre Courcele's *Recherches sur les confessions de S. Agustine* (Paris: Boccard, 1950) and *Les confessions dans la tradition litteraire* (Paris: Etudes Augustiniennes, 1963). The most valuable single introduction to the life and work of Augustine I have found is that of Peter Brown, *Augustine of Hippo* (Berkeley: University of California Press, 1968). Brown's fidelity to his subject and his hermeneutic

sophistication encouraged me to believe that it is possible to read and to learn from Augustine. The text of the *Confessions* upon which I have relied is that translated by R. S. Pine-Coffin (Baltimore: Penguin Books, 1961), where the breakdown is offered into books and chapters. Hence, 1.13 signifies book I, chapter 13.

2. "If language is to be a means of communication there must be agreement not only in definitions but also (queer as this may sound) in judgments. This seems to abolish logic, but does not do so" (Ludwig Wittgenstein, *Philosophical Investigations* [New York: Macmillan Co., 1953], paragraph 242).

3. For example, Robert J. O'Connell writes, "The solution here proposed will both test and confirm previous suggestions that the Plotinian sources active in the Saint's earlier works are still exerting their influence in the *Confessions*, and that, in their light, the sense and structural unity of the work is laid bare" (*St. Augustine's Confessions: The Odyssey of Soul* [Cambridge, Mass.: Belknap Press, 1969], p. 5)

4. For the place of Augustine's autobiography in the history of autobiography see Georg Misch, *A History of Autobiography in Antiquity* (London: Routledge & Kegan Paul, 1950), 1:17; 2:625 ff., 681 ff. Also Roy Pascal, *Design and Truth in Autobiography* (Cambridge, Mass.: Harvard University Press, 1960), pp. 21 ff. I am indebted to John S. Dunne (see n. 6) for these references.

5. See J. P. Audet, "La 'benediction' juive et 'l'eucharistie' chretienne," *Revue Biblique* 65 (1958): 371-99.

6. John S. Dunne, *A Search for God in Time and Memory* (New York: Macmillan Co., 1969).

7. One is reminded of Jung's observations about method in *Aion;* "Once metaphysical ideas have lost their capacity to recall and evoke the original experience they have not only become useless but prove to be actual impediments on the road to wider developments. . . .If metaphysical ideas no longer have such a fascinating effect as before, this is certainly not due to any lack of primitivity in the European psyche, but simply and solely to the fact that the erstwhile symbols no longer express what is now welling up from the unconscious" (*Collected Works* [New York: Pantheon, 1959], 9, pt. 2:34, 35).

8. Albert Outler, *Augustine: Confessions and Enchiridion*, Library of Christian Classics (London: SCM Press, 1955), 7:19-20.

9. The principal references are to a symposium under the direction of Paul Pruyser appearing in the *Journal for the Scientific Study of Religion*, vol. 5 (1965-1966), and an earlier article by Charles Kligerman, "A Psychoanalytic Study of the *Confessions* of Saint Augustine," *Journal of the American Psychoanalytic Association* 5 (1957): 469-84.

10. James Dittes, "Continuities between the Life and Thought of

Augustine," *Journal for the Scientific Study of Religion* 5 (1965):132; David Bakan, "Some Thoughts on Reading Augustine's *Confessions*," ibid., p. 151.

11. O'Connell, pp. 35-36.

12. Erik Erikson, *Young Man Luther* (New York: W. W. Norton & Co., 1956).

13. Philip Woollcott, Jr., "Some Considerations of Creativity and Religious Experience in St. Augustine of Hippo," *Journal for the Scientific Study of Religion* 5 (1966): 282.

14. Walter Houston Clark, "Depth and Rationality in Augustine's Confessions," *Journal for the Scientific Study of Religion* 5 (1965): 145.

15. Dittes.

16. Ibid., p. 133.

17. Ibid., p. 136.

18. Ibid., p. 138-39.

19. Woollcott, pp. 276-77.

20. Bakan, pp. 149-50.

21. Ibid., pp. 150-52.

22. Woolcott, p. 278.

23. Paul Pruyser, "Psychological Exmination: Augustine," *Journal for the Scientific Study of Religion* 5 (1965-66): 288-89.

24. Ibid., p. 288.

25. Kligerman, p. 483.

26. Joseph Havens, "Notes on Augustine's *Confessions*," *Journal for the Scientific Study of Religion* 5 (1965-66): 143.

27. Especially relevant here are the latter chapters of Brown's study, as Augustine exercises more and more authority as bishop, against a background of crumbling Roman authority.

PART TWO

Formulating Transcendence

2: ANSELM
Formulating the Quest for Understanding

Saint Anselm took up brick-making without straw. This comment of a theologian well versed in the philosophical sophistication of the thirteenth century aptly illustrates Anselm's pioneering role in the development of a systematic unravelling of religious issues. His formal education at the monastery of Bec was focussed on logical grammar under the wary eye of Lanfranc. The authorities referred to, so far as we can tell, include the Latin versions of Aristotle's *Categoriae* and *De Interpretatione,* along with Boethius' commentaries. The *Peri Hermenias* of Apuleius, Isidor's *Etymologiae,* the grammatical works of Priscian and Donatus as well as Cassiodorius' *Institutiones* were in circulation during Anselm's formative period.[1] Anselm himself wrote a work on dialectic entitled *De Grammatico*—a work which foreshadowed medieval treatises on philosophical grammar.[2] His early education evidently provided him with background in the Latin authors, and his monastic studies clearly opened to him the entire corpus of Augustine. Yet though his teacher was celebrated, the logical sources were few, so that we cannot help but see

him as making a little go a long way. He was writing,
furthermore, before the development of the cathedral
schools and a full century before the growth of university
culture. The prevailing monastic output of his time was
what we might call "devotional literature," and Anselm
wrote his share of that.

Even though he was later prevailed upon to become
Archbishop of Canterbury in the wake of his teacher
Lanfranc, Anselm's place was the monastery. The monastic
way of life forms the context for his living and his thinking. Dialectic, then, is a tool which he puts to careful use
that it might further the basic aim of his own life: the
strengthening and bolstering of that personal orientation
toward God, the world, and fellowmen called *faith*. A
monastery considered itself to be a microcosm of the
world as it tried to respond to the good news of God's
coming in Christ. In this world different people were
entrusted with different roles. Those gifted with more
refined intellects placed these talents at the service of the
Gospel. It is in this spirit that Anselm undertook to study
dialectic and would put it to use to enhance their shared
understanding of a common religious heritage. Hence the
full title of his second theological work: *Faith in Quest of
Understanding*.

There is no hint in his writing of a narrow concern with
orthodoxy, but rather of amplifying our human capacities
to better possess a heritage of riches. As he describes his
first short tract (the *Monologion*): "an example of meditation on the meaning of faith from the point of view of one
seeking, through silent reasoning within himself, things he
knows not."[3] The *Proslogion* moves within the same perspective yet relies more explicitly upon dialectic: "reflecting that this (the *Monologion*) was made up of a connected
chain of many arguments, I began to wonder if perhaps it
might be possible to find one single argument that for its
proof required no other save itself, and that by itself
would suffice to prove that God really exists, that he is the
supreme good needing no other and it is he whom all

things have need of for their being and well-being, and also to prove whatever we believe about the divine being" (*Proemium*, 103).

The focus of this intent is clearly on "one single argument." It is this fascination with formulae which we recognize at once to be the strength as well as the potential weakness of one formed in logic. The program presages both the glory and the downfall of what was to become the scholastic era. Yet there is no way to reflect responsibly upon the role of language in theological understanding than to offer a close analysis of one who tries to put his logical talents to use in expounding a common deposit of faith. This study of Anselm's *Proslogion* is taken up with that modest aim in view: to let us in on the process whereby a believer employed a few well-honed logical tools to enhance a common religious understanding.

The advantage of such a contextual reflection on Anselm will be to place his own fascination with dialectic into the monastic context from which it emanates. This will allow us to examine the more important logical moves as he *uses* them, and so examine a specifically theological use of dialectic.

The focus of this study will be to assess the import of a distinction which Anselm both makes and unmakes between "thinking a thing" by "thinking the word signifying it" or by "understanding the very object which the thing is" (IV, 121). Theologians are prone to remark about the limitations of language, but these remarks are more respected the more careful and impressed a man is with the necessity for formulae. So our discussion of this unstable distinction will involve taking a position on the role of the master formula: "a being than which nothing greater can be conceived," attempting a fresh look at "necessary existence," and finally assessing Anselm's use of dialectic as presaging what some have come to call a "transcendental method" in ontological reflection.

But before taking up these issues directly, some general hermeneutical remarks about the nature of this work are in

order, lest we allow ourselves to be so bewitched by
formulae that we overlook the way in which Anselm's
argument moves and is guided by his original intent. The
intent, we recall, was originally supplied by the monastic
context of his own life.

1.1 A Context for Interpretation

The observations in this preliminary section are designed
to engage us in that particular form of self-consciousness
which helps us to position ourselves with respect to the
eleventh-century Anselm. It is a delicate exercise, designed
finally to return one to himself with a better understanding of his own relative historical position. Although I shall
bolster my remarks with arguments where that seems necessary, they must on the whole display their accuracy to a
reader more or less accustomed to this exercise.

It is convenient to begin by asking oneself what the
work is and what it is not intended to be. I shall contend
that it is better not construed as a *proof* but rather as an
argument. The method employed, while not that of a
"mere analysis," can be construed as a rudimentary form
of what some prefer to call a "transcendental analysis":
exposing the conditions for understanding. The early chapters of the work are better not construed as a *proof* simply
because our usage tends to reserve this term for what the
medievals more properly called *demonstrations.* We speak
of proofs normally in those domains where there can be no
gap between proving a point and convincing someone of it.
"Prove" carries for us the expectations which the medievals associated with *demonstrare* rather than with their
more generic *probare*. That is, it functions in such a way
that it would be redundant to prove that p is q and then to
have to go on to prove *to* someone that p is q.

That a proof might work yet not be convincing would
be a strange outcome, giving the expectations we attach to
the term. Appropriately enough, Anselm does not use
demonstrare to announce his intent, but rather two dis-

tinctly weaker expressions: *ad probandum* and *ad astruen-dum*.[4] This is not to claim that Anselm's hold on reason was looser than we would be in the habit of demanding. On the contrary, he placed rigorous requirements on formulation and, if anything, expected greater results from rational inquiry into matters of faith than we would normally be prepared to hope for. It is not the stringency so much as the *use* of reason which requires an explicit effort of interpretation on our part. This observation may be clarified by reminding ourselves that Anselm expressly offered his formula as an argument. He labored over the formulation since grasping the movement from premise to conclusion turns on the capacity of a precise formula to render explicit what one hitherto understood only implicitly. The formula plays the role of exhibiting what was latent in one's understanding.

We can get another angle on the role Anselm reserves for reason if we look more closely at his method. I suggested that we ought not to think of him as performing a "mere analysis," but should rather expect something different, something more akin to a "transcendental analysis." These remarks were suggested by Charlesworth's commentary, which argues that Saint Anselm did not think of what he was doing "as a simple conceptual analysis of the notion 'that than which nothing greater can be thought' or 'that which necessary exists,' but rather as a genuine inference or argument in which [each premise] is an indispensable element" (92). What Charlesworth means by a "genuine inference" is not simply as well-formed concatenation of indispensable premises, but rather one *through* which we are brought to understand, as a result of the proof, what we were unable to see before (95).

A genuine inference, then, leads us to a new way of grasping a formula already understood in another sense. I have dubbed this process a "transcendental" analysis, in an accommodation of Kant's use of that term. For if meaning is a function of context, then the genuine inference succeeds in making one aware of what was presupposed to his previous understanding. The process of bringing to light conditions or presuppositions for understanding is one which Kant termed "transcendental." What Anselm claims to do through the argument carried by his "single formula" is to make us aware of what is presupposed to a proper understanding of God.

It is, I realize, somewhat tendentious to oppose these two forms of analysis, for analysis has always pretended to be a method whereby one exposes what we *really* understand by a particular expression. Analysis has always purported to make explicit what was implicit, yet the very vagueness inherent in our understanding of *that* process feeds the opposition I have drawn. In fact, the so-called "paradox of analysis" arises from the very same source: Does the analysis of a proposition merely lay it out or does it provide us with more than the original proposition? If it provides us with *more*, how can it also be said to supply the meaning of *that* proposition?

By way of concluding these initial and inescapably vague remarks, we might think of Anselm's efforts as failing to supply what we would call a *proof* and yet achieving that understanding for which he aimed. Or we could think of him providing a singular if rudimentary example of that kind of analysis which moderns have come to associate with metaphysical or "transcendental" analysis: one designed to lead the inquirer beyond the limits of his prior understanding by eliciting a keen awareness of its presuppositions.

It is these general considerations which have led me to characterize the *Proslogion* as an exercise. It means to discipline our minds in that form of analysis appropriate to thinking about what transcends the mind. This reading will save us from assimilating Anselm's concerns too quickly to those of an age of rationalism, which limited itself to examining proofs for the existence of God. On Anselm's own account, as reported by Eadmer: "it came into his mind to try to prove [*probari*] by one single and short argument the things which are believed and preached

about God, that he is eternal, unchangeable, omnip-
otent . . . and so on; and to show how all these qualities
are united in him."[5] If what Anselm does is ontological,
what he offers is not so much a proof as an argument, and
an argument designed to exercise us in the skill of thinking
responsibly about the one who poses the very conditions
for our thought.

1.2. Arguing for This Interpretation

These general hermeneutical remarks were designed to
keep us from asking Anselm to do something other than
what he himself intended to. Yet one could execute a
maneuver of this sort in so sophisticated a fashion as to
end up misleading himself. In speaking of Anselm's
Proslogion as an exercise I could be accused of blunting his
purpose. Did he not want to achieve something quite
definite? Show something quite specific, namely that
"God really exists, that he is the supreme good needing no
other and is he whom all things have need of for their
being and well-being?" Furthermore, has not most of the
critical literature around the early chapters of the
Proslogion followed that intent, and properly assessed the
success or failure of Anselm's primary aim? Of course,
achieving something like this involves skills, so that the
entire essay is also an exercise in those philosophic skills
Anselm considered requisite for theology. But all that is
quite secondary. A piano sonata also involves finger exercise, but critics assess the sonata as a musical composition,
not its capacity to give the pianist a workout.

My response to this objection is at once philosophical
and historical. It regards the kind of work Anselm was
engaged in as well as his manner of engaging in it. I have
suggested that the *Proslogion* exhibits a reflective philosophical analysis of a religious question. What is true of
philosophical arguments in general is notably true here: we
cannot succeed in showing anything to anyone lacking the

skills to follow the process of argumentation. To have arrived at a conclusion—to have tethered it down with reasons—is to be able to do so. Hence to assess whether Anselm is successful in achieving what he tried to do does not come to assessing whether his conclusion is true, but rather whether the process which he outlines leads inescapably to the conclusion which he draws. That is, we can only fault him in the use of logical skills or in the use of those more generic critical skills which lead us to choose one formulation in favor of another.

There may be other and even better ways of tethering down the conclusion in question, but what is of interest to the critics is the manner in which the author tries to tether it. For it is this manner which exhibits and exercises certain reaches of human reason, and these reaches may be useful in other researches as well. Hence a philosophic appraisal of an argument is inevitably itself an exercise in argumentation.

One might retort that these arguments for this way of reading Anselm simply show that I have allowed my interpretation of this text to be skewed by paying too much attention to the concerns of philosophic critics. In the case of Anselm, however, the argument for considering his work to be an exercise rests on more solid grounds. For Anselm rational argument is well circumscribed within the context of gratitude and praise to God. Within the monastic environs the intellectual life is always more of a means than an end, better considered an exercise than a profession. Anselm could never propose his dialectical procedure as the only way to arrive at the conclusion which he proposes. The final chapters of the *Proslogion* are replete with references to an experience of God which far transcends anything to which his arguments might lead us.[6] Nonetheless, there remains a valid role for dialectic, precisely because argument can tether down a conclusion in a way no other process can, including that of divine illumination. Assenting to the conclusion of an argument involves a different sort of assent than that elicited by revelation. Understanding, then, adds something precious to one's faith, precisely by making explicit what previously lay inchoate.

These considerations show us how odd it is to ask whether "mere dialectic" can succeed in establishing that God exists. For "mere dialectic" would certainly prove to be a starvation diet. At any rate, an attempt to use "mere dialectic" to tether down such a conclusion would be incomprehensible to Anselm, who everywhere presupposes a rich context of life, love, and fidelity to reality seen and unseen.[7] The real question for Anselm is rather: How can rational argument help us to respond to those realities in a genuine fashion? It is precisely to evoke the context which Anselm's monastic life gave to his use of logic, as well as to make a philosophic point about the interrelation of results and skills in any analysis, that I style this work as an exercise in theological understanding. The promise of the exercise is to give fresh access to that faith-orientation which one already professes by providing him with a new kind of hold upon those same realities. One of the results of this essay should be to put us in a position to assess that promise, and so Anselm's exercise becomes another opportunity for us to study the role of language and formulation in philosophical theology.

1.3. Plan of the Essay

By way of showing how skill and content interpenetrate I wish to concentrate on three issues germane to Anselm's argument which demand greater precision if they are to function as he wishes them to. This issues open up key areas in philosophical theology and serve as object lessons of the need for logical and semantic discipline in that area of discourse. In this way Anselm's exercise serves its purpose by becoming an exercise for us. The key issue, as I have mentioned, regards the viability of Anselm's distinction between understanding a thing and thinking its formula. In the process of examining this distinction, about which Anselm is himself of two minds, we shall consider the role of the master formula: "a-being-than-which-nothing-greater-can-be-conceived," take a fresh look at "necessary existence," and assess Anselm's use of dialectic as offering a "transcendental" method for ontological reflection.

I am heavily indebted to Max Charlesworth and to Desmond Henry for their critical studies on Anselm, as well as to R. W. Southern's studies on Anselm's life and work.[8] Since this essay proposes to be as much one of interpretation as of criticism, I have found these authors most helpful. One of course cannot fail to profit from careful philosophical discussion of the notions Anselm raises. But rather than use Anselm's argument as a springboard myself, I should rather help others to grasp it as it stands: an early example of respect for the authority as well as the limitations of reason which came to characterize so much of medieval intellectual life. And so recovering Anselm, we may be richer not simply in raw skills but in ways of putting them to use which cannot really be separated from the skills themselves.

2. The Role of Argument

The movement of Anselm's argument is direct and perspicuous. His prolonged and despairing search for a succinct formulation was justly rewarded.[9] Painstaking formulation brings its own reward: to pose the issues this clearly is to allow others to take issue with what one has said, and so *ipso facto* to advance the question. Presuppositions of which one has been quite innocent can be brought to light more effectively the better his formulation allows them to show through. The formula, then, is the thing with which to catch one's own conscience by engaging the reader's critical wit. There is a trick to finding a formula sufficiently perspicuous, but formulae themselves cannot be written off as tricks—if only because the tricks in them will soon out, as a reward for precise formulation.

Anyone familiar with biblical belief and worship—even if he has foolishly resisted commiting himself to it—will recognize the expression: "that-than-which-nothing-greater-could-be-thought" (*aliquid quo nihil maius cogitari possit*) to be a shorthand for "God." "Greater" (*maius*) is pregnant with the praises of the psalms, and the absolute sway over nature and over history is insured by the unyielding modal: "nothing . . . could" (*nihil . . . possit*). Once we accept the formula in the spirit in which it is intended—a distillation of the biblical rendering of divinity—the formula will do the rest. Its awkward case is designed to set up an airtight argument form to match the modal character of the premises: a *reduction ad absurdum*.

To accept the formula as a shorthand for the biblical God is to understand it, and whatever is understood can be said to be in the intellect. But it is certainly greater to be in reality than to be in the intellect. *That*, then, than-which-nothing-greater-can-be-conceived must be in reality. The formal *reductio*: assume it is in the mind but not in reality; then a *greater* can be thought, namely what is both in the mind and in reality. But this assertion generates a contradiction: that   than-which-nothing-greater-can-be-thought (assumed to be *in mente* but not *in re*) is thereby something   a-greater-than-which-can-be-thought.   So   we must deny our assumption, and the only way open to do so is to affirm: that-than-which-nothing-greater-can-be-conceived must be in the mind *and* be in reality.

To lay out the argument is to invite hostility; we cannot help but feel taken. There is an irreducible vagueness in the freewheeling way Anselm uses "greater" which cannot help but trouble us. But it is an ambiguity, latent not in the formula but in the way it is used, which will prove fatal to employing it in a *reductio*.

I shall focus on the ambiguity since it is the more incisive of the two complaints. Curiously enough, Anselm locates the ambiguity when he acknowledges that it is one thing to think (about) a thing by thinking its formula and another to understand the thing itself (IV, 121). But such a distinction is itself susceptible of so many interpretations that it would be sanguine to speak of using it to locate anything. What this essay proposes to contribute is a survey of possible senses for that distinction as Anselm employed it, and to show how one way of using it can succeed in exposing an ambiguity fatal to his argument.

Before moving to those considerations, however, it will help if we can trace movement of Anselm's thought from the final sentence of chapter two, which completes the argument, to the introduction of this distinction in chapter four. Having concluded that whatever can be described as that-than-which-nothing-greater-can-be-thought must be affirmed to be not only *in intellectu* but also *in re*, Anselm devotes the next chapter to its manner of being: "It so truly *is* that it cannot be thought not to be" (III, 118). This feature also is derived from the formula, but the result is offered, not to supplement the existence argument, but to make explicit *what* the formula has managed to turn up. The use of *cogitari* throughout this chapter confirms that we are being instructed how to *think* about this being.[10]

Furthermore, everything except God can be thought not to be, so this feature establishes the uniqueness: "and you, Lord our God, are this being." So chapter three completes the movement initiated in chapter two by deriving the most essential feature of the being there shown to exist, and by uniquely identifying it with God. All this is accomplished, furthermore, through a single formula (*id quo nihil maius cogitari potest*). Initially adopted as a shorthand, it has been used to make manifest what otherwise might not have appeared, and can now be replaced by the original expression: God.

Anselm has accomplished the first and critical stage of his announced program: to use human reason to help us understand what we believe. Having shown that God exists, that he must exist, and that such a one is unique, the rest of the attributes will follow as a matter of course. [11] Whatever difficulties lie ahead in the prosecution of his aim are bound to be local confusions which he can unravel as they come up.

3. A Central Yet Ill-Formulated Distinction

One difficulty arises immediately, however, as a result of the clarifications of chapter three. How could one who foolishly refused to respond to God ever manage to "say in his heart" that there was no God when God is such that he cannot ever be thought not to be? Certainly "to say in one's heart" is nothing but a circumlocution for "to think." How then can one be said to think what cannot be thought?

Whatever motivated Anselm to focus on this difficulty, it raises issues reaching far beyond biblical interpretation. Anselm is forced to meet it by introducing the distinction which can be understood in one way to jeopardize his generic program and used in another to lay bare a flaw fatal to his finely tempered argument. "There is not only one sense in which something is 'said in one's heart' or thought. For in one sense a thing is thought (*cogitatur*) when the word signifying it is thought (*cogitatur*); in another sense when the very object which the thing is, is understood (*intelligitur*)" (IV, 120-21). [12] One might say in his heart that there was no God in the sense of using the expression, God, to think with, but certainly not if he understood what he was thinking. "No one, indeed, understanding what God is can think that God does not exist ... [for] whoever really understands this understands clearly that this same being so exists that not even in thought can it not exist. Thus whoever understands (*intelligit*) that God exists in such a way cannot think of him as not existing" (IV, 121). [13]

The solution renders appropriate judgment on the biblical fool: he can say what he says only because he doesn't know what he is talking about. But the price may be excessively high. How can Anselm, dedicated as he is to exhibiting the indispensable role of precise formulation, drive such a wedge between "thinking the expression which signifies the thing (*vox eam significans*) and understanding the very thing itself (*id ipsum quod res est*)?" If he is invoking a facile opposition between a "merely verbal" and a "real" understanding, he is vulnerable on both counts. For his entire argument is carefully crafted to turn on a particular formula—a formula whose precise expression cost him considerable labor and disquietude.[14] And the formula is designed specifically to trip up the fool. All he has to do is to understand it: "but surely, when this same fool hears what I am speaking about, namely, 'something-than-which-nothing-greater-can-be-thought,'   he understands (*intelligit*) what he hears" (II, 117). And once he admits to understanding it, the formula itself will lead him to make the crucial affirmations about God.

If the fool's hold on the formula is "merely verbal," how can his subsequent affirmations be (really) about God? Anselm himself offers a new way of putting an old objection to the movement of his thought. Yet on the other hand we cannot demand that the fool grasp any more than the formula, for the fool cannot possibly understand the God it signifies. Anselm introduces the very distinction in question to clinch that point and so secure the biblical tradition: one who foolishly spurns God's invitation finds himself bereft of the first condition for knowing him. What is more, that same tradition so escalates the terms of "knowing God" that it is doubtful whether *anyone* could be said to "understand what God is." Any facile opposition between a "merely verbal" and a "real" understanding, then, would not only be unworthy of one trained so carefully in logical grammar as Anselm. It would also succeed in undermining his crucial argument as well as pitting him against a series of biblical and monastic statements about the inaccessible nature of God.

3.1. Import of the Distinction

What sense are we then to make of the distinction he introduces in chapter four? Did he just use it to get himself out of a hole? Apparently not, for it appears in slightly different forms elsewhere in the *Proslogion,* in his reply to Gaunilo, and is expressly treated in *De Grammatico.* Before surveying these other uses, it may be pertinent to note how critical an issue we are broaching here. On the one hand it seems facile and irresponsible to oppose thinking an expression to understanding a thing—and Anselm's remark about the fool's understanding what he hears shows how difficult it is to force a systematic difference between *cogitare* and *intelligere.* How else might we understand something than through what we say about it? However reluctant some may be to identify the knowable with what is expressible, no one would be happy about making the gap too wide between them.

On the other hand, *what* is it that we understand in properly understanding the expression which signifies the thing? Can we be said to understand the thing itself, or would it be better to keep categories distinct by saying that we understand *what* the expression says? This route leads to propositions, of course, or to meanings: we understand *what* the expression *means.* There are, however, quite sophisticated ways to handle this embarrassing question, and the medievals are wise to most of them. Desmond Henry's study shows that Anselm was possessed of a remarkable repertory of moves to deal with oblique and direct reference, and to avoid simply identifying "signify" with "standing for." His clarity about these moves exhibits a clear feel for the complexity of semantic categories.[15]

Looking at the *Proslogion,* however, Anselm seems to have been tripped up by that worrisome *what.* For it is *what* the fool understands that is in the mind and, when assumed to be only in the mind, shows itself to be in reality as well. If this *what* is the formula itself, then the proof resembles a sleight of hand, and if it is more, how much more? Here we have a preview of the way in which Anselm's distinction makes us wary of an impropriety in the formula which can prove fatal to the argument it was proposed to sustain.

3.2. Other Uses

I have fixed on the difference Anselm remarks between our thinking a signifying expression and our understanding the thing signified as a way of clarifying the movement of his argument. He offers this distinction after the fact to allow a fool room to say what an adept realizes makes no sense: that there *is* no God. Yet one obvious way of taking the distinction would undermine Anselm's entire program and threaten any proposal to lay out the world by paying careful attention to language and logic. Consequences so damaging render the obvious interpretation suspect (if not self-stultifying), so we must ask whether Anselm can lead us to a better reading. Fortunately he does, in responding to Gaunilo, who picks up the distinction himself and uses it in a familiar fashion. Anselm had already invoked something like it in chapter two as well. The similarities and differences will prove illustrative.

3.21. An Earlier Distinction

He says—just after remarking that even the fool would understand what he heard when someone articulated the formula—that what is understood is in the intellect even if it may not be understood to be. "For it is one thing for an object to exist in the mind, and another thing to understand that an object actually exists" (II, 117).[16] Translated back into terms of understanding, the distinction reads:

it is one thing to understand something and another to understand it to be.

This might be thought to be parallel to:

> it is one thing to think the expression signifying some-
> thing and another to understand the thing itself.

Gaunilo tends to assimilate the two, in wishing to reserve
intelligere for something which truly exists, as would any
Ockhamist who sought relief from ambiguity by identifying *sense* with *referent*. Then to understand something
would involve understanding it to be, and this could be
distinguished from a merely verbal grasp of the expression
used to denote it.

Without pursuing the ambiguities lurking along that
route we can simply note that Anselm does not take it. He
is careful elsewhere to distinguish sense from reference,
and here prefers to work with the unstable *what*, which
the fool understands in hearing the formula, though he
does not yet understand *it* to be. There would be only one
way, then, to harmonize the two distinctions as Anselm
uses them:

     thinking the expression signifying the thing

     understanding the thing itself = understanding something / understanding it to be

A "mere deliberation" could be contrasted with a more
existential treatment, but the link between them would lie
in understanding what one is speaking about. A highly
ambiguous linkage, to be sure, but we must feel it in a way
which Anselm could not. For his argument turns upon this
apparent point of contact.

3.22. Gaunilo's Use

Gaunilo invokes the distinction to suggest to Anselm a
more forceful way of making his point. It is not enough
for Anselm to insist in chapter three that "this supreme
being cannot be *thought* not to exist," for an assertion of
this sort affords no license at all to say that it actually

exists (since any unreal thing can be *thought*). "It would perhaps be better to say that it cannot be *understood* not to exist ... ; strictly speaking, unreal things cannot be *understood,* though certainly they can be thought of in the same way as the Fool thought that God does not exist" (G7, 165). Anselm declines the offer, of course, because it would collapse his analysis in chapter two to a tautology and lose the whole point of that chapter: to isolate the distinguishing characteristic of God. "For even if none of those things that exist can be *understood* not to exist (in Gaunilo's strict usage), all however can be *thought* as not existing, save that which exists to a supreme degree. ... Only that being ... cannot be thought as not existing" (R4, 177).

Furthermore, one cannot hope to sustain a difference between *cogitare* and *intelligere* so telling that he restricts "understanding" to what actually exists. Gaunilo himself says he would understand the story about the perfect island (G6, 165). And "if unreal things are, in a sense, understood ... , then I ought not to be criticized for having said that 'that-than-which-a-greater-cannot-be-thought' is understood and is in the mind, even before it was certain that it existed in reality itself" (R6, 183-85). Thinking, then, cannot but be a form of understanding, so the verbal difference will not sustain the distinction of chapter four. In fact, Anselm seems to have forgotten that distinction here, and is mindful only of the earlier one.

3.3. Anselm's Use

Anselm expressly adduces the distinction only twice: first to take Gaunilo to task for employing it so rigidly, and then to lay out the drift of his own argument. This time he follows his own advice and drops any attempt to force *cogitare* and *intelligere* into different roles. Quite incisively he describes his argument as moving one from understanding the formula through a grasp of its implications to making an assertion about the thing understood (R9, 187-189). The difference between understanding the formula and asserting something about the thing itself, then, is not an unbridgeable one. It can in fact be bridged by a certain kind of argument. Nor is calling attention to this difference intended to divide "real" understanding from a "merely verbal" sort in a way that would insinuate some superior, nonverbal mode of understanding. It seems rather designed to call our attention to different stages along the way to understanding anything at all.

Anselm corroborates this interpretation by the ways he uses the distinction even where he does not expressly adduce it. Summarizing the intent of the early chapters of *Proslogion,* he insists that he wanted to show in this case—that is, of that-than-which-a-greater-cannot-be-thought—"that simply if it can be thought it is necessary that it exists" (R1, 169).[17] All that is required is that we understand the formula, and the understanding we can have of it will suffice (173). In fact, the formula was deliberately crafted "to prove against the Fool that God exists, . . . since he would understand [it] in some way, [whereas] he would understand . . . [God] in no way at all" (R7, 185). The formulation is in every way essential to the argument; in fact, Gaunilo's paraphrase ("that which is greater than everything") is rejected because it cannot display the movement so perspicuously, if indeed it can carry it at all (R5, 179-183).

The nexus of Anselm's argument lies precisely in understanding the formula. Gaunilo had puzzled over the formulation. He was baffled by its abstract severity: "upon hearing it spoken of I can so little think of or entertain in my mind this being . . . in terms of an object known to me whether by species or genus as I can think of God Himself. . . . Nor can I form an idea from some other things like it since, as you say yourself, it is such that nothing could be like it." Nor is this like hearing about a man whom I have never met, for he would already be known to be a man; whereas "I know nothing at all of [this thing] save for the verbal formula, and on the basis of this alone one can scarcely or never think of any truth (i.e., assert anything to be the case)" (G4, 161).

Anselm has no feel for this puzzlement. Could it be that Gaunilo's recourse to a psychological kind of idiom baffled him? At any rate, Anselm turns the puzzlement into an objection: "but you will say that, even if the formula is in the mind, yet it does not follow that it is understood," and at once clarifies any such confusion in a tightly woven assembly of linguistic reminders (R2, 173).[18] All that remains to do is to reiterate his original contention: "I said . . . that when the Fool hears 'than-that-which-a-greater-cannot-be-thought' spoken of he understands *what* he hears."[19]

Perhaps, however, Gaunilo found the expression over-whelming because it had been offered as a shorthand for God. That would be understandable enough, but in doing so he missed the genial strategy of the argument. In his final attempt to lay out the movement of the argument, Anselm employs the distinction we have focussed on:

> But even if it were true that [the object] that-than-which-a-greater-cannot-be-thought cannot be thought of nor understood, it would not, however, be false that [the formula] 'that-than-which-a-greater-cannot-be-thought' can be thought of and understood. For just as nothing prevents one from saying 'ineffable' although one cannot specify what is said to be ineffable; and just as one can think of the inconceivable—although one cannot think of what 'inconceivable' applies to—so also, when 'that-than-which-a-greater-cannot-be-thought' is spoken of, there is no doubt at all that what is heard can be thought of and understood (R, 187-189).

And that which is understood is in the intellect . . . So turns the argument.

3.4. A Critical Look

But how does *that which* any fool can understand when he hears the formula (*quod auditur cogitare et intelligi potest*) differ from the thing which the expression signifies? Anselm must say: not at all, except that the thing may exist, and *that* need not be understood in understanding the expression (II, 117; R6, 185). Ordinary language refuses to sanction any significant difference between *cogitare* and *intelligere,* and Anselm's own semantics threaten what is left of the distinction in question. While there may well be other ways of apprehending things, the understanding which the *Proslogion* is designed to achieve comes through the efforts exhibited in formulation and argument. However inadequate this particular access may be, Anselm is anxious to show that it is nonetheless real. So to understand the formula *is* to understand the thing it signifies.

(Anselm takes up the difference between a merely verbal grasp and an adequate understanding in *De Grammatico,* where the student is counseled to look to the point of what is being said and not merely to the form [3.6313]. For since the "meaning of the words is what really binds the syllogism together, and not just the words themselves," then "it is not so much in the form of utterance [*prolatione*] as in the meaning [sententia] that the common term of a syllogism is to be sought" [3.33]. Yet one comes to understand the meaning or the point precisely by scrutinizing what has been said more carefully, and so laying out what was previously hidden to understanding [3.6313, 3.3221]. So a more precise use of words is the tool we must employ to carry us beyond a "merely verbal" grasp to understanding what was said.)

If we were to instruct Anselm in the manner in which he instructed Gaunilo, we would simply have to remind him that *what* is understood can be nothing other that the thing which is understood. For whatever is understood is in the intellect, so the thing understood and the formula by which we understand it must coalesce the very instant we understand the formula and thereby understand the thing (R2, 173). If the formula is to do its job so that we can trust what it yields, there can be no difference.

Now if the thing in fact exists *and* is known to exist,

then *what* is understood is the thing understood and now understood to exist as well. Then, of course, to understand the thing is also to understand it to be. Yet these two understandings must be kept distinct, as Anselm insists from the outset (II, 117). The role of the specific formula he employs in the *Proslogion* is to show, by way of the *reductio* argument in chapter two, that in this unique case they cannot be kept distinct: this object is such that to understand it *is* to understand it to be.

To remain consistent, however, we must also insist: in the measure that anyone grasps the formula—understanding *what* it says—he understands the object it purports to signify. So the distinction offered in chapter four between thinking the expression and understanding the thing can only work in the face of an utterly preliminary grasp of a formula—as if someone were to say: "yeah, sure" when he heard about that than which nothing greater could be thought. The understanding which the argument requires, however, is one which allows us to use the expression to draw certain implications—notably those which Anselm does!

Hence we must conclude that the distinction proferred in chapter four is unsatisfactory as formulated, and misleading in the way it is employed. Perhaps, though, Anselm's failure to show how one might coherently deny that God exists can help us pinpoint how he himself may have failed to show that God exists.

4. Limits of Formulation

In the wake of showing that a distinction which looked out of character was in fact incoherent and inconsistent, we have examined closely Anselm's program and its execution. The inquiry suggests two lines of criticism as well as a way of putting what Anselm was up to. The first criticism stems from Gaunilo's puzzlement over the import of the formula itself, the second wonders about that *what* ('he understands *what* he hears'/'*intelligit quod audit*') which

Anselm makes do double duty. The more constructive and final observation has to do with that movement or growth in understanding of which Anselm shows himself so aware. Whether he succeeded in simulating it through a *reductio* argument would seem less important than the assistance his effort gives us in trying to execute it ourselves. At least, one who views the *Proslogion* primarily as an exercise is free to understand its upshot in these terms.

4.1 Import of the Formula

Gaunilo takes Anselm's effort to formulate with complete seriousness and objects to the strategic formula: that-than-which-nothing-greater-can-be-thought. If there were ever a case of an expression being understood without understanding the thing it signifies, Gaunilo feels this expression would qualify. But the upshot of that situation is not to reclaim the distinction but to question seriously whether there is anything to be understood at all. Gaunilo's puzzlement is sophisticated: these words cannot succeed in signifying anything definite enough to be an object for understanding, for they defy locating it in a genus and expressly ward off any approaching likeness.

Failing to deliver any objective notion, all the formula can do is offer itself. Not, certainly, as an inscription (token) but as purporting to mean something (type). Yet such a maneuver comes to nothing. We are condemned to bafflement, as one "who tries to imagine what the words he has heard might mean" and can come up with nothing (G4, 161). And when the intellect reaches this impasse, when "the mind tries to imagine a completely unknown thing on the basis of the spoken words alone" and is unsuccessful (G5, 163), how can he "claim that that supreme nature exists already in my mind" (G4, 163)? For there is no nature, no objective idea, answering to these words.

There is something genuine about these observations of bafflement. They are akin to our original feeling of having

somehow been taken. Can we give them a more definite
and a less psychological rendering? I think so. The troublesome phrase is certainly 'than which nothing greater' (*quo
nihil maius*). We can note immediately that 'greater than'
requires a specified context if we want to use it unequivo-
cally as argument demands. '*X* is greater than *Y* in respect
to *Z*' supplies the syntax for the expression. In mathematics, for example, the well-ordered character of the
system furnishes the *respect*.

Without the specified respect, 'greater-than' remains inescapably vague. Vagueness does not always spell ambiguity, however, and an expression which defies definition
is often *precisely* what is needed. To be useful, however, a
vague expression must admit to being specified on demand
in any determinate context. Thus 'approximately' means
one thing for the diameter of a shotgun bore, another for a
rifle bore, yet another for the time of a dinner engage-
ment, and something else again for a wine-and-cheese
party. But when no context *can* be supplied, when the
formula expressly thrusts us beyond every possible context, how can we put the vague expression to a determinate use? Is not Gaunilo asking this sort of question
when he puzzles whether he can "think of . . . this being in
terms of an object known to me either by species or
genus . . . , nor can I form an idea from some other things
like it" (G4, 161).

This objection is not an original one, of course. It has
often been brought against the utterly unrestricted premise
in the *reductio:* it is greater to exist in reality than to exist
in the mind. It is simply economical to note the same
potential ambiguity lurking in the formula itself. We can
formulate Gaunilo's uneasiness as follows: when a vague
expression is used to carry an argument, yet in a way
which does not admit of its being given a definite sense,
then it lacks the requisite univocity. For even if one
cannot detect an actual ambiguity, a vague expression
which cannot be determined to a particular case sense *can*
mean many things. Hence the possibility of its being used

to draw other conclusions—perhaps even the opposite of that drawn—jeopardizes the uniqueness of the given conclusion and hence the cogency of the argument.

There is a way around this objection which Anselm only hints at. That would be to admit the strangeness of the formula and go on to show how an expression so strange is at once acceptable in its difference and by this very difference unique. This will be Aquinas' tack in questions three and thirteen of the *Summa*. Yet Aquinas could benefit from two centuries of fervent and careful adherence to Anselm's program of understanding faith through dialectic. Anselm had fewer logical maneuvers available to him for handling the issues peculiar to speaking of God. He was also distracted by his search for a "single argument" that would turn the screws on any fool.

Anselm does note, however, in chapter fifteen: "Lord, not only are you that than which a greater cannot be thought, but you are also something greater than can be thought" (137).[20] He hastens to note that such a one can be thought—a formidable exercise—and that if that one is not God, then something greater than God can be thought, which contradicts the original formulation. So uniqueness is preserved, and Anselm moves on, not bothering to elucidate how something greater than can be thought can in fact be thought to be. Nor does he ponder how it is that his subsequent reflections on this object led him to recognize a variant on the original formulation. Attention to queries like this would have allowed him to confront Gaunilo's fears about the formulation and to explore in a yet more telling way the role of formula in speaking of God.

4.2. *What* Is Understood?

The second objection is nothing more than an old one in new dress, plus some pregnant remarks on "necessary existence." We have seen how Anselm relies on the same *what (quod)* to move from what is understood through understanding the formula, and hence exists in the mind, to what exists in reality. Yet it is one thing to understand a formula so that one can work with it, and something quite distinct to use the formula to designate what is in fact the case. This Anselm recognized in the first distinction, proferred in chapter two: "it is one thing for an object to exist in the mind, and another thing to understand that it actually exists" (117).

How can we say, then, that it is the *same thing* now understood and later understood to be? On the other hand, how can we avoid saying it is the *same thing?* Do we not find—when we do—*what* we were looking for?

These are well-worn questions which threaten to carry us into a thicket of ontological and semantic issues. Yet Anselm's rather quaint (to us) way of speaking of whatever is understood as being "in the intellect" may actually help us find our way through. For the worn questions follow the groove offered by the surface grammar of 'what' *(quod)* to presuppose a neutral object which may exist one way or another but as understood remains existentially neutral. Anselm allows grammar to mislead him here; in fact, his argument seems to conclude so long as it aligns itself with this groove. Yet he also assumes that what is understood exists in the mind. Whatever is understood, then, partakes one mode of existence: the mental or intentional. When it is understood to be, it partakes another as well: the real.

Now "modes of existence" are not popular things, but Alston has offered a way of making them comprehensible: consider them to be like "formal features" of an objects— to adopt a *Tractatus* idiom—which license certain implications and forbid others.[21] We can be sensitized to pay attention to how we think of things, and learn to distinguish, for example, a theoretical consideration from an existential one by the implications which would be legitimate. Thus my conversation about kidnapping a government official could be either musing or conspiring. These would be quite different conversations even though facts laid out could be identical. It is even possible (though improbable) that the two conversations taped could parallel one another from beginning to end, where the final "O.K., let's go!" would mean "home" in the one case and "out to do it" in the other. But the two would differ entirely in *tone*.

"Formal features" are like tones in that they do not stand out like ordinary features. Hence we cannot predicate them of an object as we do other features; rather they are reflected in the kinds of predication that are permitted. Nor can we make them emerge from known features by way of an argument—as one can conclude from rational to risible. They can only be detected—if at all—by that kind of analysis which Kant called *transcendental*: designed to ferret out the conditions of the possibility of understanding something, the implications one may and may not be licensed to draw from the descriptions offered.

Even if Anselm is clever enough to craft a formula which concludes by a *reductio* that the object in question must be not only *in intellecto* but *in re,* then the conclusion does not succeed in giving him what he wants it to—namely, that God exists. What it does give him he sees very clearly: that such a one cannot not be. But we cannot convert the latter into the former, because the form of 'such a one cannot not be' is predicative and asserts a feature, while the form of 'that . . . exists' is impredicative and announces something like a "formal feature."[22]

The feature is not existence, of course, but the *necessity* thereof; and the sign that it is a feature is the fact that it is proved through what Anselm takes to be the distinguishing feature: "than which nothing greater can be thought." Desmond Henry supports his reading of chapter three as an elucidation and not a second argument on these grounds, and cites Anselm's shift to *cogitare* as evidence.[23] Yet Anselm does claim that the *reductio* in chapter two yields an impredicative 'to be': "*existit procul dubio . . . et in intellectu et in re*" (116).

Again, Aquinas was possessed of a sophistication sufficient to distinguish here. In question three he shows that
no descriptive predicate whatsoever can appropriately be
used of God. As a base line for whatever might be said he
offers the assertion: "to be God is to be." Yet he never
confused his statement with the assertion "God exists." It
is rather a deliberately truncated form of the paradigm for
essential predication: "to be (man) is to be (rational)."
Aquinas' way of announcing the uniqueness of God was to
forbid any term to fill the predicate place and then show
(by indirect argument) that the blank space could in this
case be suppressed. The resulting truncated form—
improper to be sure—is nevertheless more properly used of
God. For this form displays what could never be expressed: the uniquely necessary existence of God.[24]

4.3. The Germ of a Transcendental Analysis

It has been said often enough that one cannot *argue* to
the fact that something exists, and the usual alternative
offered is *encountering* it. So philosophers took to speaking of "knowledge by acquaintance"; and theologians
wanted something like this with God, so they began speaking of religious experience. We have come to see that
neither notion is a very satisfactory one. So what has
been called the "ontological argument" remains a recurrent temptation. If we have seen that Anselm could not
achieve what he desired through the analysis proper to
demonstrative argument, we have also glimpsed another
route which he might have tried: transcendental analysis.
   Here of course we depart radically from Anselm and his
grasp of dialectic to respond more directly to what seems
to be the perennial attraction of his way of proceeding. No
matter how one may suspect some sleight of hand in the
argument, this way of proceeding at least tries to display
something of the uniqueness of the God-question in a way
which accounts of "religious experiences" cannot. There is
of necessity a necessary face to God; he is not simply

adventitious, there or not there. Yet a *reductio* form of argument, appropriate to the necessity of mathematics, does not seem to be able to exhibit that necessity we associate with God.

I have tried to be faithful to Anselm's focus on formulation and dialectic in exercising our understanding on the truths of faith. As an interpretative key I used a distinction which looked odd and was found to be incoherent. But that distinction will serve us one last time if we notice *why* it was brought forward: to try to articulate the gap between a bare understanding of a theological formula and a fuller one. Something tells us that formulae of this sort are susceptible of vastly different degrees of understanding without any shift in wording. The process whereby Anselm sought to show the fool that God indeed exists was intended to awaken his understanding to the richer ways in which he could—indeed had to—understand the formula offered as a shorthand for God.

Deductive analysis is not designed to do this job. We may *use* formulae to draw out hitherto latent implications, but the conclusion is verbally different from the premises. That is normally the sign that something new has emerged. In this case, however, there is no such overt sign. What is called for is rather that the verbal formula be used in new ways. We can only do that by expanding our context, and we can only expand beyond our functioning context if we recognize there to be one. This other form of analysis, then, which I have likened to Kant's, assembles reminders to make us aware of how we are using expressions *now*. What results is a slow and awakening awareness that my statements are made within a context.

To appreciate this fact about the statements we ordinarily make already enhances our awareness. For our normal attitude takes ordinary statements to represent the norm, whereas recognizing them to be within a context calls attention to a set of norms which circumscribes these statements as well. Now if we can also articulate that context, we have in some way moved beyond it. And if any of the statements in question are framed so that none of the relevant terms are beholden to the original context, then those statements give promise of being used with an expanded significance. The terms which allow us to expand the boundaries of their use in a controlled way were called *analogous,* after Aristotle's way of characterizing expressions not restricted to a set context.

Anselm's formula certainly qualifies in expansiveness—*quo nihil maius*—yet may not be susceptible to sufficient control, as we have noted. Yet he was aware, of course, of the conditions required for such formulae. In answering Gaunilo's objection that the formula is expressly so stark that one is *ipso facto* blocked from "form[ing] an idea from some other things like it" (G4, 161), Anselm relies on our feel for the expansiveness of 'good' to insist:

> But obviously this is not so. For since everything that is less good is similar insofar as it is good to that which is more good, it is evident to every rational mind that, mounting from the less good to the more good, we can from those things than which something greater can be thought conjecture *(conicere)* a great deal about that-than-which-a-greater-cannot-be-thought.

He concludes: "there is then a way by which one can form an idea of that-than-which-a-greater-cannot-be-thought" (R8, 187). Yet his argument did not tarry to show us that way, anxious as he was to find one single formula which could do the trick.

It seems that the only way we can tease the analogous structure out of otherwise vague expressions, and exhibit how to control them, is to offer a systematic sampling of examples. Exercise with these examples helps us acquire the *know-how* we need to acquire a reflective awareness of our own operating context. The familiar *know-how* which supplies an operating context must be supplemented by another which makes us explicitly aware of the first. However this happens, philosophers have deliberately employed a method distinct from consecutive argument to help one to a new consciousness of the paradigms he is in fact employing. From Aquinas' *manuductio* to Kierke-gaard's dramatic development of "spheres of existence" and Wittgenstein's adducing examples to display the "form of life" at work, these are recognized forms of philo-sophical elucidation.[25]

The inward movement from a bare grasp to a more fully conscious use of analogous formulations asks that we ac-quire a new know-how, and deductive analysis is not designed to exercise us in that way. It seems that Anselm, in his zeal for showing the advantages of dialectic, overesti-mated the role of argument and underplayed the function of other factors in his own monastic way of life. These factors crop up in later chapters of the *Proslogion,* which adumbrate what a fully conscious use of the formula would be like. These relections corroborate those of the chapter on the inescapable character of God's existence, but also reveal this understanding to be quite unlike that yielded by even the best-designed argument. The missing factor is more like the daily fidelity to consequences symbolized in monastic discipline.

These reflections begin after he acknowledges the yet more agnostic rendering of the original formula (cf. *infra* 4.1). They begin by decrying the ironic situation: "You are within me and around me and I do not have any experience of You" (XVI, 137). That what outstrips every-thing else in import should be so intangible—every spiritual discipline from monasticism to yoga is offered to atten-tuate this paradox.[26] For the impasse is not totally a logical one; rather "the senses of my soul, because of the ancient weakness of sin, have become hardened and dulled and obstructed" (XVII, 139). The promise, moreover, carries us far beyond the serial understanding we can have through dialectic: we are promised "all in one single glance so as to delight in all at once" (XVIII, 141). Delight because "this is . . . that one thing necessary in which is every good, or rather, which is wholly and uniquely and completely and solely good" (XXIII, 147).

We are asked, then, to "consider carefully how enjoyable is that good which contains the joyfulness of all goods; not [a joy] such as we have experienced in created things, but as different from this as the Creator differs from the creature" (XXIV, 147). Something, then, must bring us to the threshold where we can experience at least the difference, or we will fail to understand his words here much as the fool failed to grasp the import of the initial formula. Dialectic can direct us where to look by calling attention to the vast difference, but we must also undertake a discipline, at least "making the motions," to place ourselves in a new position whence we can *feel* those vastly different joys.[27]

It is not unlike following a new philosophic path strewn with examples, for the discipline offers to lead us step-by-step into a new form of life. After he has employed every rhetorical skill to cite how this utterly different joy nonetheless fulfills every present aspiration (XXV, 149), Anselm goes on to outline some steps familiar to him from the monastic tradition. The first involves both asking and listening:

> Speak, Lord, tell your servant within his heart
>   if this is the joy into which your servants will enter
>   who enter 'into the joy of the Lord'?
>
> Let the knowledge of you grow in me here,
>   and there be made complete;
> Let your love grow in me here
>   and there be made complete,
>
> so that here my joy may be great in hope,
>   and there be complete in reality (XXVI, 153).

Prayer—asking and listening—is the first step then, since this growth of consciousness through a fuller knowing and loving is not presented as an achievement but as a gift: "May I receive what You promise through Your truth so that my joy may be complete." But there remain tasks "until then," so Anselm concludes by recommending to himself (and to us) the following steps:

let my mind meditate on it,
let my tongue speak of it,
let my heart love it,
let my mouth preach it.
let my soul hunger for it,
let my flesh thirst for it,
my whole being desire it,
until I enter into the 'joy of the Lord'.

Anselm's original example of the painter seems to have captured the intent of the *Proslogion* more adequately than the early focal chapters. Nothing could change the picture from one understood to one understood-to-be except his painting it (II, 117). What seems required of any fool to move from merely understanding that to be God is to be, to understanding him to be, is that he execute something. The movement called for seems to be a stepwise one, not unlike that sort of philosophical analysis which proceeds by examples and can be called "transcendental." For its intent is to make us aware of the conditions governing our habitual forms of thinking and of living. By it we are gradually brought to see that the world is, logically at least, but *a* world. Nary a feature of this world is disturbed by such an analysis, but we stand ready to ask questions *about* it. The form of the questions, of course, must differ radically from those we are accustomed to answering. Nor can we say precisely what one would have to understand to answer them. But they cannot help but arise.

Such is the function and these are the limits of that form of analysis loosely called "transcendental." The situation just described is precisely where Kant left us. It seems likely that it was this sort of analysis which Anselm intended, as a way of expanding the fool's horizons. If the early chapters of the *Proslogion* rely too sanguinely on argument, the rest of his meditation on faith in quest of understanding carries us in the direction I have sketched. Yet if we are to move beyond Kant's impasse, it seems we cannot rest with what even a transcendental analysis yields, but must go on to undertake the challenge that it offers. We are called to engage ourselves in a discipline designed to let us experience something of living at the perimeter of our world so that we can learn how to speak of it as a world. That at any rate is the upshot of Anselm's meditation.

NOTES

1. Cf. Desmond Henry, *The Logic of St. Anselm* (Oxford, 1967), 8-9, who cites as his source A. van de Vyver, "Les Etapes du développement philosophique du haut Moyen Age," *Révue Belge du Philologie et d'Histoire* 8 (1929).

2. Desmond Henry, *The De Grammatico of St. Anselm* (Notre Dame, 1964). Cf. his earlier article "Why 'Grammaticus'?" *Archivum Latinitatis Medii Aevi* 28 (1958) 165-180, which positions the questions.

3. *Proslogion*, Proemium. References will be taken from M. J. Charlesworth's edition *St. Anselm's Proslogion* (Oxford, 1965), cited by chapter in roman numerals and in Charlesworth's pagination by arabic numerals.

4. " . . . si forte posset inveniri unum argumentum, quod nullo alio ad se probandum quam se solo indigeret, et solum ad astruendum quia deus vere est, et quia est summum bonum nullo alio indigens . . . sufficeret" (Pr., 102).

5. R. W. Southern (ed), *The Life of St. Anselm by Eadmer* (Edinburgh, 1962), 29.

6. Notably chapters XXV-XXVI. John E. Smith focusses aptly on chapter XIV in his useful essay "In What Sense Can We Speak of Experiencing God?" *Journal of Religion* 50 (1970) 229-244.

7. Barth is concerned with drawing out this dimension of Anselm's life, and assessing its implications for his argument. One can better appreciate Barth's effort the more he is able to disengage Anselm from the special advocacy Barth claims for him. *Fides Quaerens Intellectum* (Richmond, Va., 1961).

8. Desmond Henry, *The Logic of St. Anselm* (Oxford, 1967), *The De Grammatico of St. Anselm* (Notre Dame, 1964); R. W. Southern, *St. Anselm and His Biographer* (Cambridge, 1963), *The Life of St. Anselm by Eadmer* (Edinburgh, 1962).

9. The classic statement of discovery in the Proemium is amplified by Eadmer: R. W. Southern, *Life*, 29.

10. Henry, *Logic*, 145-147.

11. The logic of this procedure is confirmed by the way Aquinas

organizes the *Summa:* the heart of his demonstration of the divine attributes lies in showing initially how God's very nature is to-be.

12. "Aliter enim cogitatur res cum vox eam significans cogitatur, aliter cum id ipsum quod res est intelligitur" (120).

13. "Quod qui bene intelligit, utique intelligit id ipsum sic esse, ut nec cogitatione queat non esse. Qui ergo intelligit sic esse deum, nequit eum non esse cogitare" (120).

14. Proemium, 103; Southern, *Life,* 29-31.

15. Henry, *Logic,* 108-116.

16. "Aliud enim est rem esse in intellectu, aliud intelligere rem esse"(116).

17. " . . . si vel cogitari potest esse, necesse est illud esse"(168).

18. "Vide quia consequitur esse in intellectu, ex eo quia intelligitur. Sicut enim quod cogitatur, cogitatione cogitatur, et quod cogitatione cogitatur, sicut cogitatur sic est in cogitatione: ita quod intelligitur intellectu intelligitur, et quod intellectu intelligitur, sicut intellitur ita est in intellectu. Quid hoc planius?"(172-174).

19. Italics mine: "intelligit quod audit"(172).

20. "Domine, non solum es quo maius cogitari nequit, sed es quiddam maius quam cogitari possit" (136).

21. William Alston, "The Ontological Argument Revisited," *Philosophical Review* 69 (1960) 452-474; reprinted in Alvin Plantinga (ed), *The Ontological Argument* (New York, 1965), the reference to the *Tractatus* draws from Eddy Zemach, "Wittgenstein's Philosophy of the Mystical" in I.M. Copi and R.W. Beard (ed), *Essays on Wittgenstein's Tractatus* (New York, 1966), 359-376, esp. 362.

22. The key summary statement in Alston is at 469 (Plantinga, 105).

23. Henry, *Logic,* 143-147.

24. *Summa* 1.3.4. See the chapter following.

25. Cf. M.D. Chenu, *Towards Understanding St. Thomas* (Chicago, 1964), ch. 2, 5; Paul Sponheim's introduction to S. Kierkegaard, *Stages on Life's Way* (New York, 1967); Paul Holmer, "Kierkegaard and Philosophy," in R. McInerny (ed), *New Themes in Christian Philosophy* (Notre Dame, 1968); S. Toulmin, "Ludwig Wittgenstein," *Encounter* 32 (1969) 58-71.

26. I am indebted to conversations with John Eudes, monk of Gethsemani, now abbot of the Trappist monastery of the Genesee, for pinpointing this characteristic of monasticism.

27. The phrase is Kierkegaard's, attributed to Climacus and found *passim* in the *Postscript.* It makes reference to the careful constructions of his own pseudonymous authorship, and reaches out to include all the indirect ways by which men attempt to pass from "ideality" to some form of resolution. The phrase provides an indispensable gloss on another image he used: that of a *leap.*

3: AQUINAS
Articulating
Transcendence

Pursuing my general aim of showing how relevant logical and linguistic expertise can be for clarifying theological issues, I now want to examine the way in which Aquinas manages to say what he does about divinity. He provides a cogent case in point, for while making many statements about God—explicitly proposing them as assertions—Aquinas never recants his original insistence that "we cannot know what God is, but only what he is not."[1] The task of theology has always been one of discriminating among proposed forms of religious discourse. Aquinas assumes that task and specifies it. He isolates those linguistic forms which can express the transcendence of God by deftly displaying how they work: these forms fall short of describing, yet nonetheless abide by the generic norms for referential statements. The customary philosophical parameters of experience and logic may thus take on the color of religious experience and the semantics of referring expressions.

1. Preliminary View of the Area

If anyone would respond to the invitation to change his heart, he must have some idea what he is up to—even if he cannot say what the upshot will be. He finds himself faced with something which transcends the ordinary, and acknowledging that fact introduces Aquinas' religious parameter: the transcendence of God. To be sure, this expression conveys more than a raw experience of the numinous. As Aquinas uses it, the entire Judeo-Christian scheme of interpretation is invoked. Furthermore, Aquinas' selection of suitable predicates adds another interpreting twist. Yet the precise feature that strikes a logic-sensitive theologian is the incomprehensible character of the divine, both in its activity and in men's experiencing it.

In the Judeo-Christian tradition the divine is presented as issuing an invitation. Responding to it in a responsible way normally requires some clarifications, and qualifications demand discourse. What sorts of things can be said of that which remains incomprehensible? And how can we say them in a way that is understandable yet respectful of the awesome mystery? Questions like this set the logical exigencies of the situation. Logic in its broadest reach captures the basic human demand for coherence and consistency in what we say and do.

Aquinas' introductory remarks to question three of the *Summa Theologiae* I manifest his acute awareness of both parameters: "we must consider the ways in which God does not exist, rather than the ways in which he does. . . . The ways in which God does not exist will become apparent if we rule out from him everything inappropriate, such as compositeness, change and the like." He will secure God's transcendence in specific ways designed to show to those acquainted with logic just how incomprehensible God is. *Compositeness* turns out to be that structure so utterly basic to everything that it is reflected in the form of anything we say. By denying that God is *composite,*

then, Aquinas determines that no well-formed sentence
can express his way of being. This stipulation effectively
secures God's transcendence, since nothing more can be
said.

Yet Aquinas goes to to say *much* more. I shall concentrate on the next ten questions, trying to show how
Aquinas' own procedure finds a way through the crippling
constraint of question three, until question thirteen submits that same procedure to a reflective scrutiny. The
intervening questions will illuminate *in praxi* what Aquinas' method comes to.

1.1. What of the "Ways"?

Beginning with question three allows us to sidestep the
issue of God's existence and the tangle of commentary
upon it. My strategy is deliberate, for considerations of
existence can claim no logical priority in discussing a
definite topic. Aquinas' account of the pure intelligences,
for instance, serves its purpose perfectly well whatever one
believes about angels; it remains epistemologically accurate
whether angels exist or not. Nothing which arises rests on
having settled the issue of existence, except our readiness
to use the summary expression: "beginning and end of all
things and of reasoning creatures especially." Questions
three through thirteen draw out what implications can be
drawn from that formula, which Aquinas adopts as a
shorthand for God in introducing question two.

A person's convictions about the reality of God will
certainly have some bearing on his willingness to undergo
the logical austerities demanded to elucidate that expression, but the matter itself is one for logic. The exercise
might be entitled: What, if anything, can be said about the
beginning and end of all things? The point of such an
exercise, of course, would be at least to determine the
logical neighborhood of the beginning-and-end-of-all-things,

and at best to relate to it. So engaging in the exercise as an activity with a point presupposes no doubt the existence of the object in question, but this existential precondition may be realized concomitantly with letting oneself carry out the exercise.

At any rate, the complex of factors which eventuate in one's acknowledging the reality of an object or a fact lie hidden in an alchemy well beyond my comprehension, so the scope of this essay must remain more modest: to lay out and to execute the logical notions Aquinas makes in trying to say something intelligible and coherent about the beginning and end of all things. This sort of elucidation cannot fail to engender some appreciation for the logical uniqueness of its subject.

Aquinas was simply following Aristotle in treating the question of fact before examining the nature of the object, and there is something natural about this way of proceeding. Yet it hamstrings a more hypothetical cast of inquiry, and only serves its purpose when the initial description is clear enough to identify the object without further clarifying what is at issue.[2] In Aquinas' day enough other factors were held constant to permit him to locate his God with a summary formula, and to suggest some purely intellectual ways of acknowledging his existence. Once those factors have sprung loose, it becomes painfully clear that merely intellectual inquiry cannot yield acknowledgement of this sort. So question two becomes more of a distraction than an assistance to us—both in our search for the terms of intelligible discourse and in our concern to learn from Aquinas along the way.

Any effort invested in elucidating the five ways can do one the inestimable service of sharpening his logical acumen, of course, as well as extending his philosophical horizons. I am especially grateful to Victor Preller's semantical analysis of the issues this chapter will focus on. I shall in fact be extending his program by employing his strategies.[3] I am also indebted to the editors of the particular volumes of the new edition of the *Summa Theologiae* on which I have relied so carefully: Thomas Gilby, Timothy McDermott, and Herbert McCabe.[4]

1.2. Focus: The Ways in Which God Does Not Exist

Aquinas himself lays out the order of treatment in introducing questions three through thirteen:

> Having recognized that a certain thing exists, we have still to investigate the way in which it exists, that we may come to understand what it is that exists. Now we cannot know what God is, but only what he is not; we must therefore consider the ways in which God does not exist, rather than the ways in which he does.

Question three begins the inquiry innocently enough by promising to treat of God's simplicity. Under this apparently innocuous rubric Aquinas lays down the conditions which must be met by any statement about God. And these conditions turn out to be so restrictive that apparently no well-formed statement can satisfy them. So question three sets up our specific philosophical and hermeneutical task: How can restrictions this severe be compatible with the assertions Aquinas makes in questions four through eleven? In fact, on the basis of these restrictions, how can he make any assertions at all? And given the statements he does make, what do they assert? Aquinas offers a wholesale response to the first question in 12.12; we shall examine what it comes to in each particular case. His answer to the second question is contained in the critical assessment of question thirteen. (Cf. infra #7.2.)

1.21. General Outline

In the most generic sort of epistemological considerations Aquinas concludes question twelve on "the ways in

which we know him" by sketching the contours of knowing by natural reason (12.12) and by faith (12.13). "The
knowledge that is natural to us has its source in the senses
and extends just so far as it can be led *(manuduci potest)*
by sensible things; from these, however, our understanding
cannot reach to the divine essence" (12.12). Nevertheless,
insofar as they can be taken as "effects depending from a
cause"—as Augustine heard things saying "we did not
make ourselves"—"we can at least be led from them to.
know of God (1) that he exists and (2) that he has
whatever must belong to the first cause of all things which
is beyond all that is caused. Thus we know

(1) about his relation to creatures, and
(2) about the difference between him and them:
    (a) that nothing created is in him; and
    (b) that his lack of such things is not a
        deficiency in him but due to his transcendence"

Many are loath to call so wide an overview *epistemology,* yet it is from tacit considerations just this generic that
every epistemology establishes its base line. Call it *philosophical anthropology* or whatever, but it would prove
instructive to compare Aquinas' observations about "the
knowledge that is natural to us" with, say, those of
Hempel on empirical knowledge. Hempel would have limited us to observation statements and to those assertions
which they entail (or which entail them), but entailment
proved too strong a stipulation.[5] Aquinas will allow that
we know whatever the empirical knowledge we clearly
possess can "lead us on" to acknowledge. The base lines
are similar enough, but Aquinas refuses to stipulate in
advance the forms of analysis which can responsibly extend our native knowledge. Each form—from logical to
transcendental analysis—will have to prove itself in the
execution.

The analysis that we shall assess is that which brings us
to "know of God . . . (2) that he has whatever must belong
to the first cause of all things which is beyond all that is

caused." This form of knowledge focuses on "the ways in which God does not exist: the difference between him and creatures" by showing in each case where something must be said, that "(a) nothing created is in him, and (b) that his lack of such things is not a deficiency in him but due to his transcendence" (12.12). The trick is to turn "our very inability to know God into a fruitful piece of information about him."[6] Lest the trick prove a *tour de force,* however, we cannot settle for wholesale remarks about paradox or promissory notes on analogy but must show how it works in each proposed predication.

Question three offers the paradigm. In laying down restrictions on any predication it proposes the only proper one: to be God is to be. This unusual form violates syntactic proprieties, and in any other context would be a semantic *cul-de-sac.* Aquinas transforms it into an access road in a way which offers a pattern for each subsequent instance, as we shall see. Besides being the first in the series and serving as a paradigm for the others, question three also takes its place within the series. It serves as a part of a pattern which Aquinas carefully contrives to achieve a modicum of dialectical movement in an area where the latitude of movement is severely restricted. In fact, nothing can be said of God which would succeed in "adding anything" to the normal form laid down in question three. So Aquinas has to effect a development within and among statements which must otherwise be equivalent.

He accomplishes this by carefully selecting the topics for predication, and then by treating each topic in the two ways offered in 12.12: first, in asserting what cannot be said of God, and then trying to show how this restrictive predication reveals not deficiency but transcendence. I have arranged the questions in columns to show his way of proceeding; by following the numbers one achieves an interlacing effect:

(a)	(b)
3. God's simpleness	4. God's perfection
5. General notion of *good*	6. Goodness of God

7. God's limitlessness   8. God's existence in things
9. God's unchangeableness   10. Eternity of God
                11. Oneness of God

The left column invariably elucidates what must be said, which comes down to showing us what cannot be said of God. The right column tries to suggest what one might make of that specific denial.

1.22. Method in Detail

The questions in column (a) translate the demands of logic in dealing with what is given to us by the description: "first cause of all." He is then outside *everything;* there is nothing created in him. Question three establishes the ground rules by ruling out any discourse which reflects the formal features proper to an object connatural with human understanding. Extensive work in philosophical grammar had prepared Aquinas for a view not unlike that adopted by Wittgenstein in the *Tractatus:* the very structure of a well-formed sentence reflects the formal or constitutive features of the object spoken about.[7]

If one can succeed in characterizing the structure of a well-formed sentence, then he also possesses a clue to ontological structure. Aquinas considered the structure of ordinary declarative discourse to reflect adequately that of created things in complementary ways: genus/species, substance/accident, etc. So he had to deny that this same structure was present in the first cause of all. That denial would seem to reduce him to silence as well, but we shall see how he managed to go on to speak precisely by turning the denial into an informative statement.

The other predicates were chosen carefully to achieve the same end, namely to turn a denial into a piece of information. Yet they also had to be chosen so as not to effect a characterization separate from the one established in question three: to be God is to be. In effect, question five denies that we call him good because he performs good actions (by elucidating a yet more basic sense of

'good' as convertible with 'being'), question seven denies
that God is a definite or predictable object, and question
nine says that this thing alone is not in process. The
companion question in column (b) asks what one might
make of each specific denial.

The arguments differ from one column to another, and
with them the status of the assertion. It follows logically
that one must deny of the first cause of all those formal
features constitutive of anything. Similarly, we have no
choice (given the conceptual framework we employ) but
to remove God from process. Yet as one whose very
essence is to be, or as one who is utterly and completely
what he is—at each instant, if you will—have we any
intimations what that may be like? Does our experience
offer us any analogies whatsoever that might lead us on to
some conception of God's perfection or eternity—in terms
germane to the respective denials?

Each column exhibits the effects of one's ordinary
knowledge "leading him on," yet quite distinct skills are
involved. The first column proceeds much like Wittgenstein's *Tractatus:* lay down the formal features of human
discourse, and then proceed to deny them. The second
column is more like the *Philosophical Investigations,*
though the similarity is less striking. Aquinas probes the
possibilities of different ways of thinking and speaking to
test for intimations which the outright denial might have
opened up. He makes an implicit appeal to a quality of
experience, a form of life which could prepare someone to
adopt a way of speaking quite different from that adapted
to physical objects.

1.221. Two Uses of 'Analogy'

Aquinas elsewhere calls these two ways of pursuing the
questions the *via remotionis* and *via eminentiae* respectively.[8] (Commentators since have blunted the distinction
somewhat by contrasting them as ways of negation and of
affirmation.) Genuinely analogous terms—like 'one' or

'good'—can function in both ways, so that the question on the oneness of God spans both columns. The fact that Aquinas uses different terms to signal the different ways we can be "led on," however, suggests a useful way of discriminating between analogical *expressions* and analogical *arguments* or explorations. Column (b) offers arguments by way of analogy. These are akin to the use of analogies in developing a scientific theory—they are offered in an effort to get hold of an item as yet inadequately conceptualized. They are propaedeutic rather than confirmatory, more explorations than arguments. In those areas where inadequate conceptualization remains with us either in fact (theory of light) or in principle (knowledge of God) we cannot dispense with this tentative, probing way of being led on. We can only increase our skill at using it responsibly.

Column (a) consists of expressions which deny a specific formal feature of objects as we know them. Hence the arguments proceed with logical precision. In those instances where we have one term to span both moments in the process, i.e., denial and intimation, that term qualifies as an inherently analogical expression. Such expressions will possess a syntactical structure susceptible of a wide variety of uses. One of these uses utterly denies its paradigm use (thus 'good' said of God does not assess him), and another range of uses relies on imaginative analogies to convey its import (God's activity is good despite appearances to the contrary). Note that this distinction (between *via remotionis* and *via eminentiae*) does not correspond directly to the division into columns, except that column (b) regularly employs the analogical exploration. The distinction will prove useful to head off a few misconceptions of analogy as well as to pare down some expectations of its efficacy.

1.222. Relation Between the Columns

In 12.12 Aquinas noted that the knowledge we can

claim to have of God would have to be of him as "the first cause of all things which is beyond all that is caused." We have seen how this formula translates into two distinct columns: one stating what God is not and the other showing how that denial might spell not poverty but plenitude. In lining up Aquinas' treatment pairwise into two columns I have suggested how his different ways of arguing display the difference quite clearly. This will appear as we take each pair in turn. At this point I would simply like to head off some facile ways of characterizing the disparity in approaches.

The most facile, hence the most common and misleading way of putting the difference, is to label column (a) *negative* and column (b) *positive*. This dry-cell approach gains some credibility from Aquinas' distinguishing two moments in any transcendent application of an analogous expression: *via remotionis* and *via eminentiae*. Yet to speak of the first way as negative and the second as positive quite obscures the fact that we are not sure of what we are speaking in either case, and that the denial is more (positively) secured than the intimation. One could then be tempted to contrast the two types of assertion as *hard* and *soft*. This would probably prove less misleading than negative/positive, but would miss what the hard/soft enthusiast always misses: the phenomenon of growing awareness or deepening knowledge.

The difference emerges more sharply when we ask how the columns might be related. Clearly (a) does not entail (b). One might assert (a) without any feel for what is going on in (b). Perhaps this was what Anselm was groping for in proposing the ill-fated distinction between understanding the formula and understanding the thing signified by the formula.[9] Aquinas' maneuver, which I have displayed in two columns, moves from bare statement (what *must* not be said) to suggesting how we might employ the resulting notion. By learning how to use the formula we cannot change its nature, but we can manage to allow a denial to inform us about divinity. Aquinas seems to have anticipated the central feature of Hegel's dialectic: *Auf-*

hebung.[10] Elsewhere he remarks that the mode proper to metaphysics is logical. Hence the metaphysician differs from the logician, not in a privileged access to underlying structures, but solely in his *power.*[11] One might translate 'power' as 'skill' or 'know-how' and cite the penetrating power of logic to display the limits of discourse exhibited by Wittgenstein in the *Tractatus.*

The metaphysician, it seems, cannot content himself with the bare entailment, but must try to make of the denial what he can. This relationship between the different kinds of assertions shows up more clearly where the same predicate spans both columns. Thus 'one' used to deny means 'undivided', yet 'one' employed to understand *undividedness* strains toward an idiom like "all-together" or *tout d 'un piece.* Furthermore, we only come to appreciate how inherently analogous an expression 'one' is as we employ it in ways that first appear odd or outrageously metaphorical.[12]

The very range of analogous expressions prohibits our grasping their meaning all at once. They display this fact by resisting a single formulation. Hence one must speak of a growing appreciation or deepening understanding in these cases—metaphorical as *these* expressions may be! Aquinas speaks just this way when he treats of faith deepening understanding. He uses the metaphors of light: "the stronger our intellectual light the deeper the understanding we derive from images" (12.13.2). While the context is one of faith, the principle holds for natural reason as well. To move from column (a) to (b) we must venture beyond what logic can warrant. Yet the result of that risk is a more supple wit, at once skilled and discerning.

2. God's Simpleness (3.) and God's Perfection (4.)

One is tempted to construe the title of question three—*de simplicitate Dei*—by analogy with expressions like the simplicity of doves or the simplicity of a truly great man.

'Simplicity' would be used, then, by contrast with 'complicated' (which carries a hint of deviousness), and yet most properly be said of someone who has surpassed sophistication and attained the serenity of simple vision. So simplicity would also contrast with naivete. Simplicity, used in this way, becomes a quite sophisticated notion; it has many of the earmarks of an inherently analogous term, and is susceptible of reaches that remain intimation and aspiration for most of us. On my schematic analysis a usage like this would more appropriately find its way into column (b) and the verbal exercise just sketched is not unlike Aquinas' way of operating in that column. A quick perusal of question three, however, would show this reading of *simplicitate* to be a gratuitous one.

Aquinas uses *simplicitas* rather as a technical rubric to introduce a careful metalinguistic treatise discussing how God may *not* be described. It is not offered as a descriptive predicate, even of a sophisticated sort. Hence McDermott translates the term by 'simpleness' (rather then 'simplicity') to mark its technical cast. In that role the term announces the aim of question three: to rule any ordinary descriptive statement out of order because the very syntax of such statements falsifies the mode of existence of the "primary existent" (3.1), who is the "primary source of all activity" (3.2).

To put this in grammatical terms, Aquinas held the subject/predicate construction of any ordinary sentence to reflect (and display) a similar "composition" in those things we use the sentences to talk about. This feel for a structural isomorphism between the form of a declarative sentence and that of the intended subject of discourse represents one of the main achievements of medieval philosophical grammar. After two centuries spent putting scriptural texts through the paces of Aristotelian logic, the men of the thirteenth century were well equipped to submit Aristotle's own philosophical texts to the same treatment. Furthermore, since the texts they received had passed through Arabic hands and often came in untrustworthy renderings, it was imperative to purify them by Aristotle's own methods of logical analysis. Aquinas had appropriated the tools of his forerunners well enough to bring notions still inchoate in Aristotle to greater systematic clarity.

So the analysis of sentences into subject and predicate is taken as a sign of four distinct modes of ontological composition: matter/form (3.2), individual/species (3.3), genus/difference (3.5) and substance/accident (3.6). Aquinas argues that each of these is inappropriate to the "beginning and end of all things." And since these ways of construing ontological composition are taken to be exhaustive, Aquinas must conclude that God lacks *composition* in any ontological sense of that term and hence must be said to be altogether *simple* (3.7).

Whatever his predilections may be, Aquinas does not work *from* a prior notion of *simpleness,* but concludes *to* it as he shows each way of construing composition to be inappropriate to "the first cause of all things" (12.12). His arguments, furthermore, are each appropriately indirect and austere. Indirect, since he can only show that each mode of composition fails to meet the requirements logic places on speaking of the first cause of all; and austere in that no prior characterization can control the movement of a section designed to rule out all characterizations. The only operative notion is the inherently analogous one of *actuality,* which Aquinas takes to be implicit in the notion of first-cause-of-all things. Nor would those who suspect Aquinas bedeviled by Hellenic preconceptions find much purchase here, for his use of *actuality* appears more beholden to the psalmist than to any single philosopher.

With the arguments moving at the formal (or metalinguistic) level of philosophical grammar we have little or no conception of the simpleness which must be said to characterize God. Cognizant of this fact and foreseeing the tendency to misconstrue 'simpleness' as a straightforward predicate—since "in the material world simpleness implies imperfection and incompleteness"—Aquinas had introduced question three by promising a complementary

treatment of God's perfection (4).[13] Yet there is one last
possibility for ontological composition remaining. In denying it Aquinas offers to all subsequent predication a model
which allows one both to obey and to circumvent his
ruling against using declarative sentences to speak of God.

2.1. God's Nature Is to Exist

All the modes of composition mentioned had been
formulated by Aristotle and employed in his semantic,
natural, and philosophical treatises. Medieval philosophical
grammarians took them over intact, refining them in an
effort to assimilate them and to use them as tools of
analysis. One further mode, hardly mentioned by Aristotle
and certainly never operative for him, was introduced by
the Arab commentators and explored by Aquinas in his
early opusculum, *De Ente et Essentia:* that of essence and
existence.[14] This mode of composition is not displayed in
the form of a statement, for one can make an acceptable
statement about anything without its having to exist.
Statements about unicorns and real dogs share a common
structure. What announces the essence/existence mode of
composition is rather the discrepancy between entertaining
a proposition and using it to apply to something. This
discrepancy is not a structural one, like that marking off
subject from predicate, but an existential or factual one.
Only when we reflect on the uses we make of well-formed
expressions does the discrepancy come to light. And justly
so, since it is offered as a sign of a difference between *what*
something is and the fact *that* it is. Aquinas' arguments for
a real distinction between essence and existence mean to
place this mode of ontological composition on all fours
with those modes of composition reflected in the form of
statements themselves.

The arguments denying this final composition of God
are, like all the others, indirect. They do not build on
denials of formal composition, however, but harken back

to the original formula. The first cause of all cannot be said to "receive existence" without postulating a source still more primal. Furthermore, essence taken separately is said to be "potential of existence," yet the first cause of all cannot be conceived except as actual, so it must be "God's very nature to exist" (3.4). The arguments yield no conception of what such existence would be like; we simply cannot put it any other way, given that God is the first cause of all.

Although the grammatical form of this conclusion is affirmative—God's very nature is to exist—its import remains a denial. Furthermore, it cannot amount to a covert argument for God's existence since the predicate nominative form 'to exist' is categorically different from the predicate form ' . . . exists'. This semantic fact will allow Aquinas both to employ this sentential form when every other sentential form has been judged misleading, and also to head off any attempt to turn the statement form into an ontological argument. I shall offer a scheme which elucidates this move of Aquinas in a manner designed to throw some light on the notion of *necessary existence*.

Aquinas offers an argument by analogy, in the framework of participation, which will illustrate how radical a denial is made by the apparently affirmative statement that God's nature is to exist:

> Anything on fire either is itself on fire or has caught fire. Similarly, anything that exists either is itself existence or partakes of it. Now, God, as we have seen, exists. If then he is not himself existence, and thus not by nature existent, he will only be a partaker of existence. And so he will not be the primary existent. God therefore is not only his own essence, but also his own existence (3.4).

The fire example is offered by way of analogy, yet we must throw it away almost before it has served as a ladder. For who ever heard of fire being on fire? The "fact" of the matter is—the logical or semantical fact—that anything on fire had caught fire; the 'anything' stands in the basic composition-relationship of matter to the form of fire. So we simply cannot say that fire is on fire, nor that existence exists. Hence when we do say that God exists, we must use a form which fails to do him justice, as subsequent wrangling over that expression has abundantly exhibited.

In fact, a corollary of this reading of Aquinas must note how the statement which concludes his second question—that God exists—forces us to misuse the expression ' . . . exists.' This semantic crack might appear to be the opening for an ontological form of argument: if we could get hold of the form of '. . . .exists' proper to God and be able to use it as well, it would have to be true. From the intellectual moves he makes (and refuses to make) Aquinas indicates his conviction that '. . . .exists' is always a contingent affirmation for us. There is no divine (or necessary) form of it available to us, and the most we can do is to assert that in God essence and existence cannot be distinct. [15] Here we must say—without knowing what we say—that "God's very nature is to exist."

What keeps that last statement from supplying us with a divine form for ' . . . exists' is the predicate nominative role that 'to exist' plays in it. Let me illustrate this with the following scheme, designed to display essential predication:

$$\text{(EPS) to be . . . is to be . . .}$$

EPS is clearly an essential predication scheme. That is the role played by the otherwise redundant 'to be'. Hence we can say 'to be man is to be rational', 'to be rational is to be risible' or 'to be yellow is to be colored', but we cannot say 'to be man is to be yellow'. (We can use the scheme for individuals to cite characteristic traits, since character is a kind of "second nature.")

The burden of question three comes to saying that nothing can fill the second blank in EPS when 'God' fills the first. We were able to use the formula, 'God is first cause of all things', only because this was offered as a shorthand summary of the way men use the term God. Undertaking an essential predication of the form 'to be God is to be . . .' would be quite another matter. Nor is this form prohibited simply because we can find no terms worthy of it, for Aquinas will argue that inherently analogous terms can be used in a manner worthy of God. He insists that we cannot predicate anything of God, because *the form* itself conveys a composition that would falsify the statement. (*A fortiori,* of course, one would not use an accidental predication scheme of God.)

So nothing can be said of God. Yet Aquinas has promised to go on to show him to be perfect, good, eternal, and one. How can we resolve this flagrant violation of his own rules? By suggesting that the assertion "God's nature is to exist" amounts to countenancing a *form* of predication peculiar to God. Whatever else may be said of God can be true of him only where it can be shown to be equivalent to the assertion: to be God is to be.

This acceptable form is achieved by eliminating altogether the second variable position from EPS, thus yielding the divine predication scheme:

(DPS) to be God is to be

The precise formulation is mine, not Aquinas'. Yet the arguments he offers for each subsequent predicate aim to conform each one to this scheme, in order to legitimize its application *in divinis.* Can one fracture syntax in this way and come up with a meaningful statement? Aquinas' general response would probably cite the demands each disparate subject matter makes on method. He would agree that this move is radical, yet justify it because nothing else will do for speaking of the first cause of all. Specifically, we will be invited to follow the use to which the new syntax is put and see whether we are not persuaded by the sheer beauty of coherent performance. Finally, column (b) will in each case appeal to intimations in our own experience that could predispose us to adopt so radical a program.

2.11. "Necessary Existence"

Ontological arguments seem to turn upon existence as a necessary feature of God, while objections to them tend to boggle at the very notion. I would like to offer Aquinas' scheme for as clear a characterization of "necessary existence" as may be possible. One upshot of the discussions ontological arguments provoke has been to clarify the syntax of ' . . . exists' in its impredicative or normal existential sense. It is clear that the import of this usage is *not* to announce a feature of anything, and equally clear that *necessity* of the desired sort can only be claimed where it derives from the nature of the subject in question.[16] So we have two reasons why the "necessary existence upon which ontological arguments turn cannot be parsed as ' . . . exists (necessarily)'."

Whatever it may mean to say of something that it exists necessarily, then, the only coherent way we can state it is to say of x that to be x is to be. Aquinas has argued that so radical a departure from syntax can be justified only in speaking of God. And in this unique case the departure becomes the normal form for any subsequent predication *in divinis*. It cannot serve as a covert assertion that God exists, however, simply because that is not what it says. What is does announce is that this subject is utterly unique, with the uniqueness proper to the first cause of all. That fact suggests how momentous it would be to acknowledge God to exist. But that acknowledgement stems from sources independent of such a statement.

2.2. God's Perfection (4.)

By the stipulations of question three we can say that God is perfect only if we can show that 'to be God is to be perfect' is no more than a clarification of what we mean when we say 'to be God is to be'. (As Aquinas would put it, the two notions signify the same thing, but do it in

different ways. To use a unidirectional example, something's tasting good involves its smelling good, so to say
the first means the second, even if it does not say it.)
Aquinas must then specify which among the many possible
uses of 'perfect' he wants to associate with God, and do so
by showing it to be equivalent to this unusual use of 'to
be'.

In fact, he tries to get us used to a divine sense for
'perfect' by using 'to be itself' *(ipsum esse)* as a substantive. Much as one might go on to speak of honesty after
showing how honest a man Abe was, Aquinas uses the
infinitive as an abstract singular term, asserting:

> to-be itself is the most perfect thing of all, for it is like
> *act* in comparison to everything else. Nothing achieves
> actuality except it exist, whence to-be itself is the ac-
> tuality of everything, even of forms themselves.

A statement of this sort rings suspiciously metaphysical,
yet the evidence which Aquinas gives is apparently
straightforward:

> when I say 'the to-be of man' or 'of a horse' or 'of some
> other thing', the to-be itself is regarded as something
> received like a form,. . . . So to-be is to be compared to
> other things more like what is received to the thing
> receiving than vice-versa. (4.1.3)

Or should we say it is deceptively straightforward, since
we seldom if ever find ourselves remarking on the to-be of
anything? Moreover, Aquinas acknowledges that he is
adapting 'received' to his own purposes here. One can try
translating 'to-be' as 'existence' to get the more plausible
'the existence of a horse', but this more familiar form is no
less ambiguous. For Aquinas must be using 'to-be' as an
abstract singular term to make his point. Yet we would be
prone to speak of the existence of a horse, only to mark
the difference acquiring a horse could make, say, to a
family. Here the expression would remark the fact that a
horse belongs to a family, and not, as Aquinas' example

demands, to speak of something like a feature of a horse.

Now it is clear that Aquinas must make plausible a substantive use of 'to be'. For he needs it in that form to equate 'perfect' with 'to be', as well as to assure us that he is not equivocating upon the predicate nominative sense in DPS: to be God is *to be*. The behavior of paronyms is sufficiently uncomplicated to allow a move similar to that from 'honest' to 'honesty'. Nor am I objecting in an *a priori* fashion to using 'to be' in this way. It is simply that the statement "to-be itself is the most perfect thing of all" remains elusive since the illustration failed to display a real use, and the use Aquinas offered does not apply.

Aquinas offers another pair of arguments designed to show that we must not only speak of God as perfect but as "containing, so to say, the perfection of everything else" (4.2). The first argument relies on the original formula: "Since God then is the primary operative cause of all things, the perfections of everything must preexist in him in a higher manner." Aquinas merely draws a systematic consequence from the summary statement about our use of 'God'. The second argument employs the neo-Platonic division of predicables into *per se* and *participated,* to underscore the substantive 'to-be' idiom: "because as we have seen (3.4), God is to-be itself subsisting *per se*, [he] necessarily contains within himself the full perfection of being *(essendi)*" (4.2).

Aquinas relies on this basic distinction when he needs to, without committing himself to any of the various emanation schemes designed to chart the movement of participation.[17] Nor is this an oversight, but a rigorous consequence drawn from his Aristotelian semantics. The very structure of our discourse displays *participated* (or composite) being. Hence one can never *say* what it would be like to be (or to possess something) in a nonparticipated way—that is to say, *per se.* This argument represents the burden of question three. Consequently we cannot say what it is *like* to be in a participated way either, since we have no way of getting perspective on *how* it is that we exist. *Per se* existence or possession cannot function as an effective contrast term since we have no way of *using* it; we are at best led to *posit* it.

How, then, can Aquinas permit himself the use he makes: since "God is to-be itself subsisting *per se*, [he] necessarily contains within himself the full perfection of being"? My guess would be that this argument is quite secondary for Aquinas, since the first one from causality sufficed to make his point about perfection in a properly Aristotelian fashion. This one then serves two purposes: it shows that God must also be *perfect* to the satisfaction of Augustinian purveyors in grades of perfection, and it establishes the required redundancy between 'to be' and 'to be perfect' when the expressions play a predicate nominative role. For without knowing what it might mean to say that something is 'to-be itself subsisting *per se*', we can nonetheless equate it with the 'God' in 'to be God is to be'.

In this way the *esse per se* idiom offers Aquinas a shorthand to convey the concerted denials of question three. It becomes misleading only when one is beguiled by the formula's apparently straightforward construction into thinking he can put it to use. That is why we have scrutinized Aquinas' own use so meticulously. So far each apparent use has proved just that: it has come to no more than showing that 'to-be itself' includes 'to be perfect' in a tautologous manner. Displaying a tautology is no *use* at all. And since 'perfect' cannot claim informative status, showing it equivalent with 'to be itself' cannot smuggle in a surreptitious use of either expression.

2.21. Import of Question Four

Question four will complement question three, however, in setting the parameters for legitimate predication. The earlier question stipulated the acceptable form; this question establishes the range of predicates which will be able to comply with that form: *perfections*. The effect will emerge more clearly when we consider the specifically linguistic reflections of question thirteen. Without pretending that 'perfect' is an informative predicate, however, Aquinas does count on its being more connatural than 'to be'. So he uses this question, according to the pattern I have proposed, to convey some sense for *to-be itself.*

Article three is entitled "Can creatures be said to resemble God?" and the treatment is less than rigorous. Aquinas molds causal and participation frameworks with enough license to achieve a desired effect. He begins by making the systematic point that effects bear the likeness of the agent: intraspecific effects have a specific likeness, intrageneric effects a generic one. When the agent is outside even the genus, however, as God transcends even the most remote genus of substance (3.5.1), then the only resemblance we could speak of would be "according to some kind of analogy *(aliqualem analogiam)* like that which obtains between all things because they hold to-be itself in common" (4.3).

Now Aquinas knows that *to-be itself* cannot be a characteristic, since *to be* does not determine a genus (3.5.1). That is why he expressly hedges on specifying the analogy or resemblance involved. It could only be a manner of speaking to speak of holding "to-be itself in common." Semantic propriety reinforces religious orthodoxy: there is no way of articulating how anything resembles God; no image or concept can capture him.

Yet Aquinas goes on to make a statement which, strictly speaking, he knows to be improper if not nonsensical: "and this is how things receiving existence from God resemble him; for precisely as things possessing existence they resemble the primary and universal source of all existence."[18] But there is no way of expressing *what* it is that things possess insofar as they *are.* Hence any talk about resemblance is idle, as it must be when comparing things and God (3.5.2). What, then, is Aquinas up to here? My suggestion is that he is speaking with a deliberate impropriety; the use of philosophical language here is not philosophical but rather poetic.

It is like saying: between the blueprint and the building lies something which cannot appear on the blueprint but which literally "makes all the difference," namely, whether or not the blueprint is *realized*. To say that God's very nature is to be is to say that God is unlike anything we know but most like that difference. But the difference between building and blueprint is not a feature of the building (or it would appear on the blueprints); it is more like the effort or teamwork required to get the project going. So *action* becomes the operative metaphor for achieving some understanding of to-be itself: "since nothing achieves actuality except it exist, *to-be itself* is the actuality of all things" (4.1.3).

Activity offers the normal indication that something is present, and the kind of activity serves as an index of the kind of thing it is: *actio sequitur esse*. So activity does not come in mere pushes but in kinds and qualities. If we take an appropriate set of actions, then, as both the sign and the proper effect of a specific to-be, the activity we *can* see suggests that we think of the to-be we cannot see as the playing out of a role.[19] The role itself can be formulated as the essence or nature; it is the playing-out of the role which Aquinas distinguishes as the to-be. The difference, again, between the role prescribed and the role played out cannot be found in the script.

Aquinas is trying to lead us on to some intimation of this difference: the difference each thing makes simply by being. We might want to speak of its "intrinsic worth" prior to any achievement. He is saying that each thing most resembles God simply in that it is, and in doing what is its thing to do. This terse observation in effect invites us to assume a more contemplative posture toward the world if we wish to know what God is like. For taking each thing as an object-for-me accepts its very being as a mere presupposition, and overlooks the "thing it does" in favor of what it might do for me. Perhaps statements embodying 'to-be itself' cannot help but sound mystical to us, since they reflect an habitually more contemplative attitude toward the world than is our wont.

Whatever is said about *being* is always elucidated in terms of acting or doing. Aquinas will even speak of to-be as a kind of doing *(actus essendi)*. This constant feature of Aquinas' writings gives us a handle on *to-be itself* from our experience. Even though we cannot succeed in characterizing that which "makes all the difference," something of it can be felt in a victory of resolve over lassitude. Action often makes all the difference in our lives: namely, whether we make something of them or not. Yet no formula suffices to motivate us. To act without even needing motivation, to *do* simply what one is—that's what it's like simply to be, or to be God.

2.22. Reflections on Method

The approach Aquinas takes here helps us to glean some idea of what it is simply to be, and sets the pattern for subsequent questions in column (b). He appeals, implicitly or explicitly, to a characteristically human experience to obtain some sense of what the denial in column (a) amounts to. No one can say how much sense he succeeds in conveying, since one's appreciation of such experiences varies with his appropriation of those virtues associated with a full humanity. It is most germane to a formal analysis, however, to note how Aquinas appeals to an agent's consciousness of himself as agent. By employing one's self-awareness as a focal instance, each of us can use the inherently analogous notion of *act* in a responsible manner.

This appeal represents a crucial shift: from sensible things, and the understanding to which we can be led by knowing them, to a reflective awareness of the experience of being led. The left column states what must (not) be said of God, and this is invariably established by denying a specific formal feature of things as we know them. This form of analysis is properly transcendental; it is concerned with the preconditions for any understanding connatural to the human knowing subject. The mode of this reflective analysis is logical; it comes within an extended class of those understandings to which our knowledge of sensible things can lead us—by reflecting on the conditions constituting that knowledge. The questions in the right column, on the other hand, rely less on formal analysis and more on evocation. Philosophical discourse is used with greater license, to gesture toward the experience evoked in anyone who catches some glimmer of what has been going on. The glimmer results from our becoming aware of what we have been doing.

When analysis takes this reflective a turn, it is tempting to invoke "intuition." It would be more responsible, however, simply to note how Aquinas extends his notion of *manuductio* (being-led-on). Here it includes the more typically Augustinian focus on the inner experience associated with the action itself of knowing or doing. Inner experience remains experience. It does not pretend to be a unique mode of knowing as intuition does. It stands in need of thematization and analysis. It is simply more available the more meditative and reflective a life one leads. I have tried to show how whatever use we might make of 'to-be itself' could be grounded in such an awareness. On this account one might have some grasp of what it means to assert that God's very nature is to be, recognizing all the while how tenuous a grasp that is. He need never be tempted to posit a unique act of knowing with *ipsum esse* for its proper object.

The grasp that is ours represents our own awareness of that skillful capacity to discover the formal features of a proportionate object of human knowledge. In denying one of those features of God that capacity is brought to awareness in a pointed way, for the argument depends on our grasp of what we are doing in detecting formal features.[20] We can gesture toward the import of our denial by pointing up the intellectual experience that is already ours in issuing it. Action of this sort exhibits the kind of being we are, and experience of ourselves acting provides what access we have to ourselves as existing.

2.3. Summary

One upshot, then, of stating that to be God is to be would be realizing that such a one is perfect. But that realization adds nothing to the original formula. What it represents is more like a realization of its import. So it ought to be compared more to the building that realizes the blueprints than to a revised set of blueprints. The fact that this realization is interior makes it no less real. Aquinas finds no difficulty reconciling an Augustinian sense for inner experience with a rigorously Aristotelian semantics. In fact, the experience is more poignant as we find ourselves having to live at the acknowledged limits of responsible discourse, and needing to work to understand how to use the specific denials those limits impose.

3. General Notion of Good (5.)
and the Goodness of God (6.)

Aquinas apparently intends questions five and six to clarify further God's perfection (cf. 3. *Intro.*), and the titles do not initially suggest partitioning into two distinct columns as the other pairs of questions do. Yet the treatment in each question tends to confirm that schematic decision. Question five lays out a notion of *good* equivalent to *to-be,* so that the assertion 'to be God is to be good' will at once be permitted and demanded by the stipulations of question three. This notion of good proves appropriately negative because there is no hint of assessment in it. God is not said to be good by analogy with John's being good, for John is judged to be good from his actions which are among those we assess to be good. God cannot be so judged by us: since he is good by nature, his actions cannot be subjected to assessment. They cannot but be good, and serve, if anything, as the standard for assessing. The next question intimates what it might be like to be good in this way by making the scandalous observation that "the relations that God is said to bear to crea-

tures ... really exist not in God but in the creatures"
(6.2.1).

3.1. *Good* Convertible with *Being*

We have already stumbled over an intrinsic connection
between *to be* and *to be good* in the suggestion that we
might want to refer to the difference a thing makes simply
by being as its "intrinsic worth" (#2.21). What *good* adds
conceptually to the fact of something's existing is *desirability* (5.1). This may sound curiously subjective to us,
steeped as we are in an analysis of 'good' which requires an
active assessment. Aquinas is also engaged in conceptual
analysis; he cites Aristotle in support of his claim: "good is
what all things desire" (*N. Ethics* 1094a3). I suspect that
with this initial reference to *appetite* Aristotle and Aquinas
touch somewhat closer to the grounds of assessment than
our rationalistic heritage would be able to admit.

The argument here is not informative so much as it is
clarifying: "clearly desirability is consequent upon perfection, for things always desire their [own] perfection." This
connection should make clear to us that 'desire' *(appetunt)*
is used to cover any tendency whether conscious or not,
just as perfection extends beyond the goal of conscious
achievement to take in whatever actuality is in line: "a
thing is perfect insofar as it is in act." But since "to be is
the actuality of everything, it is clear that a thing is good
inasmuch as it exists."

'Actuality' serves as a middle term to show what might
otherwise be overlooked: "being good is really the same
thing as existing." It could be overlooked because there is
an initial difference in meaning, so that "one cannot use
the words 'good' and 'existent' interchangeably without
qualification" (5.1.1). Aquinas has already located the
central difference in meaning: "good expresses a notion of
desirability not expressed by the word existent" (5.1).
Good also implies an achievement, something which we do

over and above the fact that we exist; and it is achievements that are assessed. Aquinas acknowledges that it is
more natural to use 'good' for "the actualization which
completes a thing," but reminds us that the fact that a
thing exists is already an actuality (5.1.1).

This argument is given in summary fashion: "everything,
inasmuch as it exists, is actual and therefore in some way
perfect, all actuality being a sort of perfection. [Since]
anything perfect is desirable and good (5.1), it follows
then that, inasmuch as they exist, all things are good"
(5.3). The crucial role which *actuality* plays should now be
clear, and with it, the unusual notion of *good* which
results.

God is not said to be good by assessing his achievements, which would be the ordinary way applying the
term. The only use of 'good' permissable, if one wants to
insist that to be God is to be good, would be one which
could be shown to be equivalent to the predicate nominative use of 'to be' in 'to be God is to be'. So Aquinas must
discover a way in which *good* is linked more with *being*
than with *achievement,* and must also show this meaning
to be a more basic one. We have seen how he uses the
notion of *actuality* (employing the scholastic distinction
between first and second act, or nature and achievement)
to connect *good* with *being*. This represents a sense of
'good' every bit as unusual as that associated with 'to-be
itself': "everything that is—inasmuch as it *is* is good" (5.3).
'Is' must function here as a predicate describing that "feature" by which anything which is must be said to be good,
namely, its *to-be* or *to-be itself*.

Furthermore, the *being* identified with *good* here is said
to be "the primary and distinctive object of intellect, just as
sound is the primary object of hearing" (5.2). Of course,
we do not hear sound, but sounds; just as we never
encounter nor know being, but only beings. What Aquinas
is articulating, however, is the "fact" yielded by transcendental analysis that whatever we consider must *be,* just as
hearing something presupposes the conditions for sound.
In logical terms, the fact that something exists is normally

presupposed to any formal consideration of it. In more epistemological language this use of 'being' makes implicit reference to intelligibility as such, and hence can be said to be natural to the intellect.[21]

The correlative use of 'good' intends to capture that dimension of existence coextensive with its intelligibility: its desirability. Aristotle had made reference to both when he asserted that "all men by nature desire to know" (*Meta.* 1.1). Aquinas will also hold that *good* is the "primary and distinctive object of willing," even if in fact we seek after this or that good thing. The logical point was secured by Plato: one only knowingly chooses what he thinks to be good; and the psychological aspect articulated by Augustine when he identifies the *good* with God: "our hearts are restless until they rest in Thee."[22]

So Aquinas, in asserting God to be good, is not making a contingent assessment of God, but is arguing that one who asserts 'to be God is to be' has no choice but to assert as well 'to be God is to be good.' For the second assertion is contained within the first, and stating it simply brings to consciousness the *tendency* already latent in a thing's to-be. Since that tendency or appetite is the precondition for our desiring to do or achieve anything, it underlies our more native use of 'good' to assess actions. But singling out this more basic use of 'good' does not supply us with norms for assessment; it rather recalls us to a stratum presupposed to *any* ethical use. The companion article six will have to give us some inkling of what we might mean by calling anything *good* in this sense.

3.2. Goodness of God (6.)

To make some sense of God's being good we are directed to reflect on the way each thing tends toward its originative cause, wanting somehow to be like it. The implicit model seems to be that of Aristotle's *Metaphysics,* where the unmoved mover moves all things "by being desired" (1072a25). "Clearly, then, since God is the primary operative cause of everything, goodness and desirability fittingly belong to him" (6.1). We remain far from clear, however, regarding what this could mean. Aristotle provides more of a verbal formula than a working model. He was at a loss to describe how an unmoved mover could move except by being desired, but could say little more about it.

Furthermore, the scheme Aquinas adopts here is more explicitly the archetypal one of return to origins, functioning in a neo-Platonic framework. The upshot is that "in desiring its own perfection everything is desiring God himself" (6.1.2). But what warrants Aquinas in transposing the precondition of a tendency into the object tended toward? This would seem more typically a neo-Platonic move of the sort Aquinas generally eschewed.

Finally, by way of underscoring God's *supreme* goodness Aquinas recalls that "the relations that God is said to bear to creatures . . . really exist not in God but in the creatures" (6.2.1). Many have read this as implying that God is not *really* related to creatures in the sense that we might claim his compassion or make any difference whatsoever to him.[23] If that be the case, what can 'good' possibly mean when asserted in this manner of God?

We have seen that 'to be God is to be good' cannot be rendered 'God is good' by analogy with 'John is good', for there can be no question of assessing God. Can we even oppose *good* to *evil* here? It seems not, since we are dealing with something prior to ethical discrimination. We are speaking rather of that *conatus* whereby each thing tends to its own completion without giving any thought to the right or wrong of it. If we refuse to call this innate tendency *good*, we have difficulty finding any *pied a terre* whatsoever for the ethical use, it is true. Yet this rock-bottom sense of 'good' is compatible with much moral ambiguity.[24] God's being good, then, situates him beyond (or beneath) good and evil, at least as we are accustomed to call them.

To what then can we oppose God's goodness or appetibility? Perhaps to a willful or wanton god, a god who needs to

have its own way, a god who would repulse, or, at the
other end, to an inert god who could in no way entice or
lure. The oppositions are fanciful, yet a sympathetic reading of Aquinas' statement about relations between God
and the world might guide us here. When he insists that
God's relatedness to creatures does not really exist in him
but only in them, his paradigm for "real" is not an inter-
personal relationship but a causal one.[25] It is like another
thanking us for everything we did for him, when we were
conscious simply of doing what was ours to do. He might
retort to our disclaimer: so much the better; you are an
immense help to me just by being around and being
yourself! I may not have done anything expressly for the
other person nor have been conscious of helping him at all
by what I was doing, yet he insists that I was a great help
to him. I have certainly not been oblivious of him; in fact a
firm bond may have quietly grown between us. Yet I can
still say that my being a help to him is not something
"real" in me, for his needs did not move me to some
special action. I was able to be of support to him simply
by being myself.

It would be insensitive, certainly, to label such a relationship indifferent. We are rather alluding to a level of
interaction where one is less successful the more he *tries* to
be helpful. Interaction it is, but not of a causal sort.
Furthermore this mode of offering support would seem a
most fitting way to describe the presence of the first cause
of all. For if he is the transcendent source of both the
to-be and the to-do of his creatures, as well as the one
grounding whatever tendency they exhibit, he would need
least of all to be helpful in a busybody way. His very
presence tactfully made manifest would *be* of assistance,
without any specific effort or response on his part.

In this sense, then, God's being good is more like his
being utterly desirable because he is so much himself, so
much his own being that his very presence promises to
help put me in touch with mine. The analogy here is
obvious enough among men when we meet a genuine
person. The further fact that coming into touch with my

own self means touching God's own creation assures me that his being one with himself is good for me. This remains to be acted out, of course, since nothing can be more demoralizing than someone who shames me by his genuineness, and certainly no one more terrifying than the living God. Yet Aquinas can rely at this juncture on his faith that the authentic face of God is that revealed in Jesus.

Jesus invariably upsets one's cultural accumulation about right and wrong by demanding a conversion more wrenching, it seems, for the learned than for the simple man. For a philosophical type might be tempted to presume he knew what he was saying when he succeeded in showing that God is good. Aquinas warned at the outset what an unknowing way of knowing this would have to be (3. Intro.). He adheres to these guidelines by affixing to God a sense of 'good' which neatly avoids fixing any value. It speaks rather of a native orientation than of a studied assessment; that God is good is testified by our spontaneous tendency toward what is genuine, harmonious, and otherwise beautiful. If 'good' means 'what all things desire', the first cause of all aspiring things can by rights be considered the ground of desire itself. In this utterly radical sense, God could be said to be most appetible, hence the supreme good (6.2), and we could assert (without having to imagine how) that "in desiring its own perfection everything is desiring God himself" (6.1.2).

Furthermore, since this process arrives at a notion of *good* prior to any valuation, it leaves abundant room for a revelation event in which God demands (and effects) a transvaluation of values. The way Aquinas shows how we must assert that to be God is to be good appears as the other side of the biblical assimilation of the creation story, where the God saw that what he accomplished was good. To be is to be good, before any valuation we might place upon it, just as each thing bears a significance simply by being itself, before it takes on any meaning for us (2.21). And the identical requirements hold as well: all this will remain quite hidden and meaningless until one manages to adopt a life-style increasingly consistent with what he has come to suspect is the case.

4. God's Limitlessness (7.) and God's Existence in Things (8.)

The Latin term is *infinitus,* yet Aquinas is using it here in its most austere and literal sense of lacking any limit. The argument relies solely on question three, showing that the assertion of limitlessness is a purely syntactical matter. It follows from the cumulative restrictions of question three, and is demonstrated through the single formula which expresses their upshot: God's very nature is to be.

'Limitation' might better be rendered 'definiteness' for us. It calls attention to that *composition* which spells the structural isomorphism between language and the world, accenting the fact that an object can be *defined* by the proper formula. The limits are first displayed by the form of the defining statement, and more definitely stated by the words chosen. For the medievals precision counted. Since there could be no shortcut to securing a reference, one had to state what he meant.

It should be clear, then, that this way of securing definiteness of meaning (and hence of reference) relies initially upon the syntactical composition of a declarative sentence. Since this very composition was judged inappropriate *in divinis,* there is no way in which we can make definite reference to God. Hence we must say that he is limitless. Since the upshot of that radical denial, however, was to propose a fractured form uniquely satisfying the very logic which forced a rejection of ordinary syntax, we do have a way of referring to him: to be God is to be. This special form requires a predicate nominative use of 'to be' and hence succeeds in licensing the substantive of which this use is a paronym.

So Aquinas can manage to use the expression 'to-be itself'. And the moment he does so, he realizes that to-be itself, compared with every other ontological component, is the "most formal of all" (7.1). Of course, we have no way of construing the fact that something exists as a formal feature of the thing itself, since "existence is not a predicate." Should one regard existence in that way, however, it must be said to be "like act in comparison to everything else" (4.1.3).[26] Thus nothing else can or need be said of it. Hence there is no way to limit it, so whatever it is, *to be* must be *limitless*. And since the very singularity of the formula serves to distinguish God from everything else, the statement is sufficiently definite to make sense even if we cannot ascertain what such a state of affairs would be like (7.1.3).

4.1. God's Existence in Things (8.)

Aquinas tried to secure the grammar of 'limitless' as used of God by showing that it could not be applied to the size of bodies (7.3) nor to the number of things in the universe (7.4). But a suggestion remains: "an unlimited thing ought it seems to exist everywhere in everything; we must therefore consider whether this is so of God" (8. *Intro.*). Perhaps by following this lead we may have some inkling of what it means to say that God is limitless, beyond remarking that 'to be infinite' is interchangeable with the second 'to be' in 'to be God is to be'.

The suggestion follows the quite imprecise lead of spatial metaphor: what has no limits should be everywhere and hence in everything. Yet the sense in which God was said to be unlimited simply expressed our radical inability to make a definite (and hence limiting) statement about him. Any properly spatial sense was expressly eschewed (7.3). So Aquinas is deliberately following a metaphorical lead, using philosophical notions beyond the pale of rigorous argument to explore what the denial of limitation could amount to. He tries to circumscribe a relevant sense of 'in' so that God's limitlessness can issue in his *existing in* everything without vulgarly parcelling him out. As we noted previously, he will do this by shifting to a way of speaking more typically Augustinian which appeals to a person's inward experience of himself.

The inquiry begins in straightforward Aristotelian fashion by remarking how God can be said to "exist in everything: not indeed as part of their substance or as an accident, but as an agent is present to that in which its action is taking place" (8.1). On this principle the pilot kills with bombs no less than the sniper with a bullet or the commando with a knife. Also the lawyer's hand is in the case as it progresses, just as a king is felt in his commands. God "exists in everything causing their existence" (8.3).

Using the substantive form of 'to be', then, all Aquinas need do is remind us that "since it is God's nature to be, created to-be must be the effect proper to him—just as igniting is the proper effect of fire" (8.1). The logic proper to God's activity, then, forbids us to conceive creation simply as getting something started. For whatever causes something to be "must be present to it during the whole period of a thing's existence, and present in a way in keeping with the way in which the thing possesses its existence." A thing of course does not *possess* its existence; it cannot even be said to *have* it in the austere scholastic sense of *habet*, for to-be is not a feature. But should we consider it after the manner of a feature—as we are doing in calling it the proper effect of God's activity— then we must say that "to-be is that which is more interior *(intimum)* to each thing and more deeply *in* things [than anything else]," because when considered in this way it is "like form with respect to every other component of a thing" (8.1).

The philosopher must avow that this is but a manner of speaking, of course, for strictly speaking, noting licenses us to speak of existence in this way. I have consistently rendered Aquinas' substantive *esse* literally as 'to-be' to avoid the bewitchment of the outright nominal form 'existence'. Yet on the other hand not even philosophers can rid themselves of an imperious instinct for survival. Each thing "holds onto its existence"—an observation Aquinas will make in elucidating the force of oneness as well (11.1). So we are constrained to speak of *it,* and so regard existence as a feature, even while we lack a language for doing so. Strictly speaking, of course, we do not speak of the *esse* but of the *essence* as that by which something is what it is. All the formal, structural characteristics are contained in an account of the nature of a thing, just as all the features of a building are either stated in or displayed by the blueprints. Yet what a penniless scion clings to is neither the plans nor the mortgages, but the old manor house itself.

The fact that we cannot identify *existence* allows Aquinas to speak of it as the proper effect of God while maintaining that he causes in a transcendent way. Similarly, he can affirm that each thing resembles God "in possessing existence" without betraying any determinate likeness (#2.21). So the imprecise use of language here serves a twofold purpose: it directs us to reflect on something so close to us that we can overlook it, so ingredient in the very texture of our actual thinking that we cannot even think it. Yet in doing so Aquinas preserves enough precision to elucidate the key logical features of this rarified region.

5. God's Unchangeableness (9.) and the Eternity of God (10.)

That God is unchangeable goes without saying for Aquinas. It simply means that there is no way of saying how he could change, since none of the ways in which our language is constructed to reflect change are appropriate when speaking of the first cause of all. It may be that the motivation guiding those original arguments in question three stemmed from deep-seated "hellenic" prejudices against change, but it seems more likely that so summary an interpretation may have missed the point of Aquinas's assertion. None of his arguments are designed to show that change is inimical to God, but rather that what we must affirm (and deny) of him removes God from any possibility of being in process. We simply have no way to speak of him changing, hence he must be beyond change.

Precision is capital here, for removing God from the very possibility of change does not imply that he is at rest. *Rest* belongs to the category of change; we could call it zero-motion. By the same token, we shall want to speak of God's activity, so unchangeable cannot mean inert. What is specifically denied of God is "that mode of motion and change proper to things which exist in potency" (9.1.1). The first argument appeals to a variant of the original formula—that God is the first being of all—and finds it impossible to speak of potentiality here "since actuality, simply speaking, precedes potentiality" (9.1). The next argument shows how change of this kind is conceptually linked with compositeness, and reminds us that no form of composition is appropriate *in divinis*. Strictly speaking, of course, we have no way of construing what is "sheerly actual and unalloyed with potentiality," but Aquinas crossed *that* frontier in question three. All he is stating here is what he must affirm: where we say "to be God is to be" we must also say "to be God is to be unchangeable," for the first requires the second.

5.1. The Eternity of God (10.)

To say that God is eternal, on the other hand, cannot help but add something, since this term is more properly religious than the technical 'unchangeable'. "From eternity to eternity" the Vulgate translated the psalmist—though expressions like this tend to complicate Aquinas' exposition rather than expedite it. Aquinas does not hesitate to speak of God's eternity, however, even though he knows that "eternity, in the true and proper sense, belongs to God alone" (10.3), and hence cannot be articulated for what it is. Two facts appear to smooth the way in this case, however. The first is Aristotle's painstaking analysis of *time* in the *Physics,* which allows Aquinas to make quite precise denials: "just as we can only come to know simple things by way of composite ones, so we can only come to know eternity by way of time" (10.1).

The second fact is less explicit though perhaps even more operative: it is that we have experience of operations which are not processes, and so can speak more confidently of an eternity which follows upon unchangeableness. Aquinas alludes to this fact here, asserting that "God shares his unchangeableness with other things, and reminding us that "just as we become aware of time by becoming aware of the flowing instant, so we grasp the idea of eternity by grasping the idea of an abiding instant" (10.2.1, 10.3). The allusion is to Augustine's phenomenological treatment in the tenth book of the *Confessions*; the systematic background can be found in Aquinas' precise elaboration of Augustine's trinitarian analogy. The word is the expression of the Father just as an interior formulation expresses an insight. Ideally, formulating an insight does not add to it, but it does capture it. The formulation is then the act of an act: an intelligible emanation, an operation that is not a process.[27] Although the expression "abiding instant" (*nunc stans*) gives every impression of a contradiction *in adjecto*, it speaks to us nevertheless. Not because we have ever managed to make time stand *still*, but because we can have some access to a region beyond that in process.

Aquinas characteristically relies on a traditional formula to manage this shift from the physical to the psychic: Boethius' definition of eternity as "the instantaneously whole and perfect possession of unending life."[28] There is nothing static about this description; we are clearly in another region where process is less important than constancy, fidelity, or being all together (10.1.6). Aristotle's analysis of time allowed him to deny sucessiveness and a beginning or end to eternity, but it takes quite another base to affirm that what lacks succession in fact "exists all together *(tota simul)*" (10.1). A typical physical image for what lacks divisibility (and hence succession) would be a geometric point, yet what sense would it make to say that a point "existed all together"? Clearly Aquinas is relying on another modality of experience here. As his allusion to Augustine corroborates, we are asked to attend to our experience of that awareness proper to conscious beings.

Beyond merely attending to that experience, however, Aquinas encourages us to formulate it in terms that will help lead others along to it. The terms will inevitably be taken from the behavior of things in process, and hence present themselves as metaphors and images of inner experience. While some psychic awareness is presupposed to an understanding of what is going on here, we cannot simply appeal to the experience itself as a sufficient warrant for asserting that God is in fact eternal. We must make an effort to capture the "abiding instant" in the language of changing things, for we live in the midst of them and participate in change ourselves. It simply turns out to be easier for us to get the point of these images when we are speaking of the eternity of God, for we also have direct access to an activity of understanding which is not itself in process.

6. The Oneness of God (11.)

"Oneness *(unum)* adds nothing real to any existent thing, but simply denies division of it, for to be one means no more than to exist undivided. And from this it is clear that everything existing is one" (11.1). In this utterly redundant sense we hardly need to be persuaded that 'to be God is to be one' adds nothing to the divine predication scheme. Nor would it merit deliberate treatment. The fact that the notion of *unity* has never ceased to foment discussion, however, warns that there is much more at stake.

'One' is a transcendental predicate, closely linked to that order which accounts for intelligibility. Whatever is understood must be taken as one. Any order can be traced to an ordering principle: 'order' says 'ordered to one.' The principle need not be an agent; it may be a formula—'one' is a transcendental predicate. More than a necessary condition for intelligibility, unity also expresses the aspiration of intelligence: greater unity promises better understanding. Here again, though, there can be no single paradigm. A physical theory is considered more unifying the greater range of happenings it can explain by a single model, whereas a theory of psychic activity must be able to explain how quite opposing forces manage to contribute to psychic wholeness.

To speak of *wholeness* suggests something of the range of meanings latent in an inherently analogous term like 'one', and suggests why Aquinas bothers to treat of the oneness of God so explicitly. To say that God is one intimates much more than he is an individual, though Aquinas does not fail to note that 'to be God is to be' conveys uniqueness: "so to be God is to be this God" (11.3). It seems rather that the enveloping connotations of oneness—from *undivided* to *wholeness*—serve as a fittingly symbolic summary statement of everything said of God from question three on. He ends the treatment by recalling that God is "supremely undivided because he is altogether simple" (11.4). We have already seen how misleading 'simple' could be as a predicate; it functions more like a rubric reminding us that nothing at all could be said of God if it is put in the way we must put things to say them. By linking God's being *simple* with his being *one* Aquinas enhances the shorthand of logic with a symbolic dimension.

For 'one' is a richly symbolic expression. From the fact that 'order' says 'ordered to one' we come to the further sense of *integration,* and thence to *wholeness.* It is imperative that a conscious individual discover a unitary sense in his life. The initial and minimal sense of *undivided* which serves existence as a necessary condition becomes *wholeness* to consciousness: its entire goal.[29] A statement like Aquinas makes at the beginning lies open to this range of interpretation: "clearly then everything's existence is grounded in indivision, and this is why things guard their unity as they do their existence" (11.1).

Aquinas' arguments trade on and firm up the symbolic character of *oneness* by appealing to the different modalities under which God must be considered one. We have noted the first reason: the fractured predication scheme which displays God's simpleness also conveys uniqueness. The second recalls that one whose very nature is to be by that fact "embraces in himself the whole perfection of existence" (11.3). The Platonic scheme forms the background here: everything else is what it is by participating in what God is, so he alone is utterly himself and, in this special sense, everything. The final reason offered looks empirical but turns out not to be: "because the world is one." Aquinas does not argue the fact but simply remarks that "we find all existent things in mutual order, certain of them subserving others." I take this to be less a factual than a promissory statement: hypotheses guiding our inquiry presume orderliness. And since order implies a principle of order, the one who is denominated "primary source of unity and order in the universe, namely, God, must be one himself" (11.3).

Nothing has been proved, certainly, but a web of conceptual linkages has been brought to light. Expressions like oneness have a way of calling our attention to a panoply of such connections on a variety of different levels. That accounts for the symbolic role they play. The fact itself apparently stems from these notions being ingredient in the very activity of bringing anything to light. This fact is displayed in their inherently analogous structure. Such expressions would have to recur in any language and so would be significant in every possible world. But that is simply another way of remarking how they are ingredient in the activity itself of understanding and of assessing. 'One' exhibits this structure in a remarkable way, and so serves to cap the list of divine names.

7. Reflections on Naming God

Questions twelve and thirteen wrap up our consideration of "the ways in which God does not exist" by explicitly reflecting on how it is that God might be known by his creatures, notably men (12.), and the precise import of our discourse about him (13.). The treatment is broadly epistemological. The first part sketches the outlines of a philosophical anthropology; the second takes up more specific semantic issues. The first asks how our mind is (or fails to be) proportioned to God; the second, how any statement about him—even those deemed appropriate—might be said to be a true statement. Since my concern lies more with the second type of question, I shall offer enough of a summary of question twelve to retain perspective, and move quickly to the issue of theological language in question thirteen.

7.1. How God Is Known by His Creatures (12.)

Knowledge, for Aquinas, requires two kinds of ontic similarity—to fulfill the adage "like is known by like." The first we have seen: an isomorphism between the formal features of the thing to be known and those of the formula which we use to know it. Since I take a *concept* to be a formula considered together with one's capacity to use it, and since formulas are normally so considered, I do not need to make special reference to concepts. We were unable to predicate anything of God by using an ordinary predication scheme because we could appreciate that the first cause of all would not admit of the composition displayed by such a scheme. In the terms employed by this question: "since every created form is determined to a certain meaning, whereas the divine nature is beyond any circumscription, containing to a transcendent degree every perfection that can be described or understood by the created mind, that nature could never be able to be represented by any created likeness"(12.2).

The phenomenological cast of this consideration invites us to regard the formula or concept not simply as a structure but also as a thing. Such a shift introduces another requirement for knowledge: some parity in the manner of existing between the thing known and the knower. This can be taken to apply either to the knower himself or to the formula he uses as his proper instrument of knowledge. So Aquinas announces the requirement in bold terms: "if the way of being of the thing to be known were beyond that of the knower, knowledge of that thing would be beyond the natural power of the knower"(12.4); and he applies it to the instrument: "because the essence of God is to exist, and since this could not be the case with any created form, no such form could represent the essence of God to the understanding"(12.2).

This requirement simply formulates the generally recognized fact about human cognition that "knowing [a certain class of objects] is connatural to us, namely facts about physical objects" (12.4). Aquinas tenders his observation in the broad strokes akin to what is offered today as "philosophical anthropology." Much of the discussion surrounding the verification principle, or that engaged in establishing limits for empirical knowledge, is of this sort. Here it is offered simply to remind us why we need images and models to assist us in more theoretical inquiry, and why philosophy flounders without examples.

Aquinas puts his requirements to use to give a more precise meaning to God's being incomprehensible. "To comprehend is to understand perfectly: a thing is perfectly understood when it is understood as well as it can be" (12.7). Apply the formula, whatever can be scientifically proved is comprehended when the treatment of it displays the methodical features of a demonstration, but not when the treatment amounts to offering an opinion. In trying to understand God no formula is appropriate except the peculiar fractured form, so our knowledge manifestly falls short of grasping its object. The manner of existing is relevant as well, since "each thing can be understood to the extent that it is actually realized (*ens actu*)." Since God's mode of existing is limitless, there will always remain something to be understood; or put in more anthropological terms, a knower will continually be called beyond himself.

The main use to which Aquinas puts these reflections about the structural and existential disparity between the human knowing subject and the first principle of all, however, is to give as a precise a content as possible to the promise of the Christian faith. Whoever perseveres to the end will be utterly transformed—"we know that when he appears we shall be like him and we shall show him just as he is" (I John 3:2). The knowledge, Aquinas argues, must be one of direct vision if it is to satisfy the longings of the human spirit and be as transforming as it is promised to be (12.1). But since any appropriate knowledge of God is quite incommensurate with the human condition, this transforming vision must be a gift. Aquinas employs the two ontic requirements for knowledge both to gauge the largesse of the gift and to state as precisely as possible in what it must consist: "the divine essence itself becomes the form through which the intellect understands" (12.5). Not that we could know what this would be like; there simply are no other terms available in which to clarify the promise.

This promise of faith supplies the ultimate context for Aquinas' entire effort, especially for his focus on God as an object of intellectual inquiry. He closes the question with two summary statéments regarding the knowledge of God possible to us short of the fulfillment of the promise. The first regards the knowledge available to natural reason. By reflecting on our mind's spontaneous orientation to physical objects, "we can at least be led from them to know of God that he exists and that he has whatever must belong to the first cause of all things which is beyond all that is causes" (12.12). Knowledge of this sort, we have seen, amounts to an increasingly poignant sense of the difference between God and creatures: a specific and firm denial followed by an intimation that the denial is not the end of the story. Or as Aquinas puts it, "that his lack of such things is not a deficiency in him but due to his transcendence."

Knowledge like that is more frustrating than supportive. It may prove enticing but it is certainly not transforming. There is, however, another way of knowing which Aquinas believes to be gradually transforming, and that is a knowing-by-faith.[30] Aquinas uses his phenomenology of human knowing to fasten on two ways that we might be helped to a better grasp of God: clearer images for the realities involved and a stronger light by which to read their significance (12.13). The operative notion here will also figure centrally in selecting expressions appropriate for speaking of God: the knowledge we possess must be capable of indefinitely deeper comprehension. This feature lends to Aquinas' quite intellectual treatment of knowing-by-faith a transforming cast:

> The stronger our intellectual light the deeper the understanding we derive from these images, whether these be received in a natural way from the senses or formed in the imagination by divine power. Revelation provides us with a divine light which enables us to attain a more profound understanding from these images (12.13.2).

7.2 Theological Language (13.)

Logic was a ready tool for a medieval theologian, so he seldom needed to call attention to it. Aquinas steps back in this question, however, to lay out his logical tools for appraisal. So the question not only offers a key to method in the *Summa* but also affords a glimpse of the logic embodied in "philosophical grammar," which formed

Aquinas' specific background. First the monasteries and then the cathedral schools of the previous century had all put Aristotle and Porphyry to work in elucidating the scriptures. The results for philosophy were akin to the fever of work following the publication of the *Principia* in our times: an application of the new expertise to some long-standing controversies. Since most of the controversies were theological, this could be counted a theological gain as well, though we might focus rather on the increasingly refined capacity for distinguishing among the senses of scripture. Although hopelessly ahistorical by modern standards, one could never accuse the medievals of being bound to a fundamental or literal sense. Exegesis became second nature to a culture at once weaned on the Word and increasingly skilled in the use of words.

7.21. Two Useful Tools

This heritage provided Aquinas with two specific instruments which he put to theological use. It also contributed to his sophisticated sense for words and how they signify. This expertise brought with it that *feel* so often associated with a skill, which guided his use of the tools and kept him from being sidetracked by bewitching questions. Attempts to translate this skill into a semantic theory have often been so misled by Aquinas' opening bow to Aristotle that they have neglected to note how he actually proceeds. "Aristotle says that words are signs for thoughts and thoughts are likenesses of things, so words refer to things indirectly through thoughts (*De Int.* 16a3). How we refer to a thing depends on how we understand it"(13.1). The initial idiom reminds us of question twelve; the upshot however is quite different. For how else can one discover "how we understand a thing" except by monitoring how we speak of it? And that is precisely how Aquinas proceeds. The cash value of the opening ontic scenario is simply to remind us that there is never a reference without a sense, since referring is something *we* do by performing a significant action in an appropriate manner.

The two instruments were specifically designed to meet the rigors of this semantic environment. They are, respectively, the distinction between *mode of signifying* and *what is meant (modus significandi/res significata)*, and a skilled capacity to order the various senses of certain privileged expressions in a way which tolerates the differences yet finds a focal meaning capable of gathering them together. The shorthand for this capacity is "analogy," yet the term is almost bound to mislead. For Aquinas used it in a way much more akin to Wittgenstein's "family resemblance" than to the metaphysical method claimed by later Thomists.[31] For we are speaking not of a *method* (of the sort Descartes promised) but of a *skill* demanding continual exercise to keep toned to a discriminating expertise. It focuses on expressions and the way we use them, exercising on metaphorical uses, then homing in on a set of terms which anyone can use in a vague gesturing way but which only a discriminating user can turn to a precise end. We come to recognize the skillful by the way they choose their examples.

The distinction between *mode of signifying* and *what is meant* subserves this more generic skill. Aquinas simply enlists it as part of a generally available repertory. The distinction is itself shorthand for a set of moves developed by philosophical grammarians for dealing with recalcitrant biblical texts.[32] *What is signified* does not refer directly to an existing object, of course, but rather to an intentional fact: it is *what we intend* by saying what we do. The *manner of signifying* is the way we put what we say; more precisely, the expression refers to the various entanglements in which we find ourselves by putting it that way. The more skilled we become in recognizing these entanglements and in extricating ourselves from them by bringing forth variant expressions, the more accurately do we succeed in saying what we mean. There is no magic way to deliver what is meant except by expressing it.

So the distinction between what is signified and manner of signifying remains a dialectical or programmatic one, remarking the fact that we can be made aware that putting something a certain way betrays what we intended to say. In reflecting on the statements we can make about God this distinction is enlisted to remind us that any referential interpretation will have to cope with a standing gap between what is meant and our manner of signifying it. The trick lies in turning a studied awareness of that gap into a role that we come to understand and then incorporate into the very statements themselves.

There are certain expressions which contain something of a gap in their very syntax. We need to supply examples to learn how to use them. Typically we use them to make assessments since they can be focused accurately enough on any factual situation, yet measure that situation against our aspirations. These expressions form an identifiable set which Aquinas calls "perfections." They will turn out to be the least misleading predicates for God. The use of such expressions in one context does not infect their application in another, yet neither use fails to be precise. A wise trapper and a wise judge could scarcely survive were they to exchange roles. Any of us, nonetheless, can pick out the person who is wise with respect to his particular environment, and would know to whom to go if we wanted to catch animals or receive a just decision in a case. Those terms which are "perfections" allow us both latitude and discrimination in application. Any formula which tries to capture what these expressions have in common will itself contain terms of this peculiar construction. Aquinas' more positive way of putting this is that certain words "simply mean certain perfections without any indication of how these perfections are possessed—words, for example, like 'being', 'good', 'living' and so on. These words can be used literally *(proprie)* of God" (13.3.1)..

Since any defining formula (devoid of such terms) would possess a definite *mode of signifying,* expressions admitting of such diverse use must succeed simply in

"meaning certain perfections" without benefit of definition. Here is where the ordering skill comes into play.
There is no doubt that we can and do use these expressions
to mean something definite. From those uses we derive
what understanding we have of them: "we understand
such perfections as we find them in creatures, and as we
understand them so we use words to speak of them"
(13.3). In fact, then, we can never *use* 'wise' or 'good'
simply to "mean certain perfections without any indication of how these perfections are possessed"; we must *use*
them in a definite context. Yet we use them in contexts so
diverse that no single formula could embrace all the uses.
This fact gives Aquinas enough purchase to speak of perfections as meaning something, prescinding from any specific use.

It is this *meant* that is properly predicated of God—"in
fact, more properly than of creatures, for these perfections
belong primarily to God and only secondarily to others."
But of course this *meant* is not a *use*, hence it cannot be a
sense for us; it is rather a *non*-sense. So Aquinas immediately adds: "so far as the *way of signifying* these perfections are concerned, the words are used inappropriately
[of God], for they have a way of signifying that is appropriate to creatures"(13.3).

7.22. Stating What We Know We Know Not

It feels suspiciously like a game: now you mean it, now
you don't. The way back to clarity proceeds by reflecting
on the actual ways we do use these expressions. Reflection
first suggested the distinction between *what is meant* and
one's *manner of signifying* it, simply to mark the fact that
we could submit our own way of putting something to
criticism and recognize a better one. Hence acknowledging
the distinction cannot be a way of covertly generating a
use which delivers what is meant without a hint of how we
mean it. That would be absurd, for "how we refer to a
thing depends on how we understand it." Understanding

requires formulation; and a formula, a context in which to use it. What we can understand, however is the vast compass of uses these expressions can muster. Reflection on that fact allows us to grasp that an expression like 'wise' could be put to use in an entirely different manner of signifying, one which displays an utterly different mode of realization.

Although *we* do not possess the use, we *do* possess skills requisite to reflect on the uses we do have and to recognize a set of features common enough to be gathered into a structure (or syntax). That capacity allows us to state that expressions of this sort *could be* used of God, by one who would know how to do it. We do not know how, hence we can never know precisely what we mean when we license these terms to be used of God. For their manner of realization must be entirely different: " 'wisdom', for example, [conveys] a quality when it is used of creatures, but not when it is applied to God" (13.5). When applied to God it must be made to conform to the divine predication scheme (to be God is to be) by being shown equivalent to the assertion therein.

Again, although we do not know how to speak that way, we can nonetheless state the conditions. We can also exercise our awareness by actively denying entanglements of ordinary syntax like the one mentioned above. So 'John is wise' presupposes 'wise' to be used qualitatively, whereas 'God is wise' does not. But this much awareness invites more: asserting 'God is wise' in a discriminating fashion implies that one is prepared to assert 'God is wisdom' as well. The expressions are irreducible: the first a predication, the second an identity. We cannot dispense with the predication in favor of the identity, because we are not prepared to assert simply that wisdom is God. Each taken alone proves misleading, hence a more discriminating use of one involves the readiness to use the other. In fact, Aquinas suggests that we use the *predication* to convey God's reality and the *identity* to signify that God is the norm rather than normed (13.1.2). An observation like this presumes a reflexive awareness of what we are about, without demanding access to uses which we could never legitimately claim.

The very capacity to appreciate that 'wise' would be realized in an utterly different manner in God is what allows us to mean what we say when we say that God is wise. For we can say it, conscious that we do not know how we mean it to apply to God. Furthermore, we can deliberately "not intend to signify something distinct from his essence, power or existence" so that we are explicitly aware that "what it signifies in God is not confined by the meaning of our word but goes beyond it"(13.5). In this way we can say what we mean without pretending to know what we mean when we say it of God. In fact, it is precisely by realizing that we do *not* know what it is we are saying that we are licensed to say what we do say. Such is Aquinas' solution, and the ambiguities are instructive both for semantics and for theology.

We can say what we mean. Aquinas opposes two alternative analyses of religious language by insisting that they misrepresent "what people want to say when they talk about God. When a man speaks of the 'living God' he does not simply want to say that God is the cause of our life [Alan of Lille] or that he differs from a lifeless body [Moses Maimonides] " (13.2). However numinous a range of meanings he may unleash, the believer nonetheless wants to address the living God. Yet he would be the first to acknowledge that even the term of address shades into unknown reaches. He does not pretend to know what he means when he says it, knowing that the living God realizes *life* in a totally different way than he can grasp. Nonetheless, there are analogies— leads that one can follow—which allow us to use our own experience to intimate what God's life might be like. These are expressly exploratory and tentative, and always open to correction as we acquire greater skill in ordering the uses we do possess of those expressions called "perfections."

7.23. A Clarification of "Analogy"

The two uses of 'analogy' mentioned earlier—as expressions or in arguments—should clarify this matter somewhat (#1.221). The analogies referred to here are akin to arguments by analogy. They function like the hints and suggestions of a divine mode of existence offered in column (b). Terms like being, good, alive, and wise, on the other hand, are inherently analogous expressions. Wherever they can be used they can be used properly; no allusions here. Yet the very richness of their syntax also makes some of them apt for metaphorical use—as in 'vital connection' or 'wisdom of the body'. Of course, Aquinas reaches well beyond familiar use, and even beyond the bounds of good syntax, when he insists that it makes sense to apply each such expresssion to God. Some exercise in extending our ordinary uses analogically in figurative speech can familiarize us enough with the inherently analogous structure of certain privileged expressions to be ready to put them to the conscious use Aquinas requires of us. So poetry helps to carry us to the threshold of philosophy.

The relations between these two uses of 'analogy' are real but indirect. So we notice an affinity of romantic poets for religious questions, yet find them impatient with theology. We are likewise tempted to collect appropriate predicates for God under the rubric "symbolic," until we find that rubric will not stand critical scrutiny. There must, of course, be a poetic and symbolic dimension to those expressions apt for use of God, and a theologian who fails to appreciate this has lost his sense for both the human and the divine. Yet this broad highway of analogies would avoid the abyss—the *nein*—that separates God's ways from men's. We announce that transcendence by insisting that even those things which we may properly say of God express rather "how he is not than how he is" (3. *Intro*).

Aquinas incorporates the transcendence of God by refusing to allow seductive analogies to budge him from his semantic base: "we speak of God as we know him, and since we know him from creatures we can only speak of him as they represent him"(13.2). Hence whatever we predicate of God must "fail to represent adequately what he is." But we can succeed in singling out a privileged set of terms by showing how their capacity to render precise assessment in one context after another removes any formal limitation from the expression itself. We can then use such an expression of God without pretending to grasp his manner of realizing *it*. For we can appreciate that we do not understand what *it* is as God realizes it.

Symbolic affinities keep the dialectic moving forward to an assertion, for every one of these inherently analogous expressions embodies a human aspiration. We cannot help but treasure wisdom. The precise manner of understanding that we do not know what we are saying, however, emerges as we learn to appreciate the way expressions of this sort work. That appreciation cannot be reflected in the form of the statement made, since anyone can say that God is wise. But our logical appreciation is reflected in what we make of statements like these, in the questions we entertain about them, in the problems we countenance as real. All these hidden moves distinguish a master from an apprentice, as Socrates showed his wisdom by acknowledging his ignorance.

As a way of summarizing this interpretation I want to consider in greater detail some moves Aquinas made and some questions he avoided. I can only hope that what I have said so far throws at least a modicum of light on the issue of theological language. I would be content to have offset some misunderstandings of *analogy* which have plagued dialectical, process, and Thomistic theologians alike.

7.24. Some Questions in Detail

Someone might succeed in grasping the movement of Aquinas' dialectical resolution of this issue, yet find it a

brilliant *tour de force*. The operative distinction between
the *manner of signifying* and *what is meant* seemed to
offer a handle for proper predication *in divinis*—until we
realized that no one could either formulate or use the
meant without incorporating a certain *manner*. The upshot
of that was to admit that we have no *use* ready for
speaking of God. We can only work with those we have:
using terms of the appropriate kind, realizing they will be
realized differently in God, and understanding that we
cannot understand how that will be. The terms themselves
already suggest certain analogies, it is true, but these are of
that allusive and tenuous sort that one hesitates to call
knowing.

If that is a sample of a sophisticated referential account
of religious language, why bother? How could we ever find
out if our referring expressions were successful? Especially
when they are uttered in a context declaring that they
cannot be true in the manner stated. Even granting that we
possess so acute a quality of awareness that we can judge
the manner to be misleading in the very act whereby we
assert God to be wise, so what then? So the statement is
not false as it is stated. But how informative can it be?

The answer must be: not very informative at all. And
the reason has already been given: we have no way of using
any expression commensurate with God. We do possess a
remarkable capacity for reflexively conscious employment
of the uses we have, however, and we can put this awareness to work in making statements which are true. They
are true in that they do not pretend to offer a use for
speaking of God. These statements are true also in that
what they say *can* be said of God, though we do not
know *how* to say it. Hence we cannot tell from statements
like these what God is like. So the question of successful
reference cannot even arise. (Ironically enough, the gambit
of "eschatalogical verification" would prove utterly super-
fluous for Aquinas, for at that moment discourse gives way
to vision.) Yet we *are* offered a way of heading off mis-
guided attempts to refer to God, so the issue of successful
reference is given the same twist.

There is more behind this than meets the philosophic eye, of course. Yet the move has none of the apologetic motivation we might suspect, for one so motivated would have wished more information. It stems rather from Aquinas' experience with another sort of knowing entirely—a knowing-by-faith. This is knowing of another sort because it is transforming; it represents a gift, not an acquisition. Faith offers us more felicitious images for God, notably Jesus. By increasing our command over the linguistic uses, the awareness and the analogies we do possess (12.12), faith accomplishes a growing familiarity with the ways of God which approximates more and more to a genuine use of language. Aquinas likens this increased command of language regarding God to a stronger intellectual light, but it is more akin to courage than to certitude. And the familiarity is more like getting used to a precarious job than settling into a comfortable routine.

What the philosophic treatment can do is to open the way for knowing of a very different order. It cannot offer a God to conflict with the God of faith, since it supplies no images at all and only suggests remote analogies. For Aquinas it functions more like the Hebrew prohibition against making images than like a competing doctrine. In fact, the object of Aquinas' study, God, must be said to shift from the God of these early questions to the God known-by-faith. This must be said because different kinds of acts correspond to different kinds of objects, and knowing-by-faith is not just knowing something different but knowing differently. Aquinas says as much when he admits that pagans (who may well have acknowledged the truth of the proposition 'God exists') cannot be said to believe in God.[33]

Aquinas did not make much of this difference, it is true, and as a consequence he did not clarify how the two "knowings" are related. The reason seems obvious enough: these early questions initiate a theological treatise where logical and philosophical expertise are constantly subserving faith's enterprise of seeking understanding. The God is implicitly the God of Judeo-Christian faith from the beginning. So the effort required of Aquinas is to conceive a knowledge natural to reason. Its results, as we have seen, would be quite useless to apologetics, and the endeavor is certainly too esoteric to be a preparation for receiving the gift of faith. What role, then, can his philosophical analysis possibly play?

My suggestion is that it plays the role philosophy always plays. Aquinas' mode of inquiry offers a therapy specifically designed for anyone whose *interest* in things divine tends to turn those things into questions. Such a person tends to become so preoccupied with answering these questions that he is distracted from the issues themselves, especially where they might involve himself. Put somewhat more positively, whatever exercise one gains in extricating himself from his intellectual entanglements will serve him by developing his critical powers. (Just as images and analogies predispose the more symbolic-minded to attend to what is different in the ways of God.) More positively still, by attending carefully to a set of expressions whose very syntax opens the way to a growing understanding one can become increasingly sensitive to the open texture of our ordinary ways of understanding. Thus he can come to appreciate knowing as a contemplative as well as an organizing activity. In this way we can see more precisely how intellectual exercise of the sort Aquinas offers may effectively predispose a philosophical type of person for knowing of an altogether different sort.

8. Summary

That, so far as I can see, is a handy way of summarizing these attempts to render Aquinas accessible. Philosophers inevitably take a longer way around, writing (as everyone does) for themselves first of all. Others may be able more simply to accept those spontaneous tendencies of their natures which Aquinas calls perfections. And accepting them, they will follow wherever they lead. But then such a spontaneous picture does not really reflect our condition, for culture has made philosophers of us all. Our natural tendencies run amuck, so we begin to fear them as temptations, while perfections are imposed to the point of tyranny. And this situation breeds cynics only too ready to believe that all talk of perfections masks a complicated set of "projections."

So the critical expertise of a philosopher could be helpful, even if he cannot claim to provide much information or manage a successful reference to God. The philosopher might even be cherished for not pretending to offer those things. He would then be sought for what he does offer through his effort at teaching: an exercise field, an obstacle course, a studied sequence of postures. If we take up the challenge, we shall acquire a discipline, *a yoga,* which will help us negotiate the way as it opens before us. The ideologist promises a map; the philosopher passes on an invitation, offering what assistance he can to help us respond to it.

NOTES

1. *Summa Theologiae,* Introduction to question 3. References to Aquinas will be to the *Summa* (unless otherwise indicated) and will be in text as follows: 3.2 = question 3, article 2 of the first part; 3.2.1 = question 3, article 2, response to the first objection. Any parts of the *Summa* other than the first will be indicated by roman numerals at the beginning, e.g., I-II 2.3: first part of the second part, etc. References to sections of this chapter will be set off by an #: (#3.2); and similarly for other chapters, where the chapter itself will be indicated by roman numerals: (#II.4.1).

2. *Posterior Analytics* 1.1 (71a10-25); see also Bernard J.F. Lonergan, *Insight* (London, 1957), 366, and *Verbum: Word and Idea in Aquinas* (Notre Dame, 1967), 11-16.

3. Victor Preller, *Divine Science and the Science of God* (Princeton, 1967). A common background can be traced to the theory of knowledge developed by Wilfrid Sellars, through a series of essays, largely collected in *Science, Perception and Reality* (London, 1963). For an appreciative study of Preller see my 'Religious Life and Language," *Review of Metaphysics* 22 (1969) 681-690, and for

a more critical appraisal of his approach see Donald Evans, "Victor Preller's Analogy of 'Being'," *New Scholasticism* 45 (1971) 1-37.

4. The volumes of the *Summa* which form the focus of this study are (in the Eyre and Spottiswoode/McGraw-Hill series): Vol. II: *Existence and Nature of God* (2-11), ed. Timothy McDermott; Vol. III: *Knowing and Naming God* (12-13), ed. Herbert McCabe (New York, 1964). Vol. 1: *Christian Theology* (1), ed. Thomas Gilby (New York, 1964), provides useful general background material to a study of the *Summa Theologiae*.

5. A classic statement can be found in Carl G. Hempel and Paul Oppenheim, "Logic of Explanation," in H. Feigl and M. Brodbeck (ed), *Readings in Philosophy of Science* (New York, 1953), 319-324.

6. McDermott (ed), *Existence and Nature*, 18, note a.

7. M-D. Chenu, *La Théologie au Douzième Siècle* (Paris, 1957), esp. chapter, "Grammaire et Theologie"; and Desmond Henry, *The Logic of Saint Anselm* (Oxford, 1967).

8. Cf. Gilby's note 88, p. xxxv, in McCabe (ed), *Knowing and Naming God;* and McCabe's appendix: "Analogy," 106-8; and Preller, 168, note 72.

9. Anselm, *Proslogion,* IV (cf. above, II.3).

10. Emil Fackenheim offers a clarifying treatment of *Aufhebung* in religious issues in *The Religious Dimension in Hegel's Thought* (Bloomington, Indiana, 1967).

11. *In Metaphysicorum Aristotelis Expositio* (Turin, 1950) IV.4 (574).

12. For an historical and systematic study of the uses of analogical discourse in philosophy, with special attention to models and metaphors, see my *Analogy and Philosophical Language* (New Haven, 1973).

13. He also promises there to investigate God's limitlessness, unchangeableness, and oneness. Yet the first and second mentioned each comprise two questions. My scheme of two columns finds its initial support in Aquinas' schematic introduction to questions 3-13.

14. See the critical edition of Joseph Bobik, *Aquinas on Being and Essence* (Notre Dame, 1965).

15. Preller, 172-73.

16. Cf. the discussion of William P. Alston, "The Ontological Argument Revisited," *Philosophical Review* 69 (1960), reprinted in Alvin Plantinga (ed), *The Ontological Argument* (New York, 1965), 86-110.

17. Cf. Louis-Bertrand Geiger, *La Participation dans le Philosophie de S. Thomas d'Aquin* (Paris, 1942).

18. "Et hoc modo illa quae sunt a Deo assimilanter ei inquantum sunt entia, ut primo et universali principio totius esse" (4.3). Note how the translation captures the intent of the Latin by careful syntactic transpositions.

19. "To exist, as St. Thomas sees it, is to have significance, to have point, to play out a role. Such an idea of being is indeed the seminal idea of his philosophical view of the world: an idea of being, that is, not just as an arbitrary thereness of things for sense-experience, but as a logical and significant thereness in a community of the universe revealed to man by knowledge and love. The model or image that St. Thomas uses to express this idea of being is the model of an action: being is playing out a role, realizing a significant conception." Timothy McDermott, *Existence and Nature,* xxiii.

20. It is Bernard Lonergan who has developed in a systematic fashion this conception of metaphysics as a disciplined appropriation of what one is up to in the activity of coming to know. The basic locus is *Insight* (London, 1957), though the process is summarized in his latest work: *Method in Theology* (London, 1972) as a shift from philosophy as theory to philosophy as thematizing interiority (259-265).

21. For the logical point see P. F. Strawson, *Introduction to Logical Theory* (London, 1952), 173-78; and for Lonergan's interpretation of the classical use in Aquinas see *Verbum:: Word and Idea in Aquinas,* 44, note 201.

22. Meno 77d; Confessions 1.1.

23. Charles Hartshorne in *Divine Relativity* (New Haven, 1948) and in *Philosophers Speak of God* (Chicago, 1953); also Schubert Ogden, *The Reality of God* (New York, 1966), title essay.

24. Jung tries to make this point by distinguishing *ethical* decision from *moral* evaluation, in *Memories, Dreams, Reflections* (New York, 1961), 331. See chapter 5, 4.22, for a discussion relating Aquinas and Jung.

25. The clearest article on this subject which I have found is that of Merold Westphal, "Temporality and Finitism in Hartshorne's Theism," *Review of Metaphysics* 19 (1966), 550-64. I have attempted to locate the real divergencies between Aquinas and "process" theologians in chapter 7 of my forthcoming *Aquinas,* in the Arguments of the Philosophers series (London: Routledge and Kegan Paul, 1975).

26. Cf. #2.2. The strategy is the one which Preller formulates: although we are not in possession of the comprehensive language wherein *esse* would be a feature, we can nevertheless know something of its structure. In McDermott's language (note 19) we can have an idea of the role itself from appreciating its shape (to some degree) but would not know *how* to play it.

27. For a comprehensive interpretative treatment of Aquinas see Lonergan, *Verbum,* 33-45.

28. "Aeternitas est interminabilis vitae tota simul et perfecta possessio," *De Consolatione* V.

29. I am thinking of *wholeness* in the way in which Jung uses it

to characterize symbolic expressions for both God and self (e.g., in *Memories, Dreams, Reflections* [New York, 1961], 333-34). Chapter 5 *infra* shows how he comes to adopt such a language and how he puts it to work.

30. On the specific character of knowing-by-faith see Preller, 228-38.

31. See chapter 1 and the chapter on Aquinas in my *Analogy and Philosophical Language;* also Ralph McInerny, *The Logic of Analogy* (The Hague, 1961).

32. Chenu, *La Théologie au Douzième Siècle,* ch. "Theologie et Grammaire."

33. " 'Believing [in] God' cannot be said of pagans in the same way that it can of believers. . . . Hence they cannot truly be said to believe [in] God" (*Summa* II-II 2.2.3). On acknowledging the truth of the proposition 'God Exists,' see 3.4.2.

PART THREE

Experiencing
the Transcendent

4: KIERKEGAARD
Language of Spirit

We have experienced how taxing it is to take the methods of philosophic reasoning and use them for elucidating the God who relates himself to men. For philosophy does not readily offer itself to be put to such work; it comes more congenially as taskmaster.

A guide is seldom prone to take directions, of course, and whoever proffers them seems foolish. After all, do we not engage a guide precisely for his expertise, relying on him to introduce us to an unfamiliar way of life? The image is suggestive, for it accents both the *hubris* of a believer who wants to make philosophy serve his ends, as well as the jealousy endemic to philosophy which extolls the breadth and sufficiency of what it offers.

It was impossible for Augustine to study Platonism without encountering men who lived and breathed the philosophy. They exemplified and proposed a way of life: the Platonici.[1] So utilizing the words of these philosophers to elucidate the Word could not remain a purely intellectual exercise for Augustine; it brought him into open conflict with them. Anselm learned his logic within the monastery, where everything was impressed with the spirit of serving God. Yet we saw how dialectic, even as he learned it, expressed its claim to autonomy. The very formulation Anselm adopted refused to accomplish the task he set for it in his quest for understanding. Aquinas inherited more astuteness. He deliberately maimed a basic grammatical scheme—that of essential predication—to serve his ends. Then persuading a proud philosophic discourse that it was not crippled but only lame, Aquinas went on to press it to painstaking work. He managed to inspire philosophy with something of his own awe at the transcendence of a God whom "to serve is to reign." In his hands philosophy was able to limp with pride for having experienced a hand-to-hand ordeal with the divinity—and survived.

If such effort was demanded to indenture philosophy during the "ages of faith," what superhuman exertions must it have required in the full wake of the enlightenment? Kierkegaard offers testimony. And if that takes on a pitch peculiar to his personal ordeal, we cannot thereby excuse ourselves from hearing his testimony. We should rather be able to discriminate what may be hypersensitive in Kierkegaard from the sensitivity appropriate to the prophetic individual whose own life recapitulates the life of his time.

It is telling that Kierkegaard was neither parson nor professor. The others we have considered were able to be both monk and teacher, and two of them even bishops. But Kierkegaard could not count on any communal support for his task, and in fact felt constrained to follow it in opposition to the two institutions whose stated goals he passionately pursued: university and church. No doubt this opposition helped to spur him on. But whatever the personal animus, this fact will affect the manner in which Kierkegaard assumes philosophy and puts it to use in unraveling religious issues. For one thing, it puts him squarely in our time by ushering in the sensibility called *modern*.

Like Augustine, Kierkegaard could not study philosophy without confronting an academic establishment. "The System" mocks Hegel's pretensions less than the pretentiousness of Hegelians ensconced within yet another system—the university. Of Hegel's philosophy Kierkegaard avers: "I for my part have devoted a good deal of time to the understanding of [it], I believe also that I understand it tolerably well. . . . All this I do easily and naturally, my head does not suffer from it."[2] Few could say that, certainly, and reading Kierkegaard confirms his own assessment: he is possessed of acute philosophic wit.

But Kierkegaard felt constrained to put that wit to so severely dialectical a use that most readers flag somewhere along in the antithesis, consigning him to "irrationalism." Kierkegaard's remarks about understanding Hegel "tolerably well," however, were made by way of contrast to having "to think . . . that enormous paradox which is the substance of Abraham's life" (43). These two poles capture the tension which Kierkegaard felt necessary to formulate as his way of pressing reason to the service of faith. This would entail harrassing and cajoling reason to bend it to the task, for reason identified more readily with "the System."

How to wheedle reason away from a role so congenially inflated to serve in the thankless task of elucidating the paradox of an individual life before God? Did not Kierkegaard himself admit that "every moment I am repelled [in the face of it], and my thought in spite of all its passion cannot get a hairsbreadth further" (44)? Kierkegaard would constrain philosophy into a service without hope of satisfying issue, and so he did. This chapter records what issues nonetheless from a philosophy so impressed.

1. Guidelines for Interpretation

These opening comments are ranging, but an exercise demands we now restrict our compass if we are actually to make the movements rather than be content to read about them.[3] I have chosen *Sickness unto Death* to focus our efforts: first, because it is manageable, and then because it fits the overall plan of these exercises better than the expressly philosophical *Fragments* or their *Postscript.* The reason is offered by Kierkegaard himself in the pseudonyms chosen for the different works. The earlier works were philosophical in perspective as well as method, which is to say they were philosophical works attributed to Johannes Climacus. *Sickness,* on the other hand, comes from the pen of Anti-Climacus, and while it does not qualify simply as an "edifying discourse," it is offered "for edification."[4] As the subtitle of *Sickness* acknowledges, it is written from within the perspective of faith: "A Christian Psychological Exposition for Edification and Awakening." Hence *Sickness* provides an explicit display of philosophy unraveling distinctly religious issues—of faith seeking understanding.

The rubric of *exercise* permits us to focus on one work, but the mention of "philosophy" requires some statement on Kierkegaard's relationship to Hegel. Allow me to hazard one. Kierkegaard's indebtedness to Hegel shows up best in his "dialectical" use of reasoning to lead us on to what understanding we can have of the point at hand. By "dialectical use," I refer to the way Kierkegaard has of taking a notion, showing how it cannot do what we want it to do in the situation at hand, and then proceeding to use it to do that job. The notion becomes less misleading the more we are brought to appreciate how we must misuse it. This is no wholesale plea of linguistic inadequacy or easy invocation of paradox. Kierkegaard's dialectic is a specific reminder in each case how a notion may be used once we have been shown how it must not be used. Hegel reminded us that *notions* display that "inner differentiability" that allows one both to deny and to affirm them, so long as it is done in an ordered fashion.[5] Since I take this semantic fact to be the key to Hegel's dialectic, it is easy to link Kierkegaard's procedure, as well as his use of 'dialectical', to

Hegel. (I shall show in the exposition how I feel Kierkegaard surpassed Hegel in employing reason dialectically.)

The other obvious link with Hegel, however, represents quite another use Kierkegaard makes of philosophy. I take the dialectical form of exposition to be serious and this other use to be comic. The latter appears in a frame apart, sometimes is even called an "interlude," and uses Hegelian categories (like 'finitude/infinitude' or 'possibility/necessity') in a direct mode of exposition.[6] I can only understand this as a conceit, a coy display to contemporary Hegelians that Kierkegaard "understands the System tolerably well." It is as though Kierkegaard were saying: "for what it's worth, here is what it would amount to Hegelianly." In *Sickness unto Death* this "comic" treatment is a professedly abstract one. Kierkegaard treats of the self as a *synthesis* (when he has shown it to be a *relating*), and in so treating it he prescinds from consciousness. He had just announced, however, consciousness to be the decisive factor in any treatment of the self (162). In one so alert and ironic as Kierkegaard, this order must be intended to show how remote a contemporary Hegelian treatment would be.

Generally, then, I regard Kierkegaard's dialectical use of reason as his notable contribution to philosophical theology. But in the same breath I must acknowledge this use to be Kierkegaard's legacy from Hegel. It is critical to establish this linkage across the polemical gulf Kierkegaard digs between his concerns and "the System." Yet for all his indebtedness to Hegel, I cannot help but feel that Kierkegaard in fact accomplished what Hegel at best talked about. My testy assessment of Hegel is that he talked his genuine insights into the ground. Because he knew only the expository mode, Hegel had no effective way to stop talking, and so ended by turning dialectical reason into the very thing he proposed to show up: a system. In this respect Hegel turned out an Hegelian.

What Kierkegaard brought to his understanding of Hegel, however, was a keen feel for *use*. He was able to recognize forms of discourse other than the expository, and came to use them brilliantly. Employing different literary forms and pseudonyms enabled Kierkegaard to distinguish what was able to be said from what could only be shown, and to incorporate the form of reasoning into the very shape of the work itself. Philosophy became in his hands a kind of therapy, designed to exercise one in using notions expeditious for understanding his call to faith.[7] Since these achievements appear to be a *desiderata* of Hegel's dialectic, I feel that Kierkegaard *did* what Hegel talked about doing but failed to accomplish.

2. A Distinctively Christian Use of Philosophy

Although *Sickness* is offered as a "psychological exposition," it embodies no reductive intent. It is an explicitly Christian exposition. More accurately, it is Judeo-Christian, since this qualification entails two facts for Kierkegaard: "the infinite qualitative difference" between God and man, and the infinite condescension of God to man in the Incarnation (257). The first fact secures an orthodox understanding of the second, and the difference between the two is secured in turn by the *offense* which we must take at an orthodox understanding of the Incarnation. Hence Kierkegaard asserts that "the possibility of offense is the dialectical factor in everything Christian" (256), and displays what he means by "the dialectical factor" in the way he fastens on "taking offense." By attending to Kierkegaard's use of this notion, we can see how he employs reason dialectically, and come to appreciate why this might be offered as a distinctively Christian use of reason.

2.1. Offense and the Individual

If consciousness is the decisive factor in understanding despair, offense is decisive for understanding what it is to despair before God, or to sin. For we cannot help but take offense at the announcement that God stands ready to forgive sins, when it was that same revelation of himself which made of sin a fact. One is then doubly offended: first at being called a sinner, and then at being offered forgiveness (247). Hence Kierkegaard insists that "offense is the most decisive determinant of subjectivity, of the individual man, the most decisive it is possible to think of" (253). The reasons are, we shall see, cumulative: the individual self (or subjectivity) is attested by despairing, which can only be grasped properly by bringing oneself to consciousness; and the form which this consciousness assumes in the face of revelation is that of "taking offense."

Allow these conceptual connections to remain loose for the moment and note that the operative factor is not a conceptual one. *Offense* is not part of the account one gives of sin as despairing before God, nor of the good news that the God who reveals sin will forgive it. Rather, offense is something which takes place in anyone who tries to hear what has been revealed in the way it is offered to him. And since revelation is in the form of a summons (at once an invitation and a command), one grasps it only by responding to it. Hence Kierkegaard notes that "offense is related to the individual"; it tells the form of his response. Christianity "concentrates [offense] in one place" because "Christianity begins, by making every man an individual, an individual sinner" (253).

Although Christianity comes in the form of a story (and stories begin with a first sentence), it becomes what it purports to be—a revelation—when Christianity succeeds in effecting individuality. Hence it can be said to begin (not with a sentence but) by *making* one an individual. And Christianity makes an individual of a specific sort, namely, one standing in despair before God: a sinner. But it succeeds in doing this (and hence in being what it is) only in the measure that I accept it. Yet in accepting Christianity I must overcome the offense which the news first generates in me. So my acceptance, if I can manage it, will inevitably give evidence of having taken offense. Like a threshold,

offense presents at once an obstacle to faith and the entrance
to it. This is the precise sense, then, in which (speaking
abstractly) the possibility of offense is the dialectic factor in
everything Christian. And (speaking concretely) "taking
offense" knots the thread of speculation to put an end to
an endless weaving of possible alternatives (224).

2.2. A New Account of Discourse

I have had to use parentheses and roundabout ways of
speaking because expository discourse must strain severely
to include the one hearing it. And understandably so, since
exposition is meant to be read, not responded to. Or, if
you prefer, if one speaks of "responding" to a piece of
expository prose, the appropriate response is simply to
read it. Since our standard logics are tailored to exposition,
however, we have no way of accounting for that form of
discourse which includes within its reach the one whom it
addresses. If we had such an account, it would have to
correlate forms of locution with one's characteristic responses. It would have to find laws governing the relationship of discourse to hearer.

Any account of how discourse does its job is inescapably reflexive. It encroaches on the metaphysical since it
amounts to an account of accounts. Of course, there are
many ways of engaging in the type of reflection that goes
by the generic name of "metaphysics." Or one may even
eschew doing it altogether. But no one can escape following a metaphysical path simply by avoiding to map it. For
the way we construct our accounts, the way we put what
we say, evidences a set of convictions about what can
profitably be said and how an accounting is to be made.

It may be that we are not ready to articulate the
"background language" operative in our discourse; or perhaps we do not feel capable of doing so. Or it may be that
we suspect the entire enterprise is better shown than
said—shown in the care with which we put what we say.
And if we take this last tack (which I suspect would be

Kierkegaard's), then the expression 'background language' is altogether too "straight," and 'metaphysics' far too laden to convey the quality of critical self-awareness.[8] So let me simply call that reflexive process of getting what hold we can on why we do things the way we do "critical self-awareness." Paying attention to how we put things can yield just enough more awareness for one's critical faculties to get a fresh purchase.

It is such critical self-awareness that Kierkegaard is after, and what he is up to in *Sickness* betrays that fact. He traces out the background within which he expects his pseudonymous works and literary devices to function, and offers a sketch which translates the posture basic to Christianity as revelation, namely, man the responder. Some would call this task "philosophical anthropology," others "metaphysics.' Kierkegaard calls it nothing, but he duly observes a "strict" form. He adopts the "strictly scientific" form of Aristotle's *Posterior Analytics,* thereby signalling his intent to lay out his critical reflections in a systematic way (142).

2.21. Examples of Socrates

Kierkegaard's account of accounting will have to include within it the response of the one addressed. Socrates offers an advantageous starting point and a useful corrective to the "aesthetic-metaphysical" perspective of Kierkegaard's own day:

It is highly important that, instead of going further than Socrates, we simply return to the Socratic dictum that to understand/and to understand are two things—not returning to it as a result [once for all acquired], for in the end that only helps men into the deepest wretchedness, since it simply abolishes the distinction understanding/and understanding, but returning to it as the ethical interpretation of every-day life (223).

The reference is to Socrates' contention that "if they truly had understood, their lives also would have expressed

it, they would have done what they understood" (221).[9]
The difference, then, between understanding and *truly*
understanding is akin to that which Anselm reached for in
distinguishing between understanding the formula and understanding the thing it signifies. But Socrates gives a more
felicitous formulation in terms of two modes of consistency;
a minimal sort testified by a well-formed argument, and the
ideal witnessed by a well-led life. The one allows us to draw
the proper consequences; the other shows that one believes
enough in what he says to incorporate the consequences
into his actions and so live consequentially.

To understand a *true* understanding, then, we must be
able to incorporate the response of the hearer (who may
be the speaker listening to what he himself is saying). And
we must incorporate this response by expanding our *consistency* to include pragmatic as well as logical criteria.
That is Kierkegaard's concern when he admonishes us how
to read Socrates: *not* "as a result, for in the end that
. . . simply abolishes the distinction between understanding and [truly] understanding" (223). What J. L. Austin
called a "flat constative" leaves no room for factoring in
the response of the hearer which constitutes *true* understanding.[10] Rather we are to return to Socrates as offering
"the ethical interpretation of every-day life." Socrates'
dictum will prove inadequate, but at least it does not
distract from ethics as the "aesthetic and metaphysical"
speculation of the Hegelians does (224-225).

By requiring the response of the individual for a true
understanding, this distinction between understanding and
true understanding introduces a genuinely ethical form
into discourse. All that remains for Kierkegaard to do is to
specify that response by a measure yet more individual
than any available to the Greeks: the *will*.

2.22. Will, Evil, and Sin

This way of characterizing the response and responder is
offered by Kierkegaard as distinctively Christian: "Chris-

tianity goes a little further back [than Socrates] and says [that he does not do the right thing] because he will not understand it" (226). One could observe, of course, that Aristotle had come forward with a way of correcting Socrates on the discrepancy of knowing/doing what is right. For he managed to do so while retaining the basic logic of the matter—namely, that no one knowingly does what he thinks to be wrong. Thus Aristotle corrected Socrates precisely by introducing the factor of willing. [11] Yet Kierkegaard's contention could also be supported by noting that even on the Aristotelian scheme *willing* could only be a vague motivation. It appears as an undifferentiated energy source, charged by the goals by which one allows himself to be attracted, and directed in each instance by practical reason. Kierkegaard is thinking of *willing* as a more positive determinant. He offers this view as Christian, not from a survey of theologians (who more often espoused the Greek view), but rather as the background demanded for the conflicts experienced in the drama of God's revelation in Jesus.

Recall that "Christianity begins . . . by declaring that there must be a revelation from God in order to instruct man as to what sin is," and that Christianity becomes revelation the moment it makes a man conscious of his being a sinner. In that moment he realizes "sin does not consist in the fact that [he] has not understood what is right, but in the fact that he will not understand it, and in the fact that he will not do it" (226). Though a multitude of explanations are readily available, none is expedient, for each distracts from the bald fact which is not to be comprehended but accepted. Who could be rational and not take offense? So for Kierkegaard *offense* becomes *the* characteristic response, which at once increases one's sinfulness (providing a complete definition of sin), yet also readies a man to believe (227).

The key to the schematic difference Kierkegaard draws between a Greek and a Christian anthropology, as well as a clue to what guided his selection, lies in one's posture toward evil. Most Christian theologians would be Greek in their outlook inasmuch as they found themselves unable to do more than reiterate the basic logic of the matter; thus they felt compelled to characterize evil as *privatio boni.* The basic logic of the matter is, we recall, that no one can knowingly perform what he thinks to be evil: so we must always rationalize. Whatever we picture ourselves as doing we must depict as good. That means, quite literally, that we cannot *think* evil; we must always *think* of it as good. Yet in fact we perform evil deeds. But that is unthinkable! We always have an explanation. We *must* have one, for that is the logic of the matter.

Hence Kierkegaard remarks that "speculatively sin cannot be thought at all," and since it cannot, "there can be no seriousness about sin when it is merely thought" (250). That is why philosophers have felt compelled in the face of obvious facts to define evil as a privation of good, as "merely a negation"—for "so it is speculatively; but Christianity, sin is . . . a positive situation which out of itself develops a more and more positive continuity" (237). In a curious way sin weaves a pragmatic consistency bereft of logical support: "sin is within itself a consistency, and in this consistency of evil within itself it possesses a certain power" (238). What can continue to act without benefit of rationale is *will.* And will also suggests a new kind of measure—one which opens us to a way of characterizing the individual unavailable to the Greeks, yet exhibited in the person of Socrates.[12] We must try to formulate this measure if we are to make sense of Christianity as revelation, since "the category of sin is the category of the individual" (250).

2.3. Discovering a Category for the Individual

Although each individual Greek could gesture toward immortality by the deeds he performed, the only glory he could claim was that specific to men. For on the Greek scheme a man instantiates *man,* which stands as something to grow up into by conforming to the ideals one understands to go with manhood. Christianity readily adopted this scheme, of course, as early as Paul's stated aim: "to bring every man up to his full maturity in Christ Jesus," and on through Aquinas' comprehensive treatise on virtues.[13] Yet Kierkegaard finds it flat by contrast with what revelation demands and effects: an individual. Whatever is individual, however, is impervious to thought. That is why the Greek ideal is a specific one: any ideal is, for it must be shared to be an ideal. Hence Kierkegaard reaches for an utterly distinctive category, that of *spirit*. And he proposes to elucidate what it is to be spirit by using the Greek category of *relation* (πρὸς τι, *esse ad*).

If the notion operative for the Greeks was *ideal*, it becomes *relating* for a Christian. Where becoming a man meant conforming to manhood, becoming a Christian involves relating: relating to oneself in a manner which exhibits the power creating him. One who is invited to respond to God's revealing himself may, it is true, be classified as a singular species among other species. But it would seem more to the point to regard such a one in the way revelation regards him—as an image of God. And if God is revealed as Father, Son, and Spirit, then something of this relational life will be imaged in men. If furthermore we are taught to respond to this God in the interior of our hearts, we need a way of rendering that interiority. "Relating to oneself" would seem opportune.

These factors urged the category of *relation* upon Kierkegaard in an effort to domesticate the utterly distinctive one of *spirit*. (Other more precise, intrasystematic factors will emerge in section 3). There is also a hint of the medieval shift from *form* to *act* in Kierkegaard's choice. The Greek way of characterizing *spirit* was characteristically intellectual: as the norm, the paradigm, the form *(eidos)*. The medievals adopted Aristotle but shifted the center to action, agency, *esse*.[14] Kierkegaard proposes as the "ideal state" of a man, Christianity understood, that he be relating to his own self by *willing* to be himself. The shift is one of ideals: from conforming to norms understood (Greek) to responding to a summons (Christian).

And the way one speaks of the new ideal must accent the responding individual and what he manages to respond with—his will.

I remarked earlier that the notion operative for the Greeks was *ideal*, yet in characterizing the Christian I was constrained to speak of an "ideal state" and of a new "ideal." There is a lesson here: in a measure openly displayed in our discourse Greek thought *is* thought. Every declarative sentence embodies a substance/accident ontology. Kierkegaard knows perfectly well that there is no way around this fact. He shows his appreciation of it in the way he continually invokes Socrates and chides those who would "go beyond him."[15]   For S. K. as for Aquinas there are no basic philosophical terms other than those supplied by the Greeks, who also provided the ways to use them.

Greek philosophy defines the structure of possibilities; it cannot be "overcome" short of the actual combinations offered by revelation. Yet these are combinations of which men could never have dreamt. So Aquinas uses Aristotle's characterization of the intellect as *capax omnium* as an index of its spiritual nature, but supplies an unheard-of reach to that nature in speaking of the vision of God. He does the same with man's natural desire to know, by expanding and focussing it into a desire to see God.[16]

2.31. Dialectical Use of Notions

Unlike Aquinas, however, Kierkegaard feels that in the case of man—the addressee of God's summons—a new philosophical grammar is required. It is required not because Hegel has bested Socrates, but required in fact by the revelation of God in Jesus. That revelation at once presupposes and "makes every man an individual" (253). When biblical texts are subjected to the kind of analysis we would give an expository text or theory, they turn out *not* to offer an exposition or theoretical formulation of the individual. Rather they *presuppose* a responsive individual.

(We might say that revelation presupposes an individual somewhat analogously to the way atomic theory presupposes electrons.) Then considering revelation as a summons addressed to each person individually, I can experience its *making* me an individual in the measure that I receive it.

But Kierkegaard is wary of offering an account of this way of speaking and of responding in the form of discourse left by the Greeks. So he proposes, not a new philosophy, but a rather more negative or dialectical *use* of Greek forms of thinking and speaking. In this proposal he would go further than even Aquinas.

Kierkegaard's manner is clearly exhibited in the way he uses Socrates' conception of sin as ignorance to begin his own dialectical search for a Christian way of putting it. Explicitly, "I do not by any means intend to dispose of the Socratic definition on the ground that one cannot stop with it; but, having the Christian definition *in mente,* I would make use of it [the Socratic] to bring the other out sharply (just because the Socratic definition is so genuinely Greek)" (219). While a Christian sense of sin can be acutely present to us, we will never be able to formulate it except in terms borrowed (even if to be rejected) from the Greeks. We might think of it this way: even though this particular definition may prove hollow in the face of revelation, we would never be able to manifest that fact without recourse to the peculiar mode of philosophic reflection that framed it.

There seems to be no other way of describing how Kierkegaard uses classical thought forms except as a *dialectical* use. For example, he takes over the medieval notion of *relation* only to give it a novel twist. Kierkegaard's own explicit remarks on the role played by Socrates' definition of 'sin' offer as clear a picture as possible of this dialectic. Inadequate as it is to capture sin for a Christian, that very inadequacy helps us understand where we stand. One is at loss to characterize a dialectical use precisely because it must incorporate an awareness of inadequacy into the very notion one is said to employ dialectically. Since that inadequacy is precisely what cannot be *expressed* (for every expression of a situation *eo ipso* purports to be adequate to it), then a dialectical use can only be signalled indirectly. And this is inevitably lost on the unaware.

Of course, anyone who proposes to speak about God must select expressions (like 'wise' or 'just') which admit of a dialectical use and then employ them dialectically. Yet this is a precarious undertaking because we lack precise indications whether we are proceeding appropriately. It is all the more precarious given the acute pitch of awareness we must sustain to pick up what indications there might be. Yet that awareness is precisely what cannot show up in any formulation. It belongs not to the treatise but to the individual, though his awareness will show through what he says in many indirect ways. In the ways he proceeds or refuses, say, to take God to task for what happens to him. In the measure that one has become an individual, then, by letting the word of God be the revelation it is, he should prove more able to sustain such an awareness. This would be a more precise way of putting Aquinas' statement that faith "strengthens the power of understanding."[17]

We can also begin to see why the specifically Christian items in revelation—notably the Incarnation and the forgiveness of sins it brings—escalate the dialectical differences to the limit of taking *offense.* If God's ways cannot be explained or justified to men, we must simply confront them. For the difference we have spoken of as ingredient in a dialectical use of a notion is nothing other than the "infinite qualitative difference" reflected into the very form of a discourse which seeks to elucidate God's revelation of himself in Christ. What cannot be said—and infinitely much cannot—must somehow be translated into the *form* of the discourse so that the inadequacy *shows.* This is the demand which the subject of theology, God, places on any philosophic idiom which we would use to speak of him. If we manage it properly, we will succeed in speaking *of* him (as the object of discourse) without "objectifying" him. If we do not, we fail to speak of *him,* of course, and deliver instead an idol.

In this there can be no hard and fast criteria for success, since all the indicators are indirect. But a set of indications do accumulate, whereby we can test how acute our aware-ness of the "difference" or the inadequacy may be. One of the aims of these essays is to gather up such criteria. Kierkegaard offers an example of someone *so* acutely aware of the difference, and with such refined acumen, that his dialectical use of language verges on the self-de-feating. However, careful attention to the signals he gives will reward the patient investigator with a crafted example of a distinctively Christian use of philosophical wit. Let us examine the definition Kierkegaard offers of the self des-tined to be addressed by the good news, examining it precisely as a dialectical use of philosophic reason.

3. Speaking of the Individual

Sickness unto Death opens:

Man is spirit.
  But what is Spirit?
Spirit is the self.
  But what is the self?
The self is a relation . . . (146).

The book begins with a statement—as an exposition should. But the opening statement begins an inquiry de-signed to show how revelation can begin as it does: "by making every man an individual" (253). The exposition will take a language which locates particulars within uni-versals by subordinating individuals to species and species to genera, and put that language to a new use. For it aims to exhibit how "man is distinguished from the other ani-mals: . . . [namely] by the fact that the individual is more than the species" (251).

The motivation was announced in the Preface: "The

Christian heroism . . . is to venture wholly to be oneself, as
an individual man, this definite individual man, alone before the face of God, alone in this tremendous exertion
and this tremendous responsibility" (142). What singles
out such a one is *seriousness*—though he will appear less
singular the more individual he lets himself become. And
what this serious man feels is *fear*.

So the mark of spirit in facing the burden of becoming
an individual is *despair*. Not a mark like childhood diseases
leave, this is an inward mark and an essential one. This is
not the *despair* we find in a theological catalogue of sins; it
is more like despairing of ever finishing the race or despairing of getting through to a friend trapped, say, in a rock
slide or perhaps in his own importance. It is the inability
to make a connection, so often a feature of one's dreams.
This despair is like Sisyphus' always having to begin over
again.

All this comes with conceiving one's life not as an
instance of a pattern but as a task: the task of becoming an
individual. Yet this task did not clearly emerge until we
were summoned to it—invited to stand "alone before the
face of God." So it was in history and so it is with a
person's own history. "The Greek intellectualism was too
happy, too naive, too aesthetic, too ironical, too witty" to
experience the anxiety proper to becoming an individual
(220). Kierkegaard likens "the relation between the natural man and the Christian" to the difference "between a
child and a man: what the child shudders at, the man
regards as nothing." But "the child does not know what
the dreadful is; this the man knows, and he shudders at it"
(145). The early Christian apologists celebrated men's liberation from the powers of superstition and idolatry;
Kierkegaard reminds us how we have been freed to a
"tremendous responsibility" and taught to fear what is
"truly dreadful."

For the glory which distinguishes man from all the other
animals, that destiny revealed in summoning him to individuality, "is again dialectical, it means that the individual
is a sinner, but then again that it is perfection to be the

individual" (251). With a childlike naivete, Greek intellectualism was unable "to get it into its head that a person
. . . knowingly, with knowledge of what was right, [could]
do what was wrong" (221). Awareness of our capacity for
willfulness and sin had to await the summons to become
an individual—before God. To take offense at such an
invitation and so despair of ever becoming the self we have
now been shown to be, that is sin; yet it represents an
inevitable human response. Beyond this lies the offer of
forgiveness, a yet greater offense. And with it the invitation to live by faith, the greatest offense of all. Yet
through it all one can discern the promise of a peace
beyond despair, with the task not completed but delivered
over to the one who originally posed it.

The formula which *Sickness* offers to articulate a man
called to become an individual embraces the entire reach
of the summons all the way to the promise. In its final
form "This then is the formula which describes the condition of the self when despair is completely eradicated:

> by relating itself to its own self
> and by willing to be itself
>   the self is grounded transparently
> in the Power which posited it" (147).

The dense form is that proper to exposition, for it is
carefully constructed from classical elements designed for
an expository account. I have announced the elements
from revelation which Kierkegaard has *in mente* as he
crafts his exposition: the summons, sin, offense, forgiveness, faith. It remains to show how a strictly expository
language may be used to display an utterly novel use to
which our language can be put: that of summoning us and
of our responding to the summons.

3.1. A Language of Spirit

The two pages intervening between Kierkegaard's opening statement that "man is spirit" and this culminating

formulation of the individual spirit-self amounts to an outline of the syntactical shifts necessary to use our language for speaking of what is *spirit*. The sections following teach us how to use this language *as* spirit, by "describing psychologically the forms of despair as they display themselves in reality, in actual men" (134). As we learn how to speak *about* spirit, we need to be reminded that we who are speaking *are* spirit; and even more, that we need to be summoned to become spirit. This last point is the subject of the second part of the treatise where Kierkegaard brings out what he has had *in mente,* and he speaks openly of despair before God, or sin.

Socrates can point ironically to the ways we find ourselves forgetting what we are in speaking about what men are, but Christianity finds us refusing to become what we are called to be. Kierkegaard's analysis must lay out the structure which makes such a refusal possible. Then he must bring us to an understanding of ourselves sufficient to grasp all that prevents us from responding to the summons which promises us ourselves. More than this analysis cannot do; it can do this, however, by proposing certain structural permutations in the language we possess and then teaching us how to use it in this new way. With the understanding such a new idiom affords we will not have advanced beyond Socrates, but we will have acquired some of that "Socratic ignorance [which] defends faith against speculation, keeping watch to see that the deep gulf of qualitative distinction between God/and man may be firmly fixed" (230). By such a dialectical use of the forms of reason imbedding themselves in our language we can be brought to a quality of consciousness poised in readiness for faith.

3.11. Systematic Shifts in Word Use

Spirit is not a category amenable to systematic analysis. In fact, it tends to stand over against those categorical features which Aristotle distinguished in ordinary discourse and which provide the predicates for initiating systematic inquiry. Whatever is impervious to being located, measured, or otherwise situated remains opaque to further examination. So Hegel felt constrained to develop a new method, dialectic, to articulate spirit by laying out the successively different features he found it assuming through time. Doubtless from his study of Hegel Kierkegaard developed an eye for delineating the various forms assumed by consciousness. But in his initial attention to syntax Kierkegaard pins the analysis more directly to Aristotle.

The method derives from the *Posterior Analytics:* a scientific exposition is one which succeeds in demonstrating the essential attributes of a subject to be just that, essential. It does this by deriving those attributes from a definition stated in canonical terms of genus and specific difference.[18] It is understood that we can recognize essential attributes; a scientific account is designed to confirm that skill as knowledge by showing how they follow logically from a formula for the thing itself. And so the attributes must be essential to the thing. Aristotle also assumes that we have a way of knowing the initial definition to be a true one, but that assumption is independent of the demonstrative method itself. We are free to employ it more hypothetically. What results in either case is a working framework of discourse, or a science. Such a framework represents an especially handy and illuminating way of discoursing about a certain range of things, and so becomes a specialized use of our language.

My contention is that Kierkegaard adopts this general pattern to elucidate what it is to be a man when he is taken to be spirit—with an eye to what makes him able to respond to God's summons. The result will prove to be a much more radical shift than the "specialized use" of language associated with different sciences. Yet the reason why this shift which Kierkegaard employs is so radical is systematically announced by his choice of a genus: *rela-*

tion. The essential attribute of spirit, despair, proves a correspondingly radical departure from easily recognizable ones. Kierkegaard will need to show us how to use the language which articulates it, leading us by examples to recognize despair in its successive forms. But the general outlines of Aristotle's demonstrative account shape Kierkegaard's strict expository form: the thing itself is understood through its attributes, and an analysis of it leading to firm understanding will show the essential attributes to be essential.

3.12. The Self as Relating

"Man is Spirit. . . . Spirit is the self. . . . The self is a relation . . . " (146). So much for the genus: *relation*. But 'man' is a substantive term, which means its genus is a type of substance. One may quarrel with the Greek formula "rational animal," but one cannot tamper with substantives. This is one of those ways in which our thought is inescapably Greek thought, since theirs is imbedded in the very syntax of the language we use. Kierkegaard would certainly not have put it this way, but he moved with a keen awareness of these niceties of philosophical grammar. Aware enough of them, in fact, to choose the category of *relation* deliberately, to announce a radical departure in the way we use our language (of substantives) in speaking about ourselves.

The use he wants to introduce is so different that he must incorporate it at the very beginning. This is Kierkegaard's way of reflecting into the expository form the change Christianity effects, beginning as it does by making an individual of each man who responds to it. And the syntactical change is related to this change which Christianity effects by providing the language in which to speak about it. Kierkegaard deliberately substitutes the category of *relation* for that of *substance* in the case of man because he wants to transform every statement regarding a person's human development from an ' . . . is . . . ' form to an

' . . . is becoming . . . ' form. Only the statements regarding development are affected. But the effect of the transformation is to give every one of the statements a "self-
realizing" form. So the Greek ideal of conforming to an
ideal becomes, Christianly speaking, one of becoming what
one is called to be. And this situation is never overcome.
So one can never claim to *be* a Christian (except in the
banal use of registry), but at best that he is *becoming*
one.[19] And the same can be said for the Christian use of
such terms as 'individual', 'God-fearing', 'humble', etc.

Merely announcing the genus *relation* will not effect this
change, of course, but it does prepare the way for one as
far-reaching as this. The formula presses on to establish
what kind of relation man must be. The successive formulations it takes to do this show how precarious a hold we
have on this new way of using language. But we must use it
immediately, nonetheless, for a genus as strange as *relation*
has already introduced it. Collapsing the sorites, we can
say *man* is the self, where the self is

> a relation which relates itself to its own self,
> or it is
> > that in the relation [which accounts for it] that
> > the relation relates itself to its own self;
> the self is
> > not the relation but [consists in the fact] that
> > the relation relates itself to its own self (146).

What "distinguishes man from all the other animals,"
then, is that he can also be conceived as spirit or a self. He
may still be *classified* among the animals, but if we want to
speak of what he can become, then (grounding ourselves in
the phenomenological categories of Aristotle) man is not a
thing so much as a relation. More succinctly, he is a
relation relating. And not just one which happens to be
relating, for man is a relation which is constituted by
relating, and which in relating relates itself to its own self.

The self, then, is the relating, not the relation which
relates. This clarification does all that can be done to
exorcise the ghost of *substance* lingering in the noun

'relation'. By offering a participal form instead, Kierkegaard is trying to secure the new use from that inertial
tendency of our language toward substance. He courts
paradox by insisting that the relating-self does what it is by
relating itself to its own self. We must, of course, resist the
temptation to take this formula descriptively, and rather
accept it as offering a general scheme for any statement
regarding one's personal growth. Taken in this way, its
own paradoxical form legitimizes the shift from 'is' to
'becomes': so Christianity *can* "begin by making every
man an individual" because each (individual) person is
called to become an individual. Besides the manifold roles
thrust upon us, each of us inherits an inbuilt task: to
become the individual we are (called to become). Each of
us can only do this himself, by so relating to himself that
the result is himself. Such a one feels and is felt to be "at
home with himself."

This is how I would interpret the dense formula Kierkegaard offers to define the self. It works like a metalinguistic scheme, offering a normal form for any statement
attempting to describe the self's essential task of becoming
itself. Like any definition introducing a scientific inquiry
after the model of the *Posterior Analytics,* this one adum-
brates a specialized way of using our language to talk
about the subject defined, although in this case the use
introduced is so radical a departure that it could hardly be
called "specialized." As the progressive clarifications of the
definitions showed, this new use will require a high pitch
of alertness to keep oneself from backsliding into more
congenial substantive forms. Kierkegaard contrasts this
new way of speaking with the classical scheme, which he
summarizes by

> Man is a synthesis
>   of the infinite and the finite,
>   of the temporal and the eternal,
>   of freedom and necessity,
> in short it is a synthesis (146).

But "a synthesis is a relation between two factors. So

regarded, man is not yet a self." This scheme represents Kierkegaard's highly abstract way of telegraphing how Hegelian philosophy dealt with the antinomies Kant left behind him. (Making the formula so absurdly abstract allows him to announce his dissatisfaction at the same time. He expands this strategy in the "Hegelian interlude" in *Sickness* [III.A.].) This scheme of S.K.'s might be regarded as an advance on Aristotle's classification scheme (genus/species), for it does present man in relational terms. But it stops there, and since it does no more, the relation reverts to a substantial mode. And something so described is not yet a self. It may do many things, but the description offers no way of marking its *inbuilt* task.

3.13. The God-Relation

Kierkegaard offers one further clarification which makes a more properly theological point. This relating-relation "must either have constituted itself or have been constituted by another" (146). He takes it as having been constituted by another; thus the perspective of this work is frankly theological. In that case this very relating-relation must also "relate itself to that which constituted the whole relation [the self]." That is, there cannot be a distinct relation to express the dependency, precisely because not relations but substances terminate relations. Hence one must say (since he can say no other) that the relating-relation itself expresses the dependency.

This final nicety yields the finished definition: "Such a derived, constituted, relation is the human self,

a relation which relates itself to its own self,
and in relating itself to its own self,
    relates itself to another" (146).

The upshot of this clarification is critical for theology. It offers one of those indices of which I spoke earlier—it is a sign of religious penetration and hence of theological sophistication. For it says that "relating to God" is not something else one is called upon to do, over and above the inbuilt task of becoming oneself. The "God-relation" *could* not be formulated since it is a transcendent one; and what is more, it *need* not be formulated because there really is no "relation" between God and man.

Religiously this says that one does not need to "reach out" to God. Prayer is not so much a dialogue as it is attentiveness to the shape of the inbuilt task. It is the very transcendence of God as the "source of all things" which guarantees his utter immanence to everything. So "the formula which describes the condition of the self when despair is completely eradicated" speaks not of 'relating to God', but says that

> by relating itself to its own self
> and
> by willing to be itself
> the self is grounded transparently in the
>   Power which posited it (147).

Note that this is not offered as a description of "the achieved self," for there can be no such thing: 'is' has been replaced by 'is becoming'. It is, however, noted that "this same formula is also the formula for believing" (182); it is in fact "the definition of faith" (262). What faith overcomes, then, is not becoming, for one is ever *becoming* as believer as well; but there is a real sense in which it can overcome despair.

3.14. Despair Qualifies the Self in Becoming Self

Nothing short of faith can overcome despair, however, for despair belongs to the essential structure of self becoming itself. Since Kierkegaard has already altered the way we speak about the self by insisting it is not substantial but relational, a correlative shift is called for in treating of its essential attribute. For one thing, despair will not be an *accident* of its subject, for its subject is not a substance. Kierkegaard calls our attention to this fact by ridiculing anyone who would "talk about it meaninglessly as of something which befell him" (147). Then he goes on to explain that were despair "something inherent in human nature as such, . . . it would not be despair, it would be something that befell a man, something he suffered passively, like an illness into which a man falls. . . . No, this thing of despairing is inherent in man himself" (149).

Kierkegaard contrasts 'human nature' (or 'a synthesis') with 'man himself', whom he asserted to be spirit and articulated as a relating. These are two grammatically distinct ways we have of speaking and thinking of ourselves. The first is irretrievably abstract because it has no grammatical resources for handling consciousness. It can articulate a structure of possibility—"if [man] were not a synthesis he could not despair" (149), but this way is not able to show how those possibilities come to realization. It can only speak of structures and their modifications. And despair, while logically an attribute, is not for all that an accident.

The formal reason, of course, is that "despair is a qualification of spirit", and spirit, categorically speaking, is not a substance but a relating. That much we "know" already. Yet Kierkegaard counts on us knowing something about despairing as well. On the Greek pattern of demonstration that he is following, attributes manifest what the subject is like, while some of them are shown to be essential by the formula we hit upon to define the subject. And Kierkegaard retains the pattern even when the subject and attribute call for a language quite different from that of substance and accident. In fact, one suspects that he employs the classic pattern precisely to accent the difference between man as *human nature* and man as *spirit*.

What do we know about despair, however, that would predispose us to recognize it as a "qualification of spirit" (150)? (If proposals for grammatical revision are to recommend themselves, we must have experienced some need for them.) As we might expect, there is a vulgar misconception which readily accepts the report: "I'm fine." By this reckoning "despair becomes a rather rare phenomenon, whereas in fact it is quite universal" (155). This view (and usage) takes despair to be a state like feeling ill, "completely overlooking the fact that one form of despair is precisely this of not being in despair, that is, not being aware of it" (156). Despair, then, can be hidden completely from view, notably so for one who manages to regard himself as an instance of human nature. We begin thinking of it like a sickness, only to realize that despair "is much more dialectical than what is commonly called sickness, because it is a sickness of the spirit" (157).

We must have at least a working familiarity with this logical neighborhood of *spirit,* then, for Kierkegaard's inquiry to proceed. We have to be able to lay hold of his examples, recognizing the attribute, despair, in the strange ways in which it manifests itself. Then the grammatical dictates will help explain why it appears that way by providing a language to give greater coherence to that experience. Of course, schema and instance reinforce each other; that is what powers an ongoing inquiry, especially when the region is relatively unexplored. This is notably the case with *despair.* It seems at first sight a lugubrious choice—just the sort of suspicious selection an overly existential type would engage in. Kierkegaard's own awareness of this objection regarding despair, however, forces us to look further: "it is not gloomy; on the contrary, it seeks to throw light upon a subject which ordinarily is left in obscurity. It is not depressing; on the contrary it is uplifting, since it views every man in the aspect of the highest demand made upon him, that he be spirit" (155).

That we are spirit is neglected in fact by distraction, and left in conceptual obscurity by speaking of 'human nature'. So S.K., beginning with the category of *relation* introduced the new idiom of *relating.* The upshot of this, we have noted, was to change every appropriate 'is' to 'is becoming' and to leave each of us with an inner task. But this task, curiously enough, is *not* something I can do. There is nothing I can *do* to become myself. This may sound paradoxical, and of course it is, for there are many things which I know I must do. But at the same time I can never ascertain whether the effect of these actions will be myself. And this is a fact not only of experience but now of grammar as well. For one becomes himself, we have been instructed to say, by relating himself to his own self. Yet this relating *is* the self, and so cannot be construed as something *I* do. I *am* a relating and become myself in relating myself to myself.

What the formula shrewdly prohibits is a conception of self where *I* become a project for myself. I am called to *become* myself, not to *do* myself. Hence the despair. Not *failure,* as in failing to achieve a goal I set out to accomplish; but *despair* at even knowing how to go about accomplishing it. So *despair* accompanies *relating* as an indispensable way of elucidating its meaning, just as the more I sense myself possessed of an inner task, the further I feel from achieving it. Although I may spontaneously think of this gap as a failure—since *doing* seems a more congenial way of construing *my* life than *becoming*—I can be helped to see that such an accusation is not quite accurate. But that leaves me no less desperate than before, despairing at being so far from being what I feel called to be.

Kierkegaard focuses this point by remarking that despair is not properly despairing "over something" (152). Despair, in other words, has no object. Experientially this harkens to the fact that desperation cannot be alleviated by removing some item or by offering the right charm. Grammatically it reminds us that despairing is not an *action,* for if it were, it would demand an object. This is perhaps the most acute of Kierkegaard's grammatical observations. Having eschewed the category of substance and adopted the participial form 'relating', the handiest way of conceiving the *relating* and the concomitant *despairing* would be as actions. But then, of course, they would have to be thought of as actions *of* a subject, and we would quickly revert to substance.

Rather, Kierkegaard wants to say that spirit is *active,*

certainly, but it cannot be thought of as an action. The
basic grammatical shift is from 'is' to 'becomes', not from
'is' to 'does'. And since Kierkegaard's analysis was made
with a view to elucidating the *individual* and *willing*, the
way has been prepared for a conception of *will* singularly
free from willfulness. For it looks as though willing is less
something I do than an activity I participate in. Kierkegaard does not develop this consequence that explicitly.
To distinguish despairing from doing, however, will help us
interpret a quite basic grammatical point he makes early in
the analysis.

In the case of an ordinary illness we say that "he
contracted it, but one cannot say that he *is contracting* it.
Not so with despair: . . . every instant the man in despair is
contracting it, it is constantly in the present tense. . . . This
comes from the fact that despair is a qualification of spirit,
that it is related to the eternal in man" (150). It is not
because one is *busy* contracting it that "every instant he is
in despair he contracts despair," but rather because the self
is a relating to itself.

Despairing, then, is not something one chooses to do. In
fact, it is not something we do at all. Nor is it something
that happens to us. Hence it is not something we can do
anything about, either by ceasing to despair or by correcting what might cause it. And realizing *that* makes us even
more desperate. Although we cannot help but refer to it as
a state (since every noun promises a state-description),
despairing is not a readily recognizable one.

More than anything else despairing is a sign—a sign that
the self is more than a "synthesis." It is a sign to each of us
that man is something else, something which makes "the
highest demand . . . upon him, that he be spirit" (155).
Despairing is not to be confused with "transitory dejection
or grief" (156), or even contrasted with happiness. If we
think of health as immediate effervescence, it might help
to compare despair with sickness, as Jesus used the phrase
"sickness unto death." But only if we contrast it as well,
for "despair, just because it is wholly dialectical, is in fact

the sickness of which it holds that it is the greatest misfortune not to have had it" (159). For otherwise one would never know himself to be spirit but remain an instance of human nature.

'Dialectical', we recall, is Kierkegaard's expression for anything that characterizes *spirit*. The term, together with directions for developing the awareness requisite to a dialectical account, came from Hegel. S.K. has given us directions for modifying the way we speak of despair, and so put us in a better position to recognize it as a "qualification of spirit." I have tried to show how he does this by keying into the classical categorical scheme of Aristotle, and even following Aristotle's pattern for scientific inquiry. Thus Kierkegaard proposes a radically different idiom for manifesting to men that we are spirit. He calls this treatment *abstract,* for it lays out a grammar for the new way of speaking.

In the third section of part one (after the "Hegelian interlude") Kierkegaard "describes psychologically the forms of despair as they display themselves in reality, in actual men" (134). The result, in Hegelian terms, is to manifest spirit as it appears in its successive stages. In terms of Kierkegaard's analysis, however, the point is to teach one how to use the language of spirit already sketched out. Further commentary would be reprehensible since Kierkegaard proposes to lead each of us to speak in our own voice, take our own steps, and embrace our particular destiny. The way is solitary and fearful. But keeping to an abstract voice one may assert that

> The possibility of this sickness is man's advantage over the beast, and this advantage distinguishes him far more essentially than the erect posture, for it implies the infinite erectness or loftiness of being spirit. The possibility of this sickness is man's advantage over the beast; to be sharply observant of this sickness constitutes the Christian advantage over the natural man; to be healed of this sickness is the Christian's bliss (147-148).

3.2. Reflections on the Method

What has S.K. accomplished by laying out a grammar—a set of rules—for thinking of ourselves as spirit? A *tour de force,* really; or so he himself suggests by offering us that involuted definition: "such . . . is the human self, a relation which relates itself to its own self, and in relating itself to its own self relates itself to another" (146). Quite a task to keep that set of directions in mind along the way to becoming oneself! Hearing a formula will not even teach us how to think of ourselves as spirit, much less help us to live consistently with the way we think. Learning how to use a language involves living one's way into it and testing it out where it comes in handy. The expository mode, of course, hardly lends itself to such exercises.

But Kierkegaard understood this better than any philosopher from Socrates to Wittgenstein. He deliberately espouses a variety of different angles on this inner task of becoming an individual, adopting diverse authorships and employing a range of poetic impersonations. And he never shrinks from thought-experiments. As one at home with language, he senses how pretentious it would be to propose a "new grammar." Nonetheless he knows precisely how we must modify the grammar at our disposal to shape our language to a new use. One only succeeds in modifying anything so basic as grammar by rigorously respecting its demands: only the poet who knows his grammar intimately can fracture it well. Kierkegaard deliberately adopts the strict form of exposition to manifest his respect for a substantive grammatical form in the very act of altering it.

Exposition enlarges into a paragraph the consequential structure of the ordinary declarative sentence. For predication can be interpreted as 'if . . . then', and sentences are meant to follow as consequences one of another.[20] Kierkegaard is concerned to edify. His imaginative elaborations of the forms of despair help exercise us in the new grammatical modes, yet he deliberately chooses a form which "will seem too strict to be edifying" (142). The reason is, I suggest, to show that it can be done—that one can speak Christianity with impeccable rigor. Such a move was destined to be mistaken, of course, as Kierkegaard has so often been accused of irrationalism. Inevitably some will find this sort of writing "too edifying to be strictly scientific." But such an attitude has nothing to do with the values proper to philsophic inquiry; it simply offers a different conception of what one ought to do with his intellect.

Like the *Platonici* whom Augustine confronted, philosophy can offer itself as an alternative way of life. In Kierkegaard's time it was "the high aloofness of indifferent learning," which from a "Christian point of view, [is] jest and vanity" (142). So while he deliberately chose the literary form his exposition was to take, Kierkegaard was just as deliberate in offering it as a "Christian exposition for edification and awakening." If this form was perhaps too strict to be edifying, it nonetheless contrasts with a yet "more solemn style which is so solemn that it does not signify much, and since one is too well accustomed to it, it easily becomes entirely meaningless (143). Philosophy is ever freeing itself from the bewitchments of philosophy.

3.21. A Dialectical Exposition

I have focussed on the way Kierkegaard grounds his treatment, both in form and content, in the classical (or Greek) mode. That is one test of philosophic acumen. The other test lies in the new use to which he puts that language. It is a *dialectical* use. He begins with similarities (like despair with sickness), and then proceeds to deny them in quite specific ways. This can even be expressed in a summary fashion: the self is a *relating*. But nothing can dispense us from the intensity of awareness this new idiom demands of us. We cannot propose it as a language in its own right; it will aways be an angular use of language.

Kierkegaard exhibits the intensity of awareness peculiar to dialectic by building this angularity into the overall movement of the treatise itself. The exposition not only proceeds in a dialectical fashion; its entire argument is conceived dialectically. For despair, we recall, "is in fact the sickness of which it holds that it is the greatest misfortune not to have had it—just because it is wholly dialectical" (159). The exposition moves from despair to sin dialectically, by escalating the inner task in inwardness until it opens out "before God" (208). But this entire movement is itself "dialectically conceived in the direction toward faith." The reason here stated has been exhibited throughout: "in the life of spirit everything is dialectical" (247). We progress not by constructing theories but by coming to appreciate their limits. What cannot be said, however, can sometimes be shown. Kierkegaard borrows the term and the method from Hegel, but shows us what *dialectical* means by constructing the exposition in the literary form he does.

3.22. A Theological Intent

S. K. is an irrationalist, then, in much the same way that Tiresias cannot see. He presents himself as defending, in strict philosophic manner, the "infinite qualitative difference" between God and man. His first step involves laying out a grammar peculiar to *spirit,* the image of God. Neither man nor God, then, can be comprised by the category of substance.[21]

As one begins to live into such a language, he cannot help taking offense at what he finds himself saying. *Offense* presents itself, then, as "the dialectical factor in everything Christian" (256). By daring to remind us—in the midst of an exposition—of the way we would react were we to take what it says to heart, Kierkegaard incorporates into his speculation "Christianity's defense against all speculation: offense" (214).

In reminding us that we must take offense at what

revelation proposes to make of us, Kierkegaard does all that remains in his power to secure that this exposition be a Christian one. For Christianity begins, not by stating something, but by making one an individual. And so an exposition concerning it must work to incorporate our response. The most appropriate form is one which demands a deliberate exertion, straining to use language in a different way. That form, as Kierkegaard uses it, is called "dialectic." It aims to overcome the temptation endemic to discourse: thinking we have understood something when we have formulated it. However negative the formulation may be, all we need do is state it to feel we have comprehended it; to wit: "God is infinite."

By relying on our native wit—and taking offense—we can effectively avoid every such trap. But chances are we would also turn down God's invitation as well. So we cannot simply rely on our native wit. It must be refined to a point where that wit will help us overcome the temptation itself. We need to become so wary of the pretense of our own formulations that God's invitation will stand out from all of them in its simplicity. Kierkegaard brings every poetic and philosophic talent to his aid in ferreting out this particular source of bewitchment. He had, after all, watched his mentor, Hegel, succumb to it.

The more precise the formulation, the more tempted we are to think we have understood what it conveys. And understandably so, for the role of defining is precisely to bring a series of tentative formulations to a critical point, whence one can move on more securely. In trying to bring the reader to an awareness that he is spirit, however, the most explicit formulation remains partial. This is so because the reader's own response to the message has to be factored in before he can be said to understand it. In fact, the more complete the formulation appears, the more misleading it is. So Kierkegaard adopts an explicitly incomplete form for his key definitions—an *algebraic* form (213). One must insert himself into the variable '[one] self' to understand what is being stated. One is on the way to becoming a Christian, then, when he realizes that the opposite of sin is not virtue, but faith. Yet Kierkegaard gives no argument to back up his insistence that "for the whole of Christianity it is one of the most decisive definitions that the opposite of sin is not virtue but faith" (213). For Kierkegaard has provided algebraic formulae for sin and for faith which display the opposition in a formal way.[22] What remains will be verified as one substitutes himself for the appropriate variables.

The other devices Kierkegaard employs are more in evidence in works whose form is not strictly expository. Stories, parables, imaginary scenarios, for example, engage the reader so that his own pretenses at understanding will come home to him as he plays out the part. We could consider these devices of a piece with the algebraic definitions, for in each case the reader is compelled to take part in an exercise in order to read the book. And as often as he tries to avoid a workout, Kierkegaard will be there with an ironic prod: "the greatest danger, that of losing one's own self, may pass off as quietly as if it were nothing; every other loss, that of an arm, a leg, five dollars, a wife, etc., is sure to be noticed" (165).

Finally the most effective security against the temptation is one which a man is least able to secure: keeping alive to what he is up to when writing an exposition like this one. "From the Christian point of view everything, absolutely everything should serve for edification" (142). In the measure that one writes to display his brilliance, then, he cannot hope to overcome the temptation, for he has already been overcome by it. Yet one's writing cannot help but display his brilliance. The very exposition, then, which demands that one bring his consciousness to a fine pitch of dialectical awareness requires of its composer that specific *unconsciousness* which leaves the left hand unaware of what the right is doing. Anyone—but especially one so exquisitely self-conscious as Kierkegaard—would despair of ever meeting this requirement. And appropriately so, for despair, like spirit, is everywhere dialectical.

Of course, the only way we have of showing that fact is by reflecting it into the very form of the work itself, and even into its composition.

4. Summary Observations

The difference between man and God is qualitatively infinite. And yet a man, in becoming what he is, is called to be an image of God. Should he be alive to this inner task, he may also be graced with a summons as well: to become God's son. Curiously enough, the more attuned he is to the inner task that is his, the more he is bound to take offense at what appears to be a distracting, or at best a superogatory, invitation. But he can also understand that response of his, and let that understanding filter out the offensive static long enough to consider responding. Beyond that, understanding cannot go. The response itself is better located in the heart than in the mind—yet blessed is one who understands it so.

NOTES

1. Cf. Peter Brown, *Augustine of Hippo* (Berkeley, California, 1968).

2. *Fear and Trembling and Sickness unto Death* (Princeton, 1968), 43-44. All references to this edition henceforth will be located in parenthesis in the text.

3. What moves one beyond recollection to resolution is simply his "making the movements." S. K. confessed himself to be of such a "dialectical" nature that he felt the simple need to "make the movements" acutely: *Stages on Life's Way* (New York, 1967), 113, 269, 280; *Concluding Unscientific Postscript* (Princeton, 1941), 277.

4. From Lowrie's introduction: "The word 'psychological' was substituted in the title of this book for 'edifying.' Making a subtle distinction, S. K. declared, '*for* edification is not my category.' He meant, I suppose, that this expression implied authority, whereas when he called his Discourses 'edifying' he was asserting merely that they were of a sort that might have this effect" (134).

5. This way of putting it tries to capture what John E. Smith calls Hegel's attempt to relate logic to reality to an internal fashion—cf. "The Relation of Thought and Being: Some Lessons from Hegel's *Encyclopedia*," *New Scholasticism* 38 (1964) 22-43.

6. The "Hegelian" portions of *Sickness* are introduced in the outline as treating "the factors of the synthesis," and these are "finitude/infinitude" and "possibility/necessity" (162-174).

7. For an excellent rendition of his method see Paul Holmer, "Kierkegaard and Philosophy," in Ralph M. McInerny (ed), *New Themes in Christian Philosophy* (Notre Dame, Indiana, 1968).

8. The expression "background language" is W. V. O. Quine's, from *Ontological Relativity and Other Essays* (New York, 1969), 48-51. Recall that Kierkegaard associates a metaphysical treatment of a subject with an "aesthetic" one in that both lack seriousness: "The System is therefore merely metaphysics, and that is all right, but it is not a system which embraces existence, for in that case the ethical must be included in it, and to abbreviate the ethical is to make a fool of it" (*Stages on Life's Way* [New York, 1967], 404).

9. One of the clearest statements comes from Socrates' forceful argument with Protagoras: " . . . would you rather say that if [a man] can distinguish good from evil, nothing will force him to act otherwise than as knowledge dictates, since wisdom is all the reinforcement he needs?" (*Protagoras*, 352c).

10. The expression is J. L. Austin's. In his *How To Do Things with Words* (Cambridge, Mass., 1962) he employs it first as a contrast term with "performative" utterances, and then wonders whether the contrast will hold (132-150).

11. For Aristotle's on willing cf. *N. Ethics* III, 1-5. The basic logic of our having to choose what we regard to be our good is articulated by Plato in the *Meno:* "(Socrates) Isn't it clear, then, that this class, who don't recognize evils for what they are, don't desire evil but what they think is good, though in fact it is evil; those who through ignorance mistake bad things for good obviously desire the good?" (77e).

12. Decisiveness makes the difference, as Socrates puts it in the *Apology:* "The truth of the matter is this, gentlemen. Where a man has once taken up his stand, either because it seems best to him or in obedience to his orders, there I believe he is bound to remain and face the danger, taking no account of death or anything else before dishonor" (28d).

13. Colossians 1:28; Aquinas, *Summa Theologiae*, IIa pars.

14. The clearest if somewhat one-sided treatment is Joseph de Finance, *Etre et Agir* (2nd ed.) (Rome, 1960).

15. "It is highly important that, instead of going further than Socrates, we simply return to the Socratic dictum that to under-

stand/and to understand are two things—not returning to it as a result [once for all acquired], for in the end that only helps men into the deepest wretchedness, since it simply abolishes the distinction between understanding/and understanding, but returning to it as the ethical interpretation of everyday life" (223). "Just this, however, is doubtless what the age, what Christendom, needs, namely, a little Socratic ignorance in relation to Christianity—but I say emphatically *Socratic* ignorance" (230).

16. "The ultimate happiness of man consists in his highest activity, which is the exercise of his mind. If therefore the created mind were never able to see the essence of God, either it would never attain happiness or its happiness would consist in something other than God. This is contrary to faith, for the ultimate perfection of the rational creature lies in that which is the source of its being . . . " (*Summa* I.12.1 [tr. Herbert McCabe, *Knowing and Naming God* (New York and London, 1964), 5]).

17. "Revelation provides us with a divine light which enables us to attain a more profound understanding from these images; . . . [for] the stronger our intellectual light the deeper the understanding we derive from images . . . " (*Summa* I.12.12.2 [tr. McCabe], 45).

18. Aristotle, *Posterior Analytics* I, 1-11.

19. This point is not made explicitly in *Sickness*, but is presupposed throughout. *Sickness* provides the grammar for the *Postscript*.

20. Cf. my analysis of implication as modeling the subject/predicate relation, in "Entailment: 'E' and Aristotle," *Logique et Analyse* 7 (1964) 111-129.

21. This is adumbrated by Aquinas in *Summa* I.3.2.2.

22. "Sin is: before God in despair not to will to be onself, or before God in despair to will to be oneself" (212). "Faith is: that the self in being itself and in willing to be itself is grounded transparently in God" (213).

5: JUNG
A Language for Soul

We usually do not go the length of proposing a new language unless we are thoroughly dissatisfied with the one available. So concentrated and reflective a task simply takes too much effort. Carl Jung's dissatisfaction with the psychological language of his day was both acute and pervasive. Its immediate object was Freud and his therapeutic theory; more generally he was aroused by the rationalism dominating Western intellectual concerns. By 'rationalism' I refer to the proposal that *reason* define the *humanum,* and to the specific aspiration for a unitary method of inquiry. In his dissatisfactions Jung displays many affinities with the German romanticists, and there is certainly much of the romantic within him. Yet we cannot fix him as an instance of the romantic reaction to reason, for he continued to pursue a single goal: a science of the psyche.

It will prove more useful to note how Jung found himself adopting an Aristotelian posture: distinct subject matters demand distinctive approaches. Since we are not prepared to find a scientist respecting his material in the manner in which Jung insists one must, however, the results may seem to us to be more like art than science. And Jung found himself so criticized. Yet he demurred, insisting that his was a scientific inquiry, a "[study of] nature" (186).[1] I shall argue for the rightness of that defense: what Jung finds himself challenging is a paradigm for science, one so settled as to preempt the field. In exposing this notion of science as *one* paradigm—and a limited one at that—he also managed to expose the pretensions of a society crafted in its image (16,190).

It is quite difficult, of course, to ascertain whether a challenge like Jung's is successful or not. Does it amount to a breakthrough? Does he manage more than an articulate register of dissatisfaction? Has he succeeded in proposing a new paradigm for a science of the psyche? How can we decide whether to call what he accomplishes *science?* Finally, what has all this to do with exercising our theological understanding?

1. A Quest for a New Science

The last two questions are related. A vantage point with perspective enough to assess different paradigms would already be in metaphysical territory. More specifically, the subject matter of Jung's science is the *psyche* and its goal the *self*. In terms traditional since Augustine, there is no more acceptable model for the divinity than the self; no more perspicuous image of the transcendent creator than the creature who is creative in his own right. Furthermore, Jung respects the negative properties of theology, since the *self* remains transcendent to the science. For him the self is its goal rather than its subject (9.2,23-25).

This fact alone distinguishes Jung's *science* from the standard model. It also provides a key to specifying the subject matter, the psyche, and to correlating the several ways Jung explicitly molds his procedures to the contours of the subject. Discovering those contours and shaping the inquiry to them continue in a fashion acceptable to the canons of scientific discovery: proposing likely hypotheses and testing them out. The testing in this case is carried out in circumstances accenting the uniqueness of each person, but repeated experiences do yield a kind of know-how. What singles Jung out and contrasts him with Freud is the peculiar congruence between theory and practice. In fact, his theory is so intimately linked to practice that it has been thought not to qualify as theory. Yet on the other hand the charge of methodological schizophrenia to which Freud is so vulnerable finds no purchase here.[2]

My plan is to show how Jung worked out what he came to call "my science."[3] I shall indicate how conscious he was that establishing *his* science meant dethroning a paradigm become an idol, the idol, in fact, of Western civilization. More positively, it will involve a different sort of verification process as well as an entirely new role for method (16,254-56).

Shifts like these call for a particularly acute ear to what one is presently lacking. The arguments offered for accepting a new set of methodological priorities reveal something of the contours of the subject matter, and when they are offered in a sufficiently reflective idiom, these arguments propose an alternative epistemology. Hence Jung finds himself working at more than one level, as he argues for a science of the psyche congruent with its subject matter. His growing conviction that *self* and *individual* are more goals than fact demands a language for what transcends description or explanation. Aspiration and finality are indispensable to a science of the psyche (8,24).

Dealing with transcendence of this sort prepares him for the more demanding issues involved in speaking of what is divine. Jung, of course, is normally careful to speak of the "God-image," as befits a psychologist. But he was forced to try to articulate what men aspire to. He called it "individuation" (9.1,275). Rather than Jung's explicit statements about God, it is his language conveying the pursuit of individuation which offers the most fruitful model for discovering a religious way of speaking. For individuation is the goal of spirit, and nothing but spirit can aspire to it.

The inner pressure which drove Jung to elaborate a science for *spirit* forced him to a symbolic language (16,270). Using this language helps us to see how the "God-image" and the symbol for *self* complement one another like a casting and a coin (334). Both strike us with their power and each baffles us by its inscrutability. Jung offers us hope by sketching out the ways in which that power can be released.

Each release brings a little more understanding with it, and we can come gradually to realize the self initially symbolized (8,73-5). The God-image comes more into focus the more the self is realized. Theology knows that man is made in the image of God; psychology does not. It well might be the other way about. Jung himself refuses to arbitrate this question, but each individual has a way of responding to it if he submits to the process called *individuation*.

1.1. Sources and Method

The only test available for Jung's science is that to which we put a road map: does it succeed in getting us there? A working meaning for the term *individuation* is reserved for those who allow themselves to submit to its demands. Yet there are indications, relatively early in the process; that bring assurance. One senses when the power released is his own. A truthful admission, however unwelcome, affords its own relief. Furthermore, a certain congruence between the structure of the science and the therapy it urges recommends the science itself. It should not be surprising, then, that Jung's autobiographical reflections lead us most directly into his science. Not only do they document its genesis and show how "his science" led him to discover the self that is his own. These autobiographical reflections also exhibit that self which Jung realized, allowing us to assess the worth of the science in its paradigm instance.

I have consulted many of the essays published in the *Collected Works,* and shall cite them abundantly in support of my interpretation. The essential movement of Jung's thought and therapy, however, is captured in his *Memories, Dreams, Reflections.* Autobiography also proves a more reliable medium for understanding Jung than an expository essay, since it helps to rein in his own predilection for theorizing. In the context of the autobiography Jung can invite us to accept this penchant as part of himself (327). But outside that context it can so dominate his treatment of the subject that we might be lulled into thinking we had realized what had been presented to us so clearly. The form in which he presents his theory could tempt us to overlook what Jung never ceases to insist upon: we cannot pretend to understand our *self* by grasping a schematic outline. Schemas offer at best models for action and so must be filled in by our taking the appropriate action: "psychologically, one only understands what one has experienced himself" (9.1,270).

Jung's point is reminiscent of Aristotle's insistence that practical discourse concludes not in more talk but in action. Yet he comes even closer to Kierkegaard in the assertion Jung makes here about the human spirit. One has no access to his self except through becoming himself (9.1,287). For the self I would be, I am not yet. Hence the self is more aspiration than fact, more appropriately symbolized than referred to (8,167). This maxim so crucial to Jung's science is the performative corollary of his central dictum on method: there is no language for the psyche other than its own, no explanation of the psychic other than the living process of the psyche itself (8,223).

1.2. Contrast with Freud

This dictum signals Jung's break with Freud and the prevailing scientific paradigm, and accounts for the self-involving strategies of his own science. Where one eschews the clarity of a reductive scheme, insisting that we have no outside standpoint from which to model the psyche (9.1, 207), he must show himself imaginative enough to design strategies for gaining the perspective which understanding demands. Jung will accomplish this by recourse to *archetypes,* available to each individual through his dreams and independently in the heritage of mythology (9.1,44). Since the archetype is always expressed symbolically, Jung insists that I must discover its precise meaning by taking up the most plausible of the leads it offers. I will be able to understand what it means for me only in retrospect—by assessing the relative illumination and liberation I have come to enjoy.

The archetypes may seem to offer schemata, but they do not, for their language is many-sided. I can only understand what they are saying to me by translating their symbolic expression into a series of concrete steps which I must now take (8,82-91). I can only assess their meaning when I have undertaken those steps. So the two strategies—the apparent overview and the reflective undertaking—work hand in glove. Jung's science is only realized in therapy, and therapy is only accomplished in practice.

The aim is my self—the individual which I am called to be; and the understanding concomitant with that realization augurs a new kind of objectivity (9.2,167). Jung renounces the reductive strategy of explaining human activity in causal terms, and relies on individual performance to tether down the meaning of his explanatory schemes. Yet what results is neither willful nor arbitrary, but displays that objectivity which science has always sought (9.1,58). Such is the promise of "Jung's science." I shall focus on the alternative paradigm he offers for inquiring into the psyche.

Paradigms, of course, do not arise full-blown, nor can we argue for them directly. They stem more from dissatisfaction than from insight. It was Freud's tunnel vision that forced Jung to break with him. Freud was wedded to a mechanistic explanatory model, with the result that sexuality was confined to physiology. Yet what Freud had unearthed—the unconscious—asked to be *interpreted* before it could be *explained* (9.2, 203). The role which sexuality came to play in Freud's therapy demanded a wealth of meanings unavailable to physiology (168). Yet Freud himself could not let go of the model of reductive explanation (8,55).

What a less speculative co-worker might have let pass Jung could not tolerate: so sharp a contrast between theory and practice, between science and therapy. Furthermore, Jung's analytic eye caught an undue rigidity in Freud at this point. Sexuality—in the reductive explanatory role reserved for it—soon ceased to be an hypothesis and took on the character of a dogma (150). Jung could not help but conclude that Freud was not up to undertaking an investigation of the psyche with requisite objectivity (167). What I have elevated to a shift in explanatory paradigms was actually forced on Jung as a way of keeping his scientific conscience intact.

The way to discovering an alternative pattern and perspective proved a prolonged and harrowing journey. Jung had nowhere to turn. Freud already had been treading the very limits of scientific respectability. Jung could only keep on with his own work, and continue to test his therapeutic practice against—what? Nothing but his own sense of congruity; his own feel for language rich enough to interpret the psychic material burdening his patients (9.2,28). Chapter six of the autobiography relates this period of seven years under the heading "Confrontation with the Unconscious." Jung likened it to mythical journeys into the underworld.

Mythic literature proved, in fact, an invaluable guide (9.2,180). But Jung would be satisfied with nothing less than a scientific understanding and one that attained his goal of discovering a more comprehensive model for the self. He also accepted the penalty: never to let up in questing for his own self while he helped others find their way to theirs. Anyone else who took up "his science" would be faced with the same demands. Where the subject of inquiry is the person, the inquirer must set out to become one. Whatever understanding is granted will come in the wake of this individual pursuit. There is no other way to objectivity where subjects are concerned. That is the import of Jung's new paradigm for a scientific study of the psyche.

2. The Self

Reflective autobiography offers an account of the self congruent with its peculiar status, for the self is an objective rather than an object of inquiry. We come to understand what it is only by reflecting on our efforts to attain it. And the measure of attainment comes only gradually, as successive images for self are shattered by failure—and yet we realize that it is not all over. The process of attaining oneself is not one of achievement; the images appropriate to it are never so linear as progress. Rather the pattern is one the Gospels invoke for Jesus' death and resurrection: the seed must be buried in the ground (and "die") for the plant to emerge. "Death" amounts to exposing a particular self-image as an ego-projection and hence an idol (9.1,84). The individuation process which Jung maps out thus adopts the contours of a Judeo-Christian anthropology.

Any image we have of the self, then, will be only an intimation. The patterns we adopt to guide us in realizing our self must be capable of being realized analogously at different stages of development. We know we shall always have to prune some spontaneous shoots, but cannot know beforehand which ones these will be. Jung acknowledges this fact by noting that only symbolic language captures the reality of the self (16,265). As we need images to motivate us, so symbolic language expresses what self can become. General descriptive terms pretend to offer us a commensurate object, while schemes which offer an explanation in yet simpler terms suggest comprehension. Yet in the case of the self we can claim neither. Whatever schemes are employed arise spontaneously (9.2,268), and are understood only as they are lived through (9.1,289).

2.1. Early Intimations

Jung's autobiography illustrates how we can come to understand the self through living our way into its successive symbolic expressions. The reflections are written from the lived end of a journey of eighty-three years. The consciousness they display is wrested from the unconscious in a series of confrontations. These make up the plot of the story. It is Jung's story yet the story of everyman, since each ordeal can be described and interpreted in mythic terms. The path to individuation becomes a way to objectivity, when one is in a position to say that the wall between the conscious and unconscious is "transparent" (355).

The secret lies in the unconscious. Yet the very name suggests that we know little more about "it" than we do about "x" (336). The very suggestion that all is not ours for inspection, that there *is* an unconscious, can be unsettling. Yet everyone has the suspicion that he is not one but two—or many. Jung relates how he came to feel this "other side" to himself, and the youthful ways he had of characterizing it.

Early on—he relates from the vantage of eighty-three—he felt himself not one but two. He named his other side "number two," for it was like the underside of the more dominant "number one." Yet in some curious way he was both and both were he. From the description of Jung's early adventures in consciousness we can schematize two worlds, each associated with a self and one complementing the other. To retain the associations of 'left' with 'other', "number two" characteristics are listed in the left column, and "number one" to the right:

my secret (22-23)	I came upon myself; . . . now *I* willed (32)
the forbidden thought (36-40)	
loneliness and the secret (40-41)	
the "natural mind" (50)	
animals (67)	people
Mother (=animals, trees, mountains, meadows, running water) (90)	Father (42-43)
the country world: God's world (100)	urban world
experience (42-43, 69): grace (73, 91), God (92, 98)	belief: religion, theology (42-43, 73, 91)
God's world (112)	"monastery of the world" (=all that is probable, average, commonplace)
story (124)	Clinical diagnosis
psyche (="other half of the world") (132)	intellect (=meaingless life) (139)
adventure of the spirit (141-42)	theology (=intellect not subject to control of feeling) (145)

This youthful scheme served as a skeleton for his later elaboration. To accept the fact that he, Carl Jung, was not one but two brought relief, of course, yet also left him a task: to bring the two together. But something kept him from setting out to dc that all at once. The young man sensed a dilemma: any program of unification would be engineered by number one, for that was his forte. Yet if number one were allowed to carry through the plans, they would leave no room for number two. For number two seemed the very antithesis of plan or structure. This was certainly one reason why Jung treasured number two, and could not bear to see it eliminated.

Society, of course, values number one, and quite nearly exclusively so (8,69-71). Jung felt himself sufficiently part of a culture to respect that valuation. Yet he could also feel how one-sided it is. Neither aspect, then, could be sacrificed to the other. The only way out of the tension lay through it: accept the fact that he was two. The tensions that he felt were inevitable results of an inescapable polarity in his own makeup.

Although he would later express it in more sophisticated and enlightening ways, the bipolar structure of the self which he grasped so young will remain Jung's central metaphysical conviction (9.2,267). He will use it to frame the symbolic language which discussion of the *self* elicits; it will "explain" why every psychological assertion invites its opposite, and how psychic development occurs by a shift toward one pole or the other (169). The resulting instability gives the symbol of the self a decidedly antinomial cast (9.2,62-3,225). So the model itself forbids Jung to aim for "balance." The very force of this polarity demands a more active process of integration, and one which will never allow one self to suppress the other.

2.2. Later Elaboration

An image pattern arose spontaneously to symbolize the self as an objective and to guide one in attaining it. These images display the polarities yet bring them to focus in a center. Known for centuries as a *mandala,* such images gather the four directions of the compass into a circle whose center forms the focus of the figure. Jung's patients had a way of returning to this form, as do many unsuspecting doodlers. Without attributing anything mysterious to

the figure, we can use it to elucidate Jung's theory of the
self. By using his central image to schematize Jung's theory
I can show how Freud's becomes a privileged case. An
effective image should work in that way, and the mandala
does (9.2,209-15).

Painting becomes a way of therapy for Jung, and patients can reveal a great deal by the kinds of mandalas they
happen to sketch. I shall present a schematic one designed
to reveal the dynamic elements operative in Jung's symbol
for the self. Needless to say, this scheme does not pretend
to be an interpretative key for any mandala. Symbols do
not function in that way. I am rather using Jung's central
symbol in a schematic fashion to display the forces he
finds operative in the psyche.

The entire shaded area represents the *unconscious;* the
unshaded, what is *conscious.* We name the conscious pole

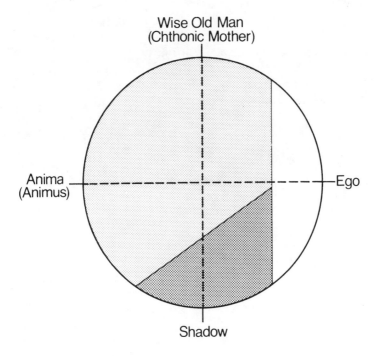

ego, though as Westerners—and thanks to Descartes especially—we normally confuse it with the self. The complementary unconsciousness pole is the *anima* (or *animus*
where the ego is feminine). The vertical poles are initially
quite unrecognizable to us since they belong to what is
unconscious. They complement one another as positive (at
the top) and negative in tone. The positive vertical pole,
the *wise old man* or the *chthonic mother*, and the negative
vertical pole, the *shadow*, normally present themselves in
the same sex as the person.

The aim of therapy can be represented as familiarizing
oneself with more and more of the shaded area, so that
one's *shadow* and the *wise old man* (or *chthonic mother*)
become recognizable members of one's own household. It
would be misleading (and therapeutically disastrous) to
depict this process as one whereby the unshaded area takes
over the shaded. The result then would not be growth as
much as a victory for *ego.* The tension Jung felt from
his earliest days would then be dissipated, and with it
psychic fertility and capacity for inward growth.

I have spoken of *anima* and *wise old man* in impersonal
terms, but not hesitated to speak of one's own *shadow.*
The *shadow* stands for the personal factors operative in the
unconscious, and takes up a relatively small region of
the vast and uncharted *unconscious* (9.2,284). It is the
first "other" that one is able to meet and to confront in
himself, precisely because it comprises the relatively accessible negative elements from his own personal history.
Facing, accepting, and befriending one's *shadow* is the
express goal of Freudian therapy. Beyond it Freud does
not tread since his reference point is the separate individual. In this way Freud's therapeutic strategy becomes a
special case of Jung's.

It may seem paradoxical that Jung insists upon the
impersonal character of the other distinguishable operating
factors in the unconscious. For they are meant to be
ingredient in personal growth, in individuation. The shorthand expression of this phenomenon—the *collective un-*

conscious—offends our western intellectual sensibilities still more. Yet there are solid reasons for Jung's adopting a language so initially implausible.

The first and most persuasive reason is that Jung was forced beyond the boundaries of his patients' individual histories to understand what was impeding their personal development and to help them discover a way through (9.2,164-67). Mythology and alchemy offered him ways of charting the *unconscious*, for he found patterns recurring in this age-old human lore. He discovered patterns common to men over space and over time, yet germane to helping *this* person find a way through to his own individual self.

The implication was clear: the uncharted part of our self that we name *the unconscious* opens us out onto a common humanity (9.2,169). Men and women have been meeting and coming to terms with the unknown since the beginning, and these recurrent themes yield what we have come to understand about it. Religious symbols, interpreted as patterns for spiritual growth, introduce us to the unknown in appropriately indirect ways (9.1,8).

In fact, Jung's notion of a *collective unconscious* looks very much like a rendition in psychic terms of the medieval notion of *spirit* (8,220-22). What distinguished spirit from matter was primarily its communicability. In a metaphysical idiom separate individuals could find themselves telling abut the "same thing" *because* their intellectual powers were of a spiritual nature. No one tried to characterize this mode of existence. Aquinas even gave arguments why a descriptive statement could not properly apply to such things. But everyone sensed that something had to account for so many individuals communicating.

Jung felt similarly constrained to assert that this otherwise quite unknown dimension of the self must be said to be *collective* rather than individual in nature. Yet it contains the wellsprings of individuality, much as the medievals used *spirit* to express uniqueness as well as communicability. The individuality which *ego* claims turns out to be quite shallow and brittle (9.2,164). It is built on assertion and protected by possessions, yet has no inner resources. The person who relies exclusively on *ego* begins before long to feel separate and isolated. Individuality as *ego* asserts itself, foments competition, and spawns division. In medieval terms, *ego* (or consciousness as a Cartesian understands it) has more affinities with *matter* than with *spirit*.

Jung's model accomplished three conceptual revolutions in one:

(a) ego cannot be thought of as coterminal with *self*, because

(b) the "other side" of *self* is *the unconscious*, which contains infinite resources for development since it opens the person out into that wider reality which he must assimilate to become him*self*, hence

(c) *self* is more an objective than an object, always transcending any particular description and appropriately expressed in symbolic language.

The result is a new form of *objectivity* attained by letting go of those clarities which *ego* demands and undertaking the fabled journey into the unknown (352).

2.3. Reality of the Unconscious

The unconscious, however, cannot help but be frightening. Anything faceless and uncharted unnerves us. Yet even as I come to accept its presence to me—as my "other side"—the particular faces it begins to assume are positively threatening. There are the traumas of one's personal history: the unresolved anxieties, the ego-fears of inadequacy, the real or imagined deprivations. And as if these factors were not crippling enough, they come dressed in legendary roles: the old witch whose hair turns into snakes, the devouring mother who may be a many-headed dog, the lecherous old man posing as a carefree youth. Personal fears become archetypal terrors.

The legendary faces enhance the fear but offer in compensation some way of charting the unknown (8,54). The ordeals of legendary heroes become the story of the unconscious, letting an individual glimpse something of what he is in for. Saga and story become *descriptive* of a new kind of reality. *Not* that they are now to be taken literally, as though they were not story or saga. Rather, they are descriptive of this reality—the unconscious—precisely by being story and saga. Once again, the *form* of the rendition reflects the reality of the object spoken about. The language *of* and the language *about* the unconscious are inherently symbolic. Then we must say that this unknown dimension of our self is real, and *symbolically* real. It is real because it is the object of a description which has an application—in this case a therapeutic one; and it is symbolically real because the form of the description is symbolic.

Although Jung does not make it in this way, the point is central to understanding him: the psyche is real. It is not "merely psychological," just as *individuation* does not spell individual fulfillment (340-41). This reality is professedly strange, however, as my schematic argument shows. We do not consider sagas to describe precisely because their idiom is expressly multivalent or symbolic. For the same set of reasons we ordinarily contrast *symbolic* with *factual,* and identify *factual* with *real.* Furthermore, we must maintain these utterly basic categories lest we find ourselves engaged in the luxuriant metaphysics which deals in many kinds of reality. Nor does this *caveat* represent a mere intellectual scruple or positivistic bias. The practical issue of that variety of metaphysics is not simply distracting speculation but destructive occultism. And Jung was not immune to this danger.

On the other hand, we can neither overlook nor minimize the influence of this unconscious dimension on our actions. And if it really affects our lives, we cannot very

well deny its *reality* (352). Jung can even show how it takes
its revenge if we do. So we may well be forced to give in a
little, loosening the identification of *real* with *factual* and
granting a symbolic idiom some access to what is *real*. Not
just any symbolic idiom, of course, but one which can
prove its therapeutic worth (8,49). Jung insists, not that
saga is descriptive *tout court,* but that it offers an appropriate way of charting a journey which can only be understood properly as we undertake it.

The therapeutic process, then, offers a way of fixing one
of the levels of symbolic meaning just long enough to
allow an individual to take the next step (9.2,18). Within
this controlling context, then, saga becomes descriptive.
And the symbolic reality of the *unconscious* is tapped to
enhance an individual's authenticity by allowing him to
appropriate that much more of his *self.* What clears that
self-appropriation from the accusation of an arbitrary and
willful self-fulfillment is the *reality* of the *unconscious*
which powers it (8,218). In similar fashion, the *unconscious* reveals its reality in the unwelcome ordeals it con-
cocts and in the power which one can feel being released as
he negotiates them (8,68-9).

2.4. Appropriation of the Self: Dynamics

Before examining that process of *self*-appropriation
which Jung calls individuation, it is worth remarking how
the process itself testifies to the reality of the *unconscious*.
For while the self is an objective to be attained, it cannot
be achieved. The reason lies in the dilemma Jung noted
early in his life. Achievement—plans, projects, goal-
directed activity—is the work of "number one," the conscious self or *ego.* If the *self* symbolized—the transcendent
self—were to be realized by our conscious efforts, the
result would necessarily complete the domestication of
"number two," the *unconscious.* Yet it is the *unconscious*
which opens an individual beyond the boundaries of his

factual self, and which contains the sources of power and fertility animating the ego's projects (16,263). Far from realizing the *self*, domesticating this resource would amount to aborting all aspirations toward it.

Western society presently finds itself in the midst of verifying this basic contention of Jung. Having set out to harness nature, and set its goals at complete control, it finds itself faced not only with diminishing resources but with a concomitant effluent which the impulse to dominate cannot control. We call it pollution, and the notion is rapidly assuming symbolic dimensions. It is the telltale of a runaway *ego*, and a glaring reminder that the conscious way of achievement—of planning and control—fails to respect the real contours of man and his world.

There is something more to reality, an other, unconscious dimension. The complete reality which *self* symbolizes can be attained only by respecting this other dimension. Attained, not achieved; and respect accounts for the difference. Whenever we feel more "together," more "at one," and are able to call upon the new power which this releases, the whole thing, Jung notes, "is felt as 'grace' " (335).

Jung adopts an explicitly religious idiom to intimate what the model will not allow him to capture: the critical integrating point in the process of individuation (8,224). The model requires that *self* be transcendent since the only idiom which can convey its contours properly is a symbolic one (16,270). Consistency then demands that the *self* outreach any efforts to achieve it, and the model can show why attainment cannot be achievement. When Jung has spontaneous recourse to the explicitly religious term "grace," some of the strains of linking *real* with *symbolic* begin to surface.

A reality which is symbolic has a contradictory ring about it, and surfaces as a paradox. An *attainment* which is not an achievement is likely to appear less secure to us than one which is, yet Jung insists that the truth lies otherwise. We have traced his arguments and shown how they can be confirmed by therapeutic experience and evidenced in our present ecological *cul-de-sac*. Yet they cannot but appear to common sense as a paradox. Like a Zen koan, they force the (conscious) mind to assume a new stance toward its world. In this case it must accept and respect the improbable reality of something which can only be rendered in symbolic language: *the unconscious*.

I have noted how Jung has recourse to a religious expression to effect a transition which his model calls for yet cannot itself describe. My intention is not to find in Jung an ally of religion. I simply want to note how "religious" is his conception of the *self* and one's becoming his *self*. I am thinking here of Kierkegaard's "religiousness A," exhibited by Socratic ignorance or a Zen koan.[4] The contrast term is "secular," where man is conceived as making or achieving himself.

As evidence, one can note how biblical sayings illumine and are themselves illumined by the paradoxes which *individuation* elicits. The gospel of John, for example, has the Baptist asserting: "a man can only lay claim to what comes to him from heaven." Furthermore he uses this maxim to differentiate his destiny from that of Jesus. Yet Western common sense would insist on just the opposite: a man can only claim that he has himself achieved. The gospel, like Jung, witnesses to a reality beyond that of our projects.[5]

3. The Method: Therapy

Since the language of the psyche is inherently symbolic, I have emphasized how appropriately definite meanings can only arise within a therapeutic exchange (8,74). And since this exchange cannot be programmed, but must allow for the mutual development of client and analyst, we are allowed at best some programmatic view of the goings-on. Freud's experience had already called attention to the phenomena of transference and countertransference. Typically, Freud was more preoccupied with "handling" it;

Jung with understanding it. Put more amply: Freud's clarity about the goals of therapy permitted him to regard transference as one procedure (albeit a key one) among a set of techniques available to the analyst, while Jung's convictions about the transcendence of the process demand that the analyst submit himself to the rigors of the journey as well.

The upshot, however, could easily upset my summary contrast: a Jungian may find himself needing to know how to *handle* the ensuing process, since there is so much to it that he does not understand; while a Freudian's clearer understanding of it allows him to handle it—if not with ease, at least without fear of being overwhelmed. Jung's extended essay "On the Psychology of Transference" indicates the kind of understanding we can hope for during the process (16,163-323). One step follows upon the next, with the earlier portending the later. The sequence can only be articulated in very general terms, however, and each stage must be described in symbolic language. So one can never quite be sure how to read the symptoms; and if he is able to recognize in what phase the relationship stands, he will not be able to tell *how* it will progress to the next one.

3.1. A Process of Transformation

Jung adopted ten alchemical plates to indicate the steps along the way, providing the psychic translation germane to each one. The process can appropriately be described as one of *transformation*. For however pretentious that may sound, it captures the aspiration common to alchemist and therapist alike. The initial stage of the process is depicted in the alchemical plates by a mercurial fountain: sheer awareness of the resources available. In the next plate the contenders enter: king and queen, presumably brother and sister. Then they appear naked, next immersed in a bath, then conjoined.

The *conjunctio* takes place in the fifth plate, assuming

the role of central symbol. The context assures that we are witnessing "instinctive energy transformed into symbolic activity," however, rather than the "mere triumph of natural instinct" (16,248-250). The *conjunctio* of king with queen (brother with sister) is not to be understood simply as copulation. It means rather to signify what "the psychologist cannot *explain*," namely, that critical juncture in the process of individuation where conscious and unconscious begin to "integrate" their complementary functions (16,256).

When each gives himself/herself over to the other, of course, both must die. The result is depicted in the sixth plate as an hermaphroditic corpse. Next follows the ascent of the soul in the stylized form of a *homunculus*. A medieval fantasy we are tempted to say, but Jung demurs. This plate represents a distinct stage in a person's coming to live with the unconscious. Just as the hermaphroditic corpse symbolized the temporary loss of *ego* and fusion with its other side, so this plate calls attention to a peculiar intensification of that phenomenon: the collapse and disorientation of consciousness (16,267). One enters a stage known to primitives as "loss of soul," where he can be left at the mercy of autoerotic affects and fantasies (16,268) or demonic incursions (16,271). Jung likens this stage to the *dark night* noted by John of the Cross, wherein one is left without light or protection, at the mercy of contending forces and shielded by nothing more tangible than the promised mercy of God (16,272).

This stage is not terminal, however, but is followed by a purification. What is chastened above all is one's understanding. By 'understanding' Jung means that faculty which affords consciousness its primacy but foments illusion as well: notably the illusion of thinking we have arrived the moment we have spied the goal (16,294-5). The purification stage symbolizes "something beyond understanding: a feeling-relationship with the contents of the unconscious" (16,279). The fruit of risking ego-death and living through its dark consequences, this "feeling always binds one to the reality and meaning of psychic contents, and these in turn impose binding standards of ethical behaviour" (16,280). It is opposed to the treacherous illusion of liberation which accompanies an intellectual understanding replete with aesthetic appreciation. Jung sees through the romantic ideal while he remains indebted to the powerful countercurrents of the romantic movement.

In the next plate the soul returns. The *ego* which had lost itself in risking fusion with the *unconscious* will recover its capacity for differentiation, but will function henceforth hermaphroditically. The new *ego* will live in a state of perpetual conflict. Joined with its other side, the ego must henceforth give it room for expression yet remain watchful lest it take too much (16,304). The price of wholeness demands one submit to this fact, for the power released is power generated from a state of perpetual conflict. Jung sees the cross as a perfect symbol for the "fundamental contrariety of human nature" and equates the gospel command to take it up daily with one's actively "accepting the fact that the psyche is at cross-purposes with itself" (16,305).

What the soul's return presages appears in the final plate: a new birth as a transformed self represented hermaphroditically. The process "ends in a paradoxical being defying rational analysis" (16,314). Using sexual imagery, the plates depict a process which outstrips the organic metaphor of *growth* by explicitly incorporating death and loss of soul. Nor is it a simple resuscitation, for the final outcome manages to conjoin what was opposed in a *complexio oppositorum.*

It is this image—the hermaphrodite—which licenses the pretentious term "transformation." What has been overcome is nothing less than that cleavage in man and in the world dramatized for the Enlightenment in Goethe's *Faust.* Jung reached the medievals like Nicholas of Cusa for a yet more comprehensive articulation and even allows himself to be guided by language of alchemy.[6] For Cusa,

God is best seen as *complexio oppositorum* since his re-
deeming activity takes that form. For Jung, what is divine
in man poses him a built-in task: to reconcile the opposites
within (16,320).

3.2. Role of Archetypes

Jung employs the alchemical plates after the fashion of
archetypes. They did mark off distinct stages and succeed
cumulatively in marking off a process. But shorn of Jung's
commentary they would do very little for us. that is to say
that Jung can make them function symbolically where
they fail to function descriptively. He does this by offering
a plausible interpretation, and one which is potentially
multivalent—guided by the plates rather than dictated by
them.

The plates *do* guide Jung's commentary, however, by
offering discriminations which prevailing thought patterns
would overlook, such as the "loss of soul" depicted in
number seven. Hence we are not simply offered a more
primitive pictorial account of a process now grasped more
accurately and scientifically. It is rather a matter of mutual
enrichment: the language of medieval imagery and scientific commentary interact in a manner strictly analogous to
the process which that interaction succeeds in symbolizing.

What we are provided with is an object lesson in how
archetypes work. They are embodied in images—recurrent
and commanding images—which can succeed in offering
illumination to one who will make the effort to try to
understand them. Understanding cannot be a matter of
simple translation, but will take the form of a commentary
linking this image with a transitional feature of human
experience so that it appears even more clearly for the
transition it is. So I will be offered some understanding of
what it is I am going through—enough to give me some
intimation of what it is I am to do next.

It will be clear why I must speak so indirectly of the

illumination which archetypes can offer when I note that the only commentary appropriate to the situation can be offered by a therapist who is working with the person concerned. And even his comments will be offered in a tentative voice, becoming an acceptable commentary on a person's experience only in the measure that person recognizes it to be. If the process is to issue in transformation, it must be directed by a higher purpose (enshrined in the archetypes), facilitated by an experienced guide, and undertaken by the person himself. Every scrap of illumination must be brought to focus on a step to be taken—a step which only the individual will recognize to be the next one for him to take (16,147).

So all of Jung's speculative flights turn out to be exercises in model building: models for examining the manifestations of the unconscious in order to learn its language (16,123). Theory is utterly subservient to therapy, as the steps outlined in the autobiography (and reiterated in other essays [8.82-91]) show:

(1) consciously submit oneself to the impulses of the unconscious (173)
(2) translate emotions into images (177)
(3) work to understand the images (178, 187-88)
(4) discover the ethical consequences (193)

The language of the unconscious is cast in images pervasive and powerful enough to be called *archetypal*. They can be harnessed, however, and made to serve a process—itself archetypal—of self-integration which issues in a genuine transformation. What is required is a willingness on the part of an individual to undertake the journey entailed, and the corresponding willingness of a skilled interpreter to accompany him. The ambivalent language of images becomes tractable and focused in the measure that we are willing to let these images guide our own footsteps along the way. If we refuse them ethical seriousness, however, and consider them a private theatrical repertoire, they will at best entertain us and at worst bewitch us (8,68). Dabblers in the occult, then, as well as hyperpractical people who find all this to be ridiculous, are on an equal footing in mistaking the archetypes and treating them as something frivolous.

A personal guide is required to glean what intelligibility the *archetypes* have to offer, and that for two reasons. The first respects their symbolic mode of discourse. Analogies function in a natural inquiry (as contrasted with *poesis*) only through an accompanying commentary.[7] The commentary does not succeed in replacing the analogy; only in directing us how to take it. In fact, it blends so unobtrusively with the analogy itself that we need to be reminded of its presence. When we think of analogies in science, we are invariably thinking of model-*cum*-commentary: of molecules as tiny bouncing balls with some explicit indications of their elasticity.

Where the effort to understand a symbolic presentation subserves the practical inquiry of an individual into the *unconscious,* the commentary had best be *viva voce.* For the capacity of *my* intellect to generate illusion is notably enhanced in this particular exercise. In fact, *neurosis* may fairly well be defined as the manner in which my relationship to the *unconscious* has come to be systematically skewed. So I need another to confront my misapprehensions by posing apprehensions which enhance my own perspective. Furthermore, since the conditions of understanding require me to leave my native land and set out on a journey, I need another like me to be my companion (16,294). For no one dare set out on such a journey alone; that is simply an archetypal fact!

3.3. Conflict: Reconciling Opposites

The opposition which Jung found within himself as a child did not subside but intensified, until his confrontation with the unconscious at thirty-eight. The fact that a man is not one but two—conscious and unconscious—and that the two begin at cross-purposes belongs to the very framework of Jung's thought. It sets the stage for every consideration and also supplies the goal of therapy: the reconciliation of opposites.[8] He seems to have been tempted from the outset toward a romantic metaphysics of *polarity*. But before long Jung recognized that such speculation could only be idle, and he sought in each opposition a kinetic impetus toward transformation. Conflict is the engine of forward movement and so can become a blessing even if it would never be welcomed for itself (9.1,272).

The threats which a young man perceives to surround him the mature person discovers within him. In fact, this very shift comes to define maturity, so that we can speak of *Romeo and Juliet* as an early attempt at tragedy when we see how *King Lear* displays Shakespeare's mature apprehension. While coincidence and happenstance may well do us in, we could not hope to be secure with these enemies eliminated, for yet more powerful ones lurk within. As Kierkegaard put it: "What the child shudders at, the man regards as nothing. The child does not know what the dreadful is; this man knows, and he shudders at it."[9] Any philosophical or religious anthropology which lauds man's ability to control or to banish the unwelcome becomes an obstacle to full consciousness. Jung views such schemes as the Hebrew prophets did idolatry.

This brings him into head-on conflict with popular rendition of the Judeo-Christian God. This God is all-good, and over against him stands Satan (9.1,103). But since God preempts all that is real, Satan's presence becomes shadowy at best. A simple translation into humanistic terms confirms the myth of progress: all that is is essentially good, and the lacunae will gradually be filled in. One is reminded of the enlightenment picture of knowledge gradually overtaking the outer darkness.

We have seen that Aquinas offered scant ground for such a reading of God, careful as he was to separate what constitutes God's goodness from the assessments we are in the habit of making. And Kierkegaard actively combated the doctrine of *privatio boni*, relegating it to the aesthetic sphere of speculation. So sophisticated theologians—classical or modern—come closer to Jung's account than to the popular one. Yet their testimony has not proved powerful enough to convince Christendom that progress is a myth and an idol. In fact, theological progress itself has often been measured in modern times by one's ability to translate the demons in the New Testament in more enlightened psychological or medical terms. Jung had the bitter consolation of finding his suspicions confirmed when this Christendom, incredulous, capitulated in the face of Nazi propoganda and power.

Jung's view began with the inevitability of conflict, and hence an inescapable admixture, if you will, of what we deem to be *good* and *evil*. Unlike *truth* and *falsity,* however, Jung finds that *good* and *evil* function more like contraries than contradictories. They are contained within the genus of "feeling," and defined relatively to one another (9.2,267; 9.1,35). This does *not* mean that 'good' is an utterly relative term; it is *evil* for me to kill in cold blood. There is no way in which *I* can mount to a perspective whence I may justify doing that. Yet the action may always be *understood* (though not performed) from yet another vantage point. The role of ethical principles is to force me to assess where it is I stand, *not* to tell me how things truly lie (331).

Jung is driven to this antinomian position by his basic picture of conflict and his project of transformation (8,207). Man is invited to transcendence, to divinization— to something which beckons from beyond the conflict of good and evil. The picture is romantic, to be sure, yet Jung insists that each man act from the consciousness he can claim now. This stricture is designed to head off a Raskolnikov, for anyone who flaunts morality in a wholesale manner simply exhibits a classic case of psychic inflation.

The metaphysical good lying beyond our ethical assessments of *good* and *evil* belongs to the resolution of opposites. Hence Cusanus speaks of God as *coincidentia opposi-torum* (16,319). Short of this ultimate situation, what appears to be good may turn out to be evil—although this fact does not license us to follow anything but the light given to us on the matter. This picture answers to Jung's therapeutic experience, where the "other side" so often confronts us as something evil. And so it may be, yet the way to integration lies through confronting it and even welcoming it as an authentic dimension of my *self* (9.1,32). Hence there can be no clear-cut "problem of evil" for Jung. Theological matters—issues, that is to say, culminating in *individuation*—cannot be that unambiguous.

4. Jung as a Religious Thinker

Jung has left us a therapeutic program along with a series of interpretative sketches designed to lend that program plausibility. The tenor of many of those sketches is explicitly religious; the upshot of his program certainly is. In that sense Jung must be said to be a religious thinker. His position here was a precarious one, however. For he never claimed to be anything but a psychologist, yet he could not resist mining the rich resources of mythology and alchemy, or of religious ritual and doctrine. He discovered here entire ranges of the psyche which outreach ordinary experience, yet which offer a key to its significance. Precisely as outreaching ordinary experience, however, these regions broach issues apparently more germane to theology than to psychology.

Psychologists, anxious to prove themselves scientists, have been more interested in uncovering factors which explain ordinary experience rather than exploring regions which transcend it. Furthermore, the current paradigm for scientific explanation demanded that one adopt reductive strategies which Jung simply could not square with the facts of human living. Jung's own therapeutic experience forced him to acknowledge that experience itself revealed dimensions transcendent to the schemes normally employed to interpret it. It was as an empiricist that he encountered the transempirical (11,247-51). This recurrent intellectual fact, together with his unwillingness to suppress it, forced Jung to reach for a new scientific paradigm—one closer to *interpretation* than to *explanation*.

Metaphysicians had developed an idiom for the transempirical, however, just as theologians had for whatever is properly transcendent. Jung never claimed to proficiency in either, yet his research constantly carried him into their domains. His strategy at such points is an ingenious one, all the more so for its ingenuous mask: "as a psychologist I can only call attention to these facts." For the metaphysical or theological *account* he professes no interest whatsoever, clearly implying that it is worthy of none. He will attend to it carefully, however, for it may well be susceptible for translation into a psychic idiom which will reveal contours of that reality which eludes direct investigation. The metaphysical or theological *affirmation,* however, makes a point which remains invariant through a shift in idioms: it asserts the reality of the regions under examination (11,247-48).

Jung's intention here is clear. It stems from an early experience (1898) documented in the autobiography:

> All in all, this was the one great experience which wiped out all my earlier philosophy and made it possible for me to achieve a psychological point of view. I had discovered some objective facts about the human psyche (107).

Whenever a metaphysical assertion makes sense it will do so because it reveals an objective fact about the human psyche.[10] Jung can afford to be patient; he will not reject an assertion because he cannot come up with an appropriate translation at the moment. Too rationalistic a temper had already written off alchemy as "nothing but an abortive attempt at chemistry" (11,296), and myths as prescientific fables. Jung of all people was too conscious of his

own relative ignorance to employ this criterion in a Pro-
crustean fashion.

Yet he did feel that he had discovered a criterion for
sifting the sense from a metaphysical assertion. This is
clear even when he formulates his method in the most
tolerant possible terms of complementarity:

> The psychological explanation and the metaphysical
> statement do not contradict one another any more than,
> shall we say, the physicist's explanation of matter con-
> tradicts the as yet unknown or unknowable nature of
> matter. The very existence of a belief has in itself the
> reality of a psychic fact. Just what we posit by the
> concept "psyche" is simply unknowable, for psychology
> is in the unfortunate position where the observer and
> the observed are ultimately identical. Psychology has no
> Archimedean point outside . . . (11,248).

As the parallel shows, the metaphysical statement has but
one point to make: asserting the reality of the object
under consideration. Whatever content the statement may
have will only be revealed when it can be translated into an
assertion of psychic fact. Whatever the statement might
presume to *say* will be respected in the hope of finding a
translation into appropriately psychic terms.

The result is, of course, a metaphysics. And the effort to
translate from a classical metaphysical idiom to a psychic
one introduces that critical factor demanded of anyone
who wants to deal with such issues after Kant. Jung
purchases critical awareness by exploiting the dialectical
relationship between the two dimensions of the psyche:
the unconscious and consciousness. Everything that comes
under the rubric of thinking, from consideration to assessment, must of course be conscious. For all of its lucidity
and pretensions to autonomy, however, this activity is
implanted in something which continually influences it:
the unconscious.

Conscious thinking is imbedded in the unconscious
much like an organism subsists in an environment. Spatial
imagery fails to convey the interaction involved at the

perimeters where an organism meets its environment. Rather we must say that one implies the other: an organism could neither arise nor persist without the context which environment supplies; and yet without the focus an organism provides, the surroundings would not function contextually and hence could not merit the name 'environment'. Biology, physics, and information theory converge at this point to remind us how fruitless it is to champion one over the other. They also suggest a logic to deal with the situation.

An organism may be represented geometrically as a point of accumulation which is neg-entropic in relation to its surroundings. That is, the negative entropy which an organism displays (in thermodynamic terms) also serves to characterize it (information-theoretically) as a distinctive configuration, thereby affording a source of order. Yet physics and biology combine to remind us that the energy which fuels the organism, allowing it to continue as an ordering principle, comes from its surroundings. And biological theory goes on to postulate that all such sources of order and of energy must be considered to have emerged from the environment they now stand over against.

Similarly, for Jung, the unconscious affords the context within which intellectual inquiry is pursued, and out of which it should be understood to have emerged. Yet the unconscious can only be understood to be a *context* in the measure that we can formulate its role, and that must be done consciously. Jung can *assert* that our thinking is imbedded in the unconscious only to the extent that he can bring the contours of that imbeddedness to light. For we have no other vantage point than consciousness, much as we cannot assume a position somewhere in the environment without that *position* turning out to be an organism.

Yet as the environment presses on an organism, and together with random mutations can account for new configurations emerging, so the unconscious impinges on inquiry. The pressure itself cannot be contested, and Jung claims that he can identify recurrent forms it takes. These forms trace the manner in which consciousness is imbedded in the unconscious. To bring them to light is to display our "sense of reality"—where objectivity is assured by the fact that these forms assert themselves, and clarity is purchased by our efforts to delineate them.

Jung calls them "archetypes." But lest the use of a noun suggest that we are speaking of objects, let us try to think of them as forms: forms of thought and of life, organizing principles which arise spontaneously to guide our activity. In this role they guide in the formation of what we take to be real, and hence might themselves be thought to constitute an "underlying" reality. But of course "in themselves" they belong to the unconscious, which is to say that are undifferentiated and hence unknown. Only in their role as configuring consciousness can archetypes be said to be what they are. Yet that role is not a role *within* consciousness. It is revealed to us only by consciously reflecting on how it is that we actually proceed.[11]

In this way Jung tries to preserve the transcendence intended by the metaphysical idiom while shedding its pretense to be describing what outreaches our capacity for investigation. There is only one way of judging whether or not he succeeds: attend to the specific translations he offers, and judge whether they illuminate that sector of human experience better than rival accounts do. Strategies may recommend themselves to us antecedently, but their only test lies in their execution.

What should recommend Jung's strategy to us, however, is the way in which it knows how to profit from Kant's radical critique, and yet is not afraid to deal with those recurrent issues which perimeter human existence and so have been termed "metaphysical." Furthermore, he deals with them in a gingerly manner reminiscent of the classical figures we have examined. It is a manner which anticipates certain key distinctions to be drawn by Wittgenstein—namely, that between *saying* and *showing*.[12]

Nothing can be said about the unconscious—the unknown—except that it is a reality which perimeters consciousness and impinges upon it: "insofar as the archetypes act upon me, they are real and actual to me, even though I do not know what their real nature is." Jung adds, "this applies, of course, not only to archetypes but to the nature of the psyche in general" (352). At best we have hints: patterns which recur in myth and in therapeutic experience, traces where the unconscious shows something of itself to the inquirer who works to assimilate it (302-304). The only reliable method, however, embraces all four steps including the practical consequences (193). There is no other way to get at what Jung is getting at than "by dealing directly with the realities of which he has written."[13] This fact above all marks Jung as a religious thinker.

4.1. Jung as Metaphysician

We have seen how one cannot take Jung's psychological demurrings at face value, since his very strategies imply a metaphysics. Nevertheless he is accurate in not claiming to be a metaphysician. When he is tempted on metaphysical forays it is not difficult to fault him. Yet if one is willing to accept his disclaimer and chalk the blundering forays up to a certain intemperance, he will be in a position to appreciate how keen a sense Jung possessed for the *point* of metaphysics and how accurately he could pinpoint the central issues.

In fact, his sense for what metaphysics is up to stems from his own picture of consciousness imbedded in the unconscious—and confirms *that* metaphysical picture by its incisiveness. For, he says, "unless metaphysical concepts are rooted in living, universal psychic processes, they are not only useless but impediments" (9.2,34). Then he assesses the cultural lay of the land (in 1950) to conclude:

> If metaphysical ideas no longer have such a fascinating effect as before, this is certainly not due to any lack of primitivity in the European psyche, but simply and

solely to the fact that the erstwhile symbols no longer express what is now welling up from the unconscious as the end result of the development of Christian consciousness through the centuries (9.2,35).

In another place, examining the doctrine of the Trinity from "a psychological point of view," he remarks how "despite all the mental exertions of the Councils and of scholastic theology, they failed to bequeath to posterity an intellectual understanding of the dogma that would lend the slightest support to belief in it" (11,153). His quarrel lies not with reason and logic—the tools of metaphysicians—but with their misapplication to symbolic realities. One feels that Jung is more effective in displaying the reality which metaphysicians purport to expound when he tries to ascertain the reasons why this doctrine made the psychic impact it did, seeking to discover therein its specifically numinous character.

Metaphysically Jung has but one point to urge, and that is *the reality of the psyche.* The problem he faced faces every teacher in the Western world daily: if everything we know is framed in one set of terms or another, and if these frameworks are merely "subjective"—that is, a matter of choice—then isn't every discussion a game and all learning a charade? Practically, of course, a teacher can ride the question out until a student becomes sufficiently exhilarated with learning something that the "framework" ceases to interpose itself. As a psychologist, however, Jung had to take it head-on, for he traced the malady of our civilization directly to this cynical issue of rationalism.

The challenge came to Jung more directly from Kant, and he tended to respond in those terms. For Kant's revolutionary rendition of *objectivity* worked only so long as one accepted the *a priori* concepts (or forms) of the understanding as given. Yet even then these concepts were to be guided in their application by the "ideas of reason." These "ideas," however, were said to be merely *subjective.* According to this rendition of *objectivity,* then, it is constituted by factors which are *subjective:* a flaw fatal to Kant's system, yet one which took its time to appear in the cultural rationalism which the system promoted. When it did appear, however, it appeared not merely as a flaw but as a deceit, and spawned a corrosive cynicism. The best educated generations the world has ever known lost contact with that very intelligence which they were supposed to be exercising and which had prepared the environment in which they could learn so much.

Jung diagnosed the malady as reason run amuck, much as a system can burn itself out when it is not supplied with compensating mechanisms. He was seeking for the negative feedback appropriate to regulate the human use of human intelligence. The romantic movement may have given him some fruitful leads, but Jung was determined to face the issue in the terms in which Kant had bequeathed it. He had to show that a plurality of mediating frameworks does not jeopardize the *objectivity* of the psyche itself. For what is *objective* about the psyche is located at a deeper level, a level from which frameworks as such emanate (not just this one or that one) and from whence we are guided in employing them.

Such an account would be a "psychological one." Not "merely psychological," as though one could map out the mind and be in a position to *explain* how such things arose. But "psychological" in the sense that one could be brought to acknowledge how the root demands of intelligibility—for unity and order—are not themselves explainable. Nor do they represent arbitrary assumptions, after the model of an axiomatic system. Rather these demands appear to be thrust upon consciousness. Not however from the outside as though from the world, but from below, as it were, from yet another dimension of that power active in consciousness. And we can sensitize ourselves to acknowledge this dimension as it makes its presence felt to conscious inquiry.

That presence—while not directly accessible to consciousness and so named *unconscious*—is nonetheless real and hence *objective.* Its full objectivity can only be appreciated, however, by the person who works to articulate the way it makes itself felt—to his conscious self. The method Jung lays out to bring the unconscious to articulation, and so to display its objective character, is an explicitly self-involving one. Modeled on a therapeutic exchange, it asks that one begin by consciously submitting himself to the impulses of the unconscious, thereby acknowledging the role it plays in constituting reality. Then he is asked to go to work to translate emotions into images (177) so that he can understand the images (187). The upshot of this understanding will be certain ethical consequences (193), which one is charged to discover and to carry out. In this way the reality of the psyche and the manner in which its unconscious dimension conspires to reveal to us how things stand become a matter both of personal experience and of objective record. It was the goal of Jung's life and work to show how the two could be brought to converge (352).

4.2. Jung as Theologian

The focus of Jung's entire activity was to lay bare the dynamics of *individuation:* the process whereby one becomes himself.[14] He presented a process, not a program; a becoming rather than a making or doing. The process he outlines is as far from a scheme for "personal fulfillment" as *self* is from *ego.* If *ego* is the me that I have a hand in making, self is what I am invited to discover. The *self* functions as a lure; it represents what I am called to become and holds the power which, released, will bring me there. The self, then, always outreaches my actual self now, yet contains the materials which intimate what I will be. And should I doubt whether that be the case, there are stores of stories which tell otherwise and which have proved to be telling in my own experience.

Hence Jung does not hesitate to identify the *self* with

the God-image—psychologically they are indistinguishable (11,160)—just as he insists that the goal of *individuation* entails transformation. Transcendence, that is being called beyond one's present self, is simply a fact of Jung's personal and therapeutic experience. In that sense his model for human development is a "religious" one (recalling Climacus' "Religiousness A") by contrast with an "ego-gratification" model, where the self, already constituted and presumably autonomous, sets out to satisfy its needs and to protect its interests.[15]

So Jung's avowedly psychological exploration moves into theological territory, and unescapably so. Furthermore, some of his essays are explicitly theological in character, even while he professes to be treating these issues "from a psychological point of view." Matters here do not lie quite parallel with those treated under the rubric of *metaphysics,* however. For one thing, Jung turns out to do theology better than he does metaphysics, even though his want of systematic training will show up here as well. (Personal as that judgment is, I doubt whether it would be contested in its comparative form. Whether Jung does theology *well* when he turns his hand to it is another question entirely.)

In fact he has greater respect for theology than for metaphysics. Respect for the enterprise, that is; not necessarily for its practitioners. He could not fail to notice how powerful religious symbols proved to be in bringing individuals to some sense of the wholeness possible to them— far more powerful than metaphysical notions. In the measure that a theologian allows himself to be guided by the symbols which form his proper subject matter he finds himself in a more favorable position than a metaphysician to appreciate the realities involved in his inquiry and to respect its objective character.

And Jung, for his part, was not so convinced that a psychological translation could exhaust what it was theologians were trying to say. What remains is more than the point of assertion. But that "more" is only discovered to faith.[16] Yet "it is dangerous if these matters are only objects of belief" (11,200), so the tradition of faith sought understanding. Yet in the measure that the understanding was proffered in metaphysical terms, Jung found it necessary to attempt a translation, for "as a metaphysical 'truth' it remained wholly inaccessible to me" (11,199).[17] He makes it very clear, however, that psychological investigations into theological matters are not meant to replace disciplined theological reflection so much as to challenge theologians to "tackle this very necessary task" of showing how religious symbols stand for psychic (and cosmic) wholeness, and in this way to articulate their objective character (11,192).

Let us look more closely at two ways in which Jung finds himself having to deal with explicitly theological issues: his identification of *self* with *God-image,* and his quarrel with characterizing evil as *privatio boni.* Both topics are utterly central to his project. The first traces the perimeters of the process to define its scope, while the second leads us into the "union of opposites" and so to the very nerve of the *individuation* process.

4.21. Self as God-Image

Jung reiterates time and again that "the self cannot be distinguished from an archetypal God-image" (11,160). Hence it is inevitable that "a religious interpretation [of] an autonomous functioning of the unconscious ... will insist that [it] was a divine revelation. In both Hebrew and Christian scriptures dreams are often taken as the voice of God. And, "so long as a mental or indeed any psychic process at all is unconscious, it is subject to the law governing archetypal dispositions, which are organized and arranged round the self." Thus "it would be equally true to say of any such arrangement that it conforms to natural law and that it is an act of God's will" (11,160).

He claims, not that the languages of psychology and of

theology are equivalent, but simply that they are indistinguishable for a therapist: "faith or philosophy alone can decide, neither of which has anything to do with the empiricism of the scientist" (11,190). In fact, Jung finds a decided therapeutic advantage in one's being able to *use* a religious idiom, for it "makes possible a much better objectification of the vis-a-vis, namely, a *personification* of it. . . . Hate and love, fear and reverence, enter the scene of the confrontation and raise it to a drama. What has been merely 'displayed' becomes 'acted' " (337). When it comes to expounding his own therapeutic model and method, however, "one can explain the God-image . . . as a reflection of the self, or, conversely, explain the self as an *imago Dei* in man. Both propositions are psychologically true, since the self, which can only be perceived subjectively as a most intimate and unique thing, requires universality as a background" (11,190).

The point Jung wishes to make is strictly analogous with that regarding metaphysical assertions. The point of God-language lies in affirming that one does not create himself, but is a part of a larger context which provides significance to his life by inviting him out of a separate individuality into full-blown individuation. Whatever might be said about God—the unknown—that does not elucidate this process remains speculative and vain.

God (or the self) functions as "a *numinosum,* filling life with something impersonal . . . ; only then is life whole" (356).

It may sound strange to us to have God, or the self, referred to as "something impersonal." Yet the expression is carefully chosen, and the choice of it testifies to Jung's theological acumen as well as elevates his goal beyond anything so banal as self-fulfillment. For this last expression employs 'self' in precisely the sense which Jung wishes to transcend by reminding us that he uses 'self' as a symbol. The self-fulfillment syndrome accentuates what is or can be mine: everything which conduces to my personal gratification. For Jung this way leads nowhere at all. It backs off from the archetypal invitation to become one's self by insisting that I already am myself, and proceeds to accentuate my separateness by gratifying my desires and protecting my rights. It can end only in death, and an unsung death because without a plot there is no story—only a sentimental narration of events. What God—or the self-symbol—provides for an individual is the background of universality wherein he can discern a pattern rich enough to make a story of his own life by affording it a plot. One becomes a person only through incorporating something impersonal.

It is true that we speak of God in personal terms, and (Jung agrees) it is appropriate that we do. Yet habituation to such usage can prove religiously debilitating and theologically misleading. It tends to make us think that we ought to relate to God as we might to another human being, and raises untold difficulties in framing the paradigmatic religious posture of prayer.[18] The God who is the source of all and who means to be "all in all" can hardly be thought of as another individual. Hence where Jung finds the self-symbol and the God-symbol to coincide is precisely in their unknown, impersonal dimensions, referred to as "the unconscious" and "the unknown" respectively. This *self* of which I have been speaking also names what each of us is called to live his way into. Socrates' irony, Kierkegaard's humor, and the Zen koan all find their purchase here, and suggest a more immediate way in which *self* and God-image are linked, namely, the way in which becoming one's self links one with the divine. True enough, we can overlook this inbuilt task, and to the extent that we do, "the self . . . corresponds to Freud's super ego and is a source of perpetual moral conflict. If, however, it is withdrawn from projection and is no longer identical with public opinion, then one is truly one's own yea and nay. The self then functions as a union of opposites and thus constitutes the most immediate experience of the Divine which it is psychologically possible to imagine" (11,261). If one undertakes the inner journey leading to individuation, he cannot fail to meet God.

Jung sketches the dynamics of this encounter in many

places, but perhaps most succinctly in the "late thoughts" which conclude his autobiography. Written in 1959, these form as near a summary statement as one can find. Harkening back to his "Psychological Approach to the Trinity," which I have cited frequently in this section, he reminds us that "the *complexio oppositorium* of the God-image enters into man . . . not as a unity, but as conflict" (334). With some assist from "analytical treatment [which] makes the 'shadow' conscious, it causes a cleavage and a tension of opposites which in their turn seek compensation in unity. The adjustment is achieved through symbols [notably the symbol of the cross]. The conflict between the opposites [i.e., what works at cross-purposes in us] can strain our psyche to the breaking point, if we take them seriously, or if they take us seriously. The *tertium non datur* of logic proves its worth: no solution can be seen. If all goes well, the solution, seemingly of its own accord, appears out of nature. Then and then only is it convincing. It is felt as 'grace' " (335).

By submitting to the process or by undertaking the journey (and both expressions are necessary) we come to appreciate that the *self* may be attained but cannot be achieved.[19] Therapy can never become a method not merely because the language is inherently self-involving but also because its successful issue can never be predicted. Something gratuitous is required, paradoxical as that may sound. In this way the person intent upon individuation *will* experience God—not however as he is himself, but in his "grace." The psychologist is not only pressed into employing religious language but finds himself doing so with a theological finesse.

4.22. Reality of Evil

The "process of becoming one's self" is never so expansive as that neutral idiom suggests. It is more like negotiating precipitous slopes and narrow defiles, or like a hand-to-hand struggle in spiritual combat. That is why stories, sagas, and tales of mythical journeys offer us more illumination than do ethical treatises or clinical diagnoses. If individuation is to occur, conflict appears to be inherent in it; so much so that Jung will insist that "the shadow and the opposing will are the necessary conditions for all actualization" (11,196). We have just seen him formulate this law in a shorthand manner when he reminded us that "the *complexio oppositorum* of the God-image enters into man . . . not as a unity but as conflict" (334). Individuation is a process (and a task) forced upon us by the presence of the opposites: *unio* only results from *complexio*, order from confusion, peace from conflict.

The reasons which Jung offers for making conflict a matter of principle and not just of fact sound plausible enough yet suspiciously generic: "life, being an energic process, needs the opposites, for without opposition there is, as we know, no energy. Good and evil are simply the moral aspects of this natural polarity. . . . The tension of opposites that makes energy possible is a universal law, fittingly expressed in the *yang* and *yin* of Chinese philosophy" (11,197). These diverse examples of opposites may form a collage illustrating a romantic *Weltanschauung*, but they hardly constitute an argument. We are hard pressed, for example, to know what to make of *good* and *evil* as "moral aspects of this natural polarity."

One has the impression that cosmic assertions like these are quite secondary for Jung. What impressed him above all was the tenacity with which men resist the light, the stubbornness with which we cling to illusion. As a therapist he experienced this human fact in a particularly pointed and vicious way. A person intent on becoming himself, or concerned to help another do so, must not simply negotiate obstacles, but has to deal with live enemies lying in wait to slay him. Whatever wholeness one may attain comes only at the risk of his life. These were the facts of Jung's life and practice. He did not mind their flying in the face of a rationalist myth of progress; in fact he seemed to relish that particular advantage. What he could not stand, however, was the way even reputable theologians had of appearing to waive this fact in favor of a theory: explaining evil as the privation of good ((*privatio boni*).

And even more fundamentally, the basic Chirstian symbol—the Trinity—seemed to be deficient as a symbol for wholeness by just this much: it failed to accord to a dark or evil principle the status of its fourth member. This failure is more acute than the other, for it marks a defect not in theory but in a central religious symbol. These above all need to be trusted to bear the secrets of the unconscious—of the divine way—to men. The fact that the central Christian symbol is a trinity rather than a quaternity represents a symbolic deficiency, since the quaternion is more conducive to wholeness. Jung traces this defect to a stubborn refusal in Christianity to admit an alternative or evil principle into the godhead.[20]

While Jung can appreciate the systematic reasons for denying the devil a place in the divinity, he nonetheless regards it as a mark of superficiality. To acquiesce to conventional moral conceptions of good/evil represents a failure of religious nerve. Anyone who has experienced God has had a brush with his dark side. Why does the presence of God in Jesus stir up the powers of evil so if they are not on a par with him (11,175)? And sofar as the theological ruse of *privatio boni* goes, one has only to experience the tenacity of evil in himself and others to question its seriousness:

> Whatever the metaphysical position of the devil may be, in psychological reality evil is an effective, not to say menacing limitation of goodness, . . . and this is the reason why the victory of the good is always a special act of grace (11,173).

One is reminded of Aquinas' matter-of-fact remark that "evil prevails for the most part." Where is the conceptual tangle and how can it be unravelled?

The conceptual issue in question is not so comprehensive as the so-called "problem of evil," though it certainly bears upon it. Jung shows that he appreciates the systematic pressure to regard evil as a privation (of good) by formulating the logical situation succinctly: "In a monotheistic religion everything that goes against God can only be traced back to God himself [as the cause of all]. This thought is objectionable, to say the least of it, and has therefore to be circumvented" (11,169). The result is a theory which absolves God of responsibility by removing evil from the status of something which is caused, and instead regards evil as privation.

Yet this shadowy status hardly does justice to the facts. Those facts are the ones which constellate to pose that larger "problem of evil." Jung puts it dramatically:

> if the devil has the power to put a spoke in God's creation, or even corrupt it, and God does nothing to stop this nefarious activity and leaves it all to man (who is notoriously stupid, unconscious and easily led astray), then, despite all assurances to the contrary, the evil spirit must be a factor of quite incalculable potency (11,169).

Jung cites with favor the tradition "which holds that the devil, though created, is autonomous and eternal." This would be "in keeping with his role as the adversary of Christ and with the psychological reality of evil."

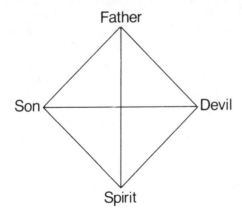

Created or not, "the devil is autonomous; he cannot be brought under God's rule, for if he could he would not have the power to be the adversary of Christ, but would only be God's instrument" (11,173). This suggests correcting the one-sided trinitarian scheme to include the devil as "equal and opposite" to Christ. The devil would then represent the dark side of God which came to light as "the opposites latent in the Deity flew apart when the Son was begotten, and manifested themselves in the struggle between Christ and the devil" (11,175). The Holy Spirit mediates this conflict as it is played out in us, holding out the promise of victory.

Jung is sensitive to the gnostic flavor of all this, and quite aware that the logic of the quaternity symbol would demand that the devil—the Son's opposite—be uncreated. He senses how far-reaching a revision he is proposing in "correcting" the central symbol of Christianity, but he sees no other way to give adequate voice to the reality of evil as well as to make up for the symbolic deficiencies inherent in a trinity. By incorporating the spirit of evil Jung at once fills out the one-sidedness of a "good God" and expands the incomplete trinitarian symbol to one more conducive to wholeness, a quaternity.

Would it not be possible to account for the reality of evil without performing so drastic an operation on an utterly basic religious symbol? If other conceptual moves were available, one senses that Jung would have found them more congenial. My contention is that these moves are available, and that Jung failed to see them precisely because he lacked the specific metaphysical discipline necessary to realize the consequences of the *privatio boni* formulation, as well as to detect the equivocal senses of 'good'/'evil' at work to confuse the issue. Furthermore, there is a more plausible and scriptural way in which the Trinity can function as a symbol of wholeness—a quaternity—and do so precisely in virtue of its incompleteness.

First it is necessary to distinguish between 'good'/'evil' as collecting a set of assessment-terms, and 'good' as it can be said of God. We have seen how Aquinas was careful when applying 'good' to God to distinguish a sense of that term prior to ethical discrimination (III. 3.2). As Jung sees them, the 'good' and 'evil' of assessment reflect "the feeling-values of human provenance," and he doubts whether we can "extend them beyond the human realm" (11,197). All the more reason to insist that when we say God is good we are predicating of him something beyond good and evil. Aquinas attempted to establish this divine sense of 'good' by calling our attention to that *conatus* whereby each thing tends to its own completion without giving any thought to the right or wrong of it.

One cannot help but find this maneuver utterly congenial to Jung, who was so acutely aware of the relativity involved in any human assessment of 'good'/'evil'. Not that we would ever be in a position "beyond good and evil" from which we could dispense with such evaluations (11,180). Nevertheless, any assessment we make has to be made from *within* the demands of the individuation process, whence "ethical decision becomes a subjective, creative act. We can convince ourselves of its validity only *Deo concedente*—that is, there must be a spontaneous and decisive impulse on the part of the unconscious" (330). In this way what began as a "subjective act" comes to enjoy that *objectivity* associated with reconciling opposites. The objectivity of the decision is confirmed by the way we live out its consequences.

In this sense, making an ethical decision of the sort described carries a person beyond the good or evil of assessment into a realm where he does what it is he must do. In this situation the evil course would have been to choose one or the other of the available alternatives without allowing a genuine decision to emerge. Once a person submits to a decision of this sort, however, we are hard pressed to identify a course of action contrary to the one decided upon, one which could be opposed to it and labeled 'evil'. (Think, for example, of any conflict-of-duty situation: fighting in this war, divorcing this man, marrying this woman, aborting this fetus or not.) For Jung these alternatives function precisely to frame the conflict. But it is only in resolving this conflict that a person can reach the decision which then defines what he must do—the *good* for him.

Jung's own discussion of *individuation* had already suggested a context within which 'good' and 'evil' play their assessment roles. The alternative to undertaking the inner journey or engaging oneself in the built-in task is not to undertake another journey or task, but simply to fail to do it. The alternative to the arduous process of assuming consciousness is simply to remain unconscious. At this level evil appears as a failure, a want, a privation, and not as an active and symmetric opposite. The result, of course, is both tenacious and destructive, for it is to be gripped by the illusion that we *know* what we are up to when in fact we do not. And Jung loves to quote the saying of Jesus found in one of the Lucan manuscripts: " 'Man, if thou knowest what thou doest, then art blessed, but if thou knowest not, then art accursed, and a transgressor of the law' " (11,197). In this sense of 'know', failing to know offers the very paradigm for what is evil—yet it is nothing more than a privation.

Considerations like these point to a level where evil is not the symmetric opposite of good, but more accurately described as the absence of what would be appropriate—in short, a privation. Furthermore, both the good and the evil we find at this level seem to be more fundamental—more archetypal, if you will—than that which we bring to bear in moral evaluations. These considerations bring Jung's simple arguments from parity—"how can one speak of 'good' at all if there is no 'evil' " (11,168)—into question, and lend greater plausibility to the scheme of *privatio boni.* Although originally countenanced for systematic reasons, this notion bears consequences which not only underscore the asymmetry of evil but can explain its power as well. What was called a *privation* so that it could not be imputed to God turns out for the same reason to have no cause at all.[21]

In a world where intelligibility is measured by sufficient reasons, an evil action—*qua* evil—can claim none at all. It is absurd. Yet the demand for reasons will not be so easily silenced, hence the impulse to rationalize, to cover up. One rationalization upon another creates a fogbank of deceit, resulting in the well-known state of aggressive illusion. Aggressive because rationalizations—unlike reasons—will not support themselves but demand constant bolstering. Illusory because one cannot afford not to believe the rationalizations himself.

Finally, Jung's generic observations about the indispensable role of conflict in releasing psychic power seem to be shrewd enough, yet need not have anything to do with *good* or *evil* in the sense which we have touched upon here. We seem always to be faced with alternatives, it is true. Nearly every human situation conceals conflicting values which compete for our allegiance. But the ethical demand, as we have seen Jung formulate it, normally does not require that we choose between them as between good and evil. It rather presents an invitation to move through the conflicting values, to ascertain their relative weight to me in the world to which I am committed and in fidelity to the task I have undertaken—and in that light to decide what I am to do. That course may or may not be one of the alternatives originally posed. But even if it should be, I have chosen it not *as* it was originally posed but as I have come to understand it. The result of taking a decisive step like this is to release fresh powers of discernment and to give one the courage to proceed along the path which the step itself has opened before us.

These conceptual distinctions can be employed, then, to give an adequate account of the reality of evil—and one which even explains its asymmetry with good—without needing to add a fourth and evil principle to the godhead. The consequences of the *privatio boni* scheme show how, despite appearances, it can offer a uniquely powerful way of characterizing evil and the illusion which evil foments.

So far as the Christian symbol of the Trinity is concerned, it does in fact seem to invite a fourth member.

Christian tradition holds out the missing place to be filled by each one who is adopted into sonship. Jung appreciates the significance of the doctrine of the Assumption of Mary in precisely these terms (11,171). And since Mary is the exemplar for all those who respond to revelation, the Assumption announces that each believer forms a quaternity with God.

As John has Jesus promise:

> If anyone loves me he will keep my word,
> and my Father will love him,
> and we shall come to him
> and make our home with him (14:23).

The intimacy promised is accomplished through one's relation to the Son, and so displays the symmetry of a quaternity:

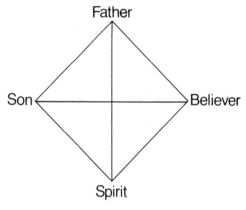

Another Johannine formulation confirms this link of the believer with Jesus as Son:

> If anyone acknowledges that Jesus is the Son of God,
> God lives in him, and he in God (1 John 4:15).

Without denying that trinity is symbolically inferior to quaternity, one can see in the deficient symbol of the Trinity a way of displaying the fact that the Christian revelation is not a mere announcement but an invitation.

God presents himself as lacking what only the faithful respondent can fill. Or more explicitly yet, what only the community of the faithful can make up for, as it fills out "the fullness of him who fills the whole creation" (Eph 1:23).

4.3. Summary Observations

The aim of this section has been to complete my exposition of Jung's singular scientific discipline by showing how it fared when it carried him into allied regions. Since all speculation must serve the purpose of therapeutic understanding, metaphysical notions and theological symbols will be asked to do the same. While he sometimes assumes an air of modesty, there is no doubt that Jung meant to apply this criterion rigorously, demanding a translation of each notion or symbol into psychic terms. He is careful to note that this represents, not a reductive move, but only a strategy to glean what is of significance for therapy.

What of the rest? Here he appears to distinguish between metaphysical notions and theological symbols. He is fairly well convinced that metaphysics leaves no remainder; at best it is therapeutically irrelevant and hence of no *objective* worth. Things lie otherwise, however, with those symbols with which theology deals. Here the remainder itself appears to have therapeutic worth: the fact that revelation is *from* God enhances its value immeasurably. Hence the Trinity enjoys a surplus value beyond puzzling philosophers.

One can never succeed in *characterizing* this remainder, of course, so that a translation into psychic terms would be able to render all that can be *said*. Such a translation could prove misleading, but probably less so than the customary speculations of theologians about that surplus, since these carry no more weight than metaphysical considerations and so must share their fate. So a "psychological point of view" cannot pretend to supplant faith— the God response appropriate to a revelation of God *from*

God. It may even succeed in predisposing one to it. On balance, Jung's work promises to prove as reliable a hand-maid for doing theology today as more metaphysical schemes proved in the past. Every such interpretative scheme must be carefully monitored and critically employed, yet that defines the theologian's task.

This hermeneutic exercise in Jung has a more modest goal: to show that the discipline of metaphysical analysis may still prove useful. Not to substitute, certainly, for the gains accomplished when one shifts to a "psychological point of view," but for unraveling the confusions which that viewpoint evokes. Along the way I have tried to underscore the challenges which Jung's "psychological point of view" poses for a metaphysics or a theology which aspires to cast some light on our common task of becoming human.

The effort he expended to discover the discipline appropriate to this inquiry became a part of the discipline itself. A constant fidelity to the experience of therapy brought Jung to recognize how inappropriate was the current reductive paradigm for scientific inquiry. But he could only succeed in challenging it to the extent that he took it upon himself to explore regions hitherto uncharted, though everywhere celebrated in story and song from their beginnings. This journey had to be a solitary one. It is recorded in the sixth chapter of his autobiography. Its results are embodied in the discipline which analytical psychology has become.

Jung's approach remains too distinctively human for a culture modeled on the scientific paradigm which he found it necessary to reject: a neutral method extending into problem-solving techniques. And the discipline proves too demanding to attract a host of practitioners or clients. Finally, it appears too "metaphysical" to be scientifically respectable. The aim of this exercise has been to bring us to a position whence we might assess these criticisms for ourselves. It is my hope that we may have increased our own critical acumen in the process.

NOTES

1. The reference scheme for Jung will be in text as follows: simple page references will be to Jung's autobiography, *Memories, Dreams, Reflections* (New York, 1961). Page references preceded by a cipher (e.g., 8,129) are to the *Collected Works*, where the initial numeral indicates the volume. (Volume 9 is bound in two volumes, hence the 9.1 and 9.2.) Jung's *Collected Works* constitute Number XX in the Bollingen Series and were originally published by Pantheon Books, New York. The series has been taken over for the Bollingen Foundation by Princeton University Press. The volumes (and editions) consulted for this study include *The Structure and Dynamics of the Psyche*, Vol. 8 (Princeton, 1969); *The Archetypes and the Collective Unconscious*, Vol. 9.1 (New York, 1959); *Aion*, Vol. 9.2 (New York, 1959); *Psychology and Religion: West and East*, Vol. 11 (Princeton, 1969); *The Practice of Psychotherapy*, Vol. 16 (New York, 1966).

2. Daniel Yankelovich and William Barrett, *Ego and Instinct: The Psychoanalytic View of Human Nature* (New York, 1970).

3. A key phrase, lifted from the central chapter of the autobiography, reads: ... "my science was the only way I had of extricating myself from that chaos" (192). This essay could be considered an extended gloss on that sentence. For a more ambitious treatment see John A. Sanford, "Analytical Psychology: Science or Religion? An Exploration of the Epistemology of Analytical Psychology," in Hilde Kirsch (ed), *The Well-Tended Tree* (New York, 1971).

4. For Kierkegaard's "Religiousness A" see *Concluding Unscientific Postscript* (Princeton, 1941). I am indebted to Sister Mary Rachel Dunne, whose dissertation "Kierkegaard and Socratic Ignorance: A Study of the Task of a Philosopher in Relation to Christianity" (Notre Dame, 1970 [unpublished]) explores these affinities with clarity and grace. For some explicit references in Jung cf. 16,190; 16,256; 16,271; 9.2,194; 9.1,27-29, 131-132.

5. John Sanford offers extensive and illustrative interpretations of the Gospel in *The Kingdom Within: A Study of the Inner Meanings of Jesus' Sayings* (Philadelphia, 1970).

6. Nicholas of Cusa: "In these most profound matters every endeavor of our human intelligence should be bent to the achieving of that simplicity where contradictions are reconciled," from *Of Learned Ignorance* (London, 1954), 173—cited in 16,320.

7. Cf. Wilfrid Sellars, "Language of Theories," in *Science, Perception and Reality* (London, 1963), where he argues that a model in science presupposes a commentary in order to function as a model.

8. "If we do not turn back to the problem of individuation, we shall see ourselves faced with a rather extraordinary task: the psyche consists of two incongruous halves which together should form a whole. One is inclined to think that ego-consciousness is capable of assimilating the unconscious, at least one hopes that such a solution is possible. But unfortunately the unconscious really is unconscious; in other words, it is unknown. And how can you assimilate something unknown?" (9.1, 287).

9. Soren Kierkegaard, *Sickness unto Death* (Princeton, 1941), 145.

10. Although Jung is moving in another direction, his program can help one understand the project of Bernard J.F. Lonergan's commentary on Aquinas, *Verbum: Word and Idea in Aquinas* (Notre Dame, 1967): "The Thomist concept of inner word is rich and nuanced: it is no mere metaphysical condition of a type of cognition; it aims at being a statement of psychological fact . . . " (46). This project becomes one of intellectual self-appropriation in his later *Insight* (London, 1957): " . . . we are concerned not with the existence of knowledge but with its nature, not with what is known but with the structure of the knowing, not with the abstract properties of cognitional process but with a personal appropriation of one's own dynamic and recurrently operative structure of cognitional activity" (xxiii); " . . . more than all else, the aim of the book is to issue an invitation to a personal, decisive act" (xix).

11. In a pregnant footnote Jung insists that " 'reflection' should not be understood simply as an act of thought, but rather as an attitude. It is a privilege born of human freedom in contradistinction to the compulsion of natural law. As the word itself testifies ('reflection' means literally 'bending back'), reflection is a spiritual act that runs counter to the natural process; an act whereby we stop, call something to mind, form a picture, and take up a relation to and come to terms with what we have seen. It should, therefore, be understood as an act of *becoming conscious*'" (11,158 n.9).

12. Note the affinities with Stephen Toulmin's interpretation of Wittgenstein's intent in the *Tractatus*, in Toulmin's "Men and Ideas: Ludwig Wittgenstein," *Encounter* 32 (1969) 58-71.

13. So writes Morton Kelsey, the guide to whom I am personally indebted, in "Jung as Philosopher and Theologian," in Hilde Kirsch (ed), *The Well-Tended Tree* (New York: Putnam, 1971), 190.

14. What follows is a representative sketch of the process of becoming oneself as Jung came to understand it: "Behind a man's actions there stands neither public opinion nor the moral code, but the personality of which he is still unconscious. Just as a man still is what he always was, so he already is what he will become. The conscious mind does not embrace the totality of a man, for this

totality consists only partly of his conscious contents, and for the other and far greater part, of his unconscious, which is of indefinite extent with no assignable limits. In this totality the conscious mind is contained like a smaller circle within a larger one. Hence it is quite possible for the ego to be made into an object, that is to say, for a more compendious personality to emerge in the course of development and take the ego into its service. Since this growth of personality comes out of the unconscious, which is by definition unlimited, the extent of the personality now gradually realizing itself cannot in practice be limited either. But, unlike the Freudian superego, it is still individual. It is in fact individuality in the highest sense, and therefore theoretically limited, since no individual can possibly display *every* quality. (I have called this process of realization the 'individuation process.') So far as the personality is still potential, it can be called transcendent, and so far as it is unconscious, it is indistinguishable from all those things that carry its projections—in other words, the unconscious personality merges with our environment in accordance with the above-named *participation mystique.* This fact is of the greatest practical importance because it renders intelligible the peculiar symbols through which this projected entity expresses itself in dreams. By this I mean the symbols of the outside world and the cosmic symbols. These form the psychological basis for the conception of man as a microcosm. . . . The term 'self' seemed to me a suitable one for this unconscious substrate, whose actual exponent in consciousness is the ego. The ego stands to the self as the moved to the mover, or as object to subject, because the determining factors which radiate out from the self surround the ego on all sides and are therefore supraordinate to it. The self, like the unconscious, is an *a priori* existent out of which the ego evolves. It is, so to speak, an unconscious prefiguration of the ego. It is not I who create myself, rather I happen to myself" (11,258-259). Or more simply in the opening sentence of the autobiography: "My life is a story of the self-realization of the unconscious" (3).

15. Cf. note 4 of reference to the *Postscript.* Chapter 4 on Kierkegaard notes how his formulation shows *becoming* to differ from *making* oneself. Behaviorism is ordinarily consistent, and the manner in which it assumes the self to be a substance underscores its resolve to avoid any characterization of what might be "distinctively human."

16. In an aside reminiscent of Kierkegaard, Jung admits: "Faith alone would suffice, too, did it not happen to be a charisma whose true possession is something of a rarity, except in spasmodic form. Were it otherwise, we doctors could spare ourselves much thankless work" (11,192).

17. Jung's concluding remarks to his essay "A Psychological

Approach to the Trinity" (1948) sum up his attitude and locate his approach: "If I have ventured to submit old dogmas, now grown stale, to psychological scrutiny, I have certainly not done so in the priggish conceit that I knew better than others, but in the sincere conviction that a dogma which has been such a bone of contention for so many centuries cannot possibly be an empty fantasy. I felt it was too much in line with the *consensus omnium*, with the archetype, for that. It was only when I realized this that I was able to establish any relationship with the dogma at all. As a metaphysical 'truth' it remained wholly inaccessible to me, and I suspect that I am by no means the only one to find himself in that position. A knowledge of the universal archetypal background was, in itself, sufficient to give me the courage to treat 'that which is believed always, everywhere, by everybody' as a *psychological fact* which extends far beyond the confines of Christianity, and to approach it as an object of scientific study, as a *phenomenon* pure and simple, regardless of the 'metaphysical' significance that may have been attached to it. I know from my own experience that this latter aspect has never contributed in the slightest to my belief or to my understanding. It told me absolutely nothing. However, I was forced to admit that the 'symbolum' possesses the highest degree of actuality inasmuch as it was regarded by countless millions of people, for close on two thousand years, as a valid statement concerning those things which one cannot see with the eyes or touch with the hands. It is this fact that needs to be understood, for of 'metaphysical truth' we know only that part which man has made, unless the unbiddable gift of faith lifts us beyond all dubiety and all uneasy investigation" (11,199-200).

18. I have made a tentative attempt to lay out the proper groundwork for prayer in "Prayer as Language of the Soul," *Soundings* 54 (1971) 388-400.

19. "Conscious realization or the bringing together of the scattered parts is in one sense an act of the ego's will, but in another sense it is a spontaneous manifestation of the self, which was always there. Individuation appears, on the one hand, as the synthesis of a new unity which previously consisted of scattered particles, and on the other hand, as the revelation of something which existed before the ego and is in fact its father or creator and also its totality. Up to a point we create the self by making ourselves conscious of our unconscious contents, and to that extent it is our son. ... But we are forced to make this effort by the unconscious presence of the self, which is all the time urging us to overcome our unconsciousness. From that point of view the self is the father" (11,263).

20. This is the burden of his late work, *Answer to Job* (1952), published in *Collected Works*, Vol. 11: *Psychology and Religion: West and East* (Princeton, 1969). For a contemporary response to

that work on the part of a sympathetic theologian see Victor White, *Soul and Psyche* (London, 1960), Appendix V: "Jung on Job." White's correspondence with Jung on this point strained their growing friendship enormously: cf. *C.G. Jung Letters I: 1906-1950,* ed. Gerhard Adler (Princeton, 1973), 383-87, 419, 539-41, 555.

21. Bernard J.F. Lonergan has explored in detail Aquinas' dark saying that evil has no cause, in *Grace and Freedom* (New York, 1971). I have tried to distinguish polemic from genuine disagreement on this matter in chapter 7 of my forthcoming *Aquinas* (London: Routledge and Kegan Paul, 1975).

CONCLUSION
Removing Obstacles
to Understanding

I have tried to present each chapter in this book as an object lesson in interpretation by offering an example of what it means to do hermeneutics. To succeed, then, the chapters must not only inform us of what Augustine, Anselm, Aquinas, Kierkegaard, and Jung thought about selected religious topics. They must also afford a glimpse of the ways each one of them proceeded to meet those issues, and so offer us a set of working exemplars for religious understanding.

The object is twofold: to display the ways reflective religious thinkers work, and, by offering a taste of apprenticeship, to suggest how we might acquire similar skills ourselves. If it belongs to hermeneutics to raise the issues attendant upon interpreting another's method, and to deal with those issues as well, then each of these exercises does some hermeneutics in doing what it does. This very approach, however, contests the claim that 'hermeneutics' stands for an identifiable discipline. It represents more of a title pretending to link together those disciplines people have relied upon to understand what another thinker is up to.

Just as skillful interpretation attends to the moves an author makes (or fails to make) as much as to what is said, so the exercise of interpretation itself gains credibility by the way it proceeds. The art of interpreting lies in displaying how the work in question manages to show what it fails to say. And by accomplishing this task the interpretation shows its own worth as well. Proceeding on that conviction, I have tried to adapt myself to each author in question, to capture his mood together with the problems he felt it necessary to grapple with. Yet I have chosen these particular ones to develop an extended lesson in philosophical theology as well. For the thinkers selected display an impressive array of refined philosophical skills as they meet the religious issues which faced them.

These issues deal broadly with man's knowledge of God, though less with the abstract possibility thereof than with diverse ways of handling what must lie beyond our grasp. None of them uses the philosophical tools available to him to construct a divinity; so none can be convicted of engaging in that brand of natural theology which the Reformers found so distracting. Rather than turning up a god who explains all manner of things, each is rather concerned to articulate what he can of a divinity which lies beyond explanatory schemes.

Augustine shows the way, as he maps a journey of progressive awareness: one scheme after another fails to explain, to the point where he himself realizes that the issue is no longer explanation but confession. His life story details how we learn how to discriminate our action from God's while discerning God's action in ours, and teaches us how to confess to each: imploring forgiveness as well as trumpeting praise.

With Anselm and Aquinas the task turns more explicitly to formulating transcendence, but the goal was the same: how to say what could be said truthfully, without thereby pretending to have defined divinity. Or how to express divine things accurately enough to forestall misapprehensions, without conveying the impression that we have succeeded in articulating what must remain simple.

For Kierkegaard and Jung the focus turns rather to experiencing the transcendent. Yet their writings proceed by developing the language required to articulate that experience. In that way we can measure their success by assessing how well their idiom manages to unravel the difficulties blocking their way to faith and understanding. But these difficulties had arisen previously in more classical dress. So the manner in which Kierkegaard and Jung each met them could display relevant analogies with Augustine, Anselm, and Aquinas, even though their own ways of working differ dramatically from classical methods and from one another.

By proceeding in this fashion, I have tried to show how similar in temper a critical employment of philosophical skills can be when they are faced with unraveling conceptual blocks to understanding in matters religious. This critical temper persists through a diversity of philosophical skills, developed to meet problems arising in quite disparate intellectual milieux. The kinship lies, I feel, in a shared understanding of philosophy itself. None of these thinkers is beholden to philosophy as a subject matter. Each rather treats it as a skill, and uses that skill to help us work our way through what appears to be an obstacle.

Like master teachers, they arrange to exercise us in the requisite skills. Like good therapists, they manage thereby to liberate our own native dispositions to insight and understanding. Their very skill at resolving specific problems keeps us from distorting the entire quest for understanding into a problem. Furthermore, their individual performances show how effective a form of therapy philosophy can become, as each offers a paradigm for engaging religious issues philosophically.

Taken as intellectual therapy, philosophy itself poses no inherent difficulties for the *élan* of human understanding that strains toward faith. Moreover, philosophy so understood and practiced may offer considerable assistance to the near-impossible tasks identified by hermeneutics. Yet it makes all the difference how well we do it. Hence this manual of apprenticeship.

Index

241